TWELVE SHIPS A-SAILING

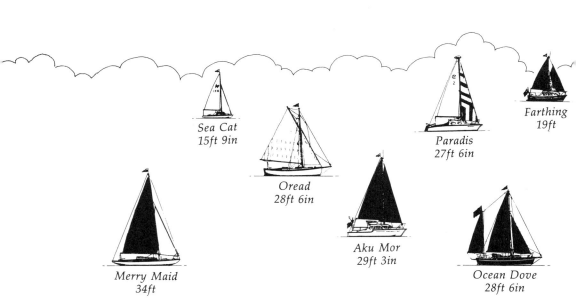

Sea Cat
15ft 9in

Oread
28ft 6in

Paradis
27ft 6in

Farthing
19ft

Merry Maid
34ft

Aku Mor
29ft 3in

Ocean Dove
28ft 6in

TWELVE
SHIPS A-SAILING

Thirty-five years of home-water cruising

JIM ANDREWS

DAVID & CHARLES
Newton Abbot   London

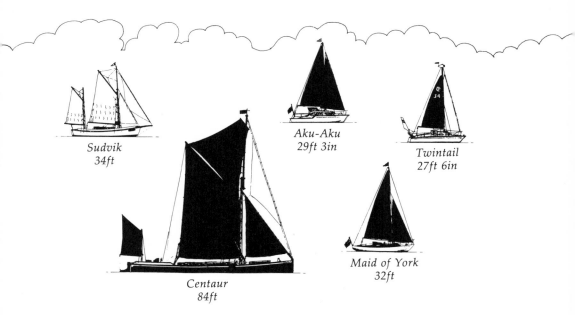

Sudvik
34ft

Aku-Aku
29ft 3in

Twintail
27ft 6in

Centaur
84ft

Maid of York
32ft

British Library Cataloguing in Publication Data

Andrews, Jim
Twelve ships a-sailing.
1. Sailing—Great Britain   2. Boats and
boating—Great Britain
I. Title
797.1'24   GV811
ISBN 0-7153-8787-1

Phototypeset by Typesetters (Birmingham) Ltd,
Smethwick, West Midlands
and printed in Great Britain
by Butler & Tanner Limited, Frome
for David & Charles Publishers plc
Brunel House   Newton Abbot   Devon

CONTENTS

'The perfect anchorage . . .'

1
THE DEEP END

'It spat a few short bursts of fire . . .'

Beyond the slow flashes of the Copeland Island lighthouse, a full moon rose from the sea and sent a lane of silver dancing towards *Oread*'s dimly nodding bowsprit. With the soft night wind ruffling our youthful hair, Malcolm, Peter and I stood gripping the cold wire shrouds, swaying to the old yacht's ponderous movements, and eagerly watching the familiar waters of Belfast Lough slipping astern.

With every yard we sailed, a long-held fantasy further unfolded, for ahead beyond the end of the moonpath the North Channel spread across our course; a vast crossroads on our way to the mighty Firth of Clyde. This, to us schoolboys, was nothing short of real voyaging – very different indeed to the round-the-buoys racing which had so far formed our sole boating experience.

It had been exciting enough that somehow we had ourselves been chosen to represent our college in the annual sailing events for schools and universities, over on the Gareloch in Scotland. The boats used for these races were in those days the sleek and

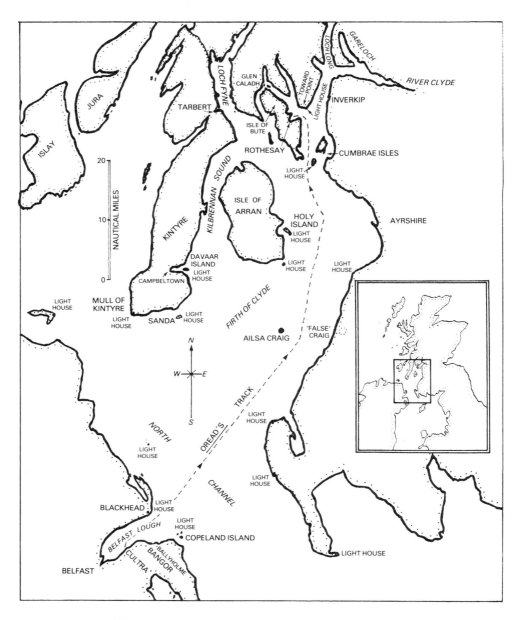

quite sizeable International Dragon Class keelboats; marvellous machines compared to the dinghies we were used to. But we could hardly believe our ears when we learned that two of our parents had got together and persuaded a mutual friend of theirs to lend us his 28ft (8.5m) gaff cutter, as a transport ship and floating hotel for the week. To make a real passage and then actually live on board a sea-going yacht for a time was a bonus almost beyond our dreams.

'Sea-going.' Why, the phrase had a ring to it that made me inflate my young chest and strike a more manly pose up there on *Oread*'s sidedeck. But then how could I know that the next twenty hours were about to teach me much more than I anticipated concerning that complex subject.

For almost an hour now, we had been watching the golden necklaces of tiny shore lights tracing out the distant streets of Bangor and Ballyholme, ever more brilliantly against the darkening background of land to starboard. Perched aft on the cockpit coaming behind the indistinct outlines of Peter's Dad and mine, our young skipper, nephew of *Oread*'s generous owner, could be seen silhouetted against the swiftly winking beacons marking the channel back towards Belfast. And in the reflected sky-glow from that already out-of-sight city, my own little 8ft (2.4m) clinker-built dinghy followed in our straggling wake at the end of her painter and a heavy sea-going (that phrase again!) warp. This was to be her first long passage, too.

We had inverted *Oread*'s own rather larger dinghy over the cabin skylight a few minutes before leaving – and what a magic moment that had been. With all sail set and the mooring buoy dropped clear to the traditional call of "All gone, forrard!", the heavy old ship had slowly eased herself round and gathered way.

That had been hours ago; and now I could see above me the outline of the mainsail's long gaff blotting out first one faint star and then another as it swung in rhythmic jerks against the night sky. Almost invisible at the masthead our burgee rippled forward as though directing us towards the empty, black horizon. But no; *nearly* empty. Low, and very small, the lights of a steamer were crawling steadily across it from the south, outward bound from Liverpool, perhaps, for maybe Canada or America.

I tried imagining what it would be like if we were about to gybe round and take *Oread* herself north-westward past Black-head, and out into the lonely vastness of the Atlantic. It really was there, just around the corner, mingling its ocean particles with this same water on which we now sailed through the darkness. And as though to prove it, the gaff jaws suddenly creaked overhead as the cutter rolled more firmly to the first beginnings of a long, slow swell.

11

But maybe *Oread* knew only too well that our course lay in what was for her a more homely direction. She had been built in Scotland by Dickie's of Tarbert, back in 1898.

"Your watch, Jim!"

The skipper's call broke into my thoughts and set my heart unexpectedly thumping as I made my way aft to take my place in the tiny cockpit. A smoky oil-lamp guttered in the brass binnacle before me as I rather self-consciously gripped the long iron tiller. At first the dim, ornately marked compass card swung widely one way and then the other as I struggled to get the feel of the huge rudder and the retarding effect of the long, deep keel on my attempts to hold her in the right direction. This was so completely unlike the highly responsive, quick-to-turn racing craft which had until then been the only boats I had steered, and it was quite a while before our young skipper felt confident that both my father and I could keep the ordered course accurately enough for him to leave us alone, and call the rest of the crew below to their bunks.

How quickly that first watch went! The breeze gathered strength as we got further out, and we were enthralled by the mystery of our passage through the moonlit seas, with the rush of the wake alongside, and the sails swaying darkly amongst the stars. There were fewer of those now, we noted, and the sky had become very black indeed further astern. Ahead we had plenty to watch, for there was a succession of ships' lights to sort out and avoid as they stole silently across our bows. The whole business was intriguing, and I was totally surprised, and disappointed, when the hatch suddenly slid back and a well-muffled Peter preceded his father into the cockpit, announcing that our two hours were up.

"How are we getting on?" they asked. It seemed a matter of some little pride to be able to point out how the Copeland Light now flashed back over our starboard quarter, and the 'Fl. ev. 3 sec.' blink of Blackhead showed that even to port the Ulster coast was dropping well astern.

That night I thrilled to the new realities of so many things which had previously belonged only in books such as Arthur Ransome's wonderful *We Didn't Mean To Go To Sea*. One typical moment was when, on handing over the helm and chanting out the course to steer, I heard Peter's father at once repeat it word for word as he settled himself in a hunch of lamplit oilskin over the binnacle. Only then did I appreciate the good sense of that ancient maritime tradition, for now I realised the value of being sure that the new watch had properly understood where to steer, particularly when you yourself were about to put your life in their hands and go below to sleep in perfect trust while they sailed you on through the night.

How much warmer it was in *Oread's* old-fashioned saloon when we climbed down the ladder and closed the hatch. A brass oil-lamp, its wick turned low, moved gently in shiny gimbals, seeming to lean this way and that as the ship rolled imperceptibly about it, and we removed our shoes and jackets and got ready for bed. Its yellow glow wandered over the mahogany panelling and twinkled on the brass locker-knobs, casting moving shadows over the huddled shapes which must be Malcolm and the skipper, cocooned like drowsy caterpillars in their sleeping-bags.

It seemed odd, turning in fully dressed – 'all standing' as sailormen say – and my bunk, a folding affair slung high under the curved oak deckbeams on the lee side, proved narrow even for a gangling youth like me, but sheer luxury of course, because it was a real bunk and not some ordinary bed ashore. As I wriggled to get myself comfortably wedged against the motion, muted gurgles and soft rushing noises came from the planking by my ear, where as each foaming crestlet passed along her topsides the aged cutter chatted quietly about her progress. Despite my excitement, it was only a minute or two before I lost the thread of what she was saying.

A deafening crash and sudden sharp pain woke me. An express train thundered past . . . I lurched again into a projection on the ship's side; the dark cabin seemed to upend, and I felt wild rolling acceleration, then a thud and a jolt as the bow was flung high and water rattled by overhead. *Overhead?* Fighting out of the restricting bedding and dropping to the clammy floor-boards, I grabbed for my shoes and was at once thrown half across the saloon. Staggering, I listened with racing heart as a surge of bilge-water sloshed loudly beneath me. There seemed a great deal of it.

With an old sports jacket slung on for warmth, I scrambled up the crazily reeling companion-ladder to tug at the hatch above. It was stuck. I banged on it, and at once it slid open with a jerk. Malcolm peered down at me, his face pale and pinched in the dawnlight that burst in, along with a gust of ice-cold sea air and the searing hissing of the wake. Behind him, the oilskinned figure of the skipper glanced at me as I struggled out.

"Breezing up a bit", said he, conversationally, and pushed hard with both hands on the tiller. I shuddered in reply, and then gasped in horror as a monstrous breaking sea reared high over our stern. It was going to sweep us from end to end! Slamming the hatch shut behind me, I turned and took a firm grip of the cockpit coaming, but, incredibly, *Oread* rose at the very last second, and to my intense relief the huge wave rumbled harmlessly under her. Surging forwards, she yawed to one side, rolling heavily, and the skipper again heaved at the tiller to hold her on course. Grey, he looked, as did almost all that I could see; the sails, the breaking wavetops, the heavily overcast sky – all except just ahead, where, as the dripping bowsprit end was briefly raised over the back of a sea, a vivid orange gleam appeared luridly through a ragged slot low in the murk.

Dawn at sea. So this was what it was like. I shivered again, and sat down wordlessly beside Malcolm in a corner of the cockpit. As I watched, the glare ahead grew, brightened hopefully, then quite suddenly faded away as ragged rolls of purple cloud closed in and engulfed it.

"Last we'll see of that, today", called the skipper, his voice oddly distorted through the wuther of the wind in my ears. He pointed beyond the port bow. "Look! There's Ailsa Craig – you can just make out the very edge of it. It's jolly misty."

At first I could see nothing except the vague leaping line where water stopped and grey nothingness took over. The strangely bitter smell of salt filled my nostrils. A gliding, very white bird with long, angular, black-tipped wings and a yellowish head slid suddenly across my view followed by several more, but of land I could find no hint at all, despite the rapidly increasing daylight.

"See? There", the skipper pointed again. "Just a single, curving line."

I saw it now. A mere shade denser on one side than on the other, a faint smudge soared up out of the sea into the low cloud – the eastern profile of a gigantic rock mass, rising from a seabed thirty fathoms below.

"Eleven hundred feet high, that is, and not much broader," the skipper continued. "Thousands of gannets nest there. Look! Did you see that one dive?"

Even as I shook my head I saw yet another of the great birds suddenly turn itself into a streamlined dart and from a great height plummet straight into the sea. A small plume of spray erupted and blew away downwind.

"After herring, he is."

"H-how do you know it's herring?" I asked, trying not to let my teeth chatter.

The skipper grinned. "Fisherman told me. If they go in almost vertically like that, it's herring. A more slanting dive means they're after mackerel. Either of you two feel like breakfast?"

I shook my head; the thought wasn't in the least attractive. One glance at Malcolm told us he wasn't hungry either.

"Never mind. You'll soon get your sea-legs." The skipper turned his gaze once more on that massive outline of rock to port. "Paddy's Milestone, they sometimes call that. Good thing we can see it so well, just now. At least we know it's it."

"W-what d'you mean?" My teeth were chattering despite my efforts.

"So we can be sure it's not the 'False Craig'. In low fog like this", he explained, "a mountain over there on the Ayreshire coast has much the same shape, and sometimes shows when the real Craig's obscured. Ships have been known to steer for that one by mistake. Very nasty. Lots of rocks over there."

I shuddered, pulled my jacket closer to my ribs, and twisted round to stare away to starboard. A crest heaved up and broke in a white explosion some distance away, but beyond that there was nothing recognisable. "Is it f-far to the c-coast?"

"Not very. We're nicely on course here, roughly parallel to it. Visibility can't be more than a mile though, so we'll hardly see it. Hang on, here comes another big one!" He leant his full weight against the tiller as *Oread* tried to swing round and her stern lifted. For a moment a roaring mass of foam tumbled level with the cockpit, then the long bowsprit sank into the trough ahead, scooping water into the foot of the jib as the wave began to overtake us. The companion-hatch slid open, and Peter's father appeared, his thin, wrinkled face smiling cheerily.

"I say! Bit lively isn't it?" he asked, then clung on tightly as the bows went soaring skywards on the back of the sea, so that water swilled aft down the tilted deck and spilled in over the curving coaming, on either side of him.

"Time we took in some sail," said the skipper through his teeth, obviously glad to see him. "She's getting jolly hard to hold. Call David, would you; and Peter. We'd best stow the main altogether, I think. No sense in messing about reefing, when in this wind she'll run just as well under the headsails alone."

Another sea burst around our stern and its edges frothed fussily on board. My dinghy – I had quite forgotten it – made its presence felt by suddenly riding up to us on the crest, towing a long loop of its warps, then drifting astern again as the yacht surged on, so that it was viciously snatched after her when the painter sprang taut.

The business of getting the big sail and its heavy spars down and secured was fraught with difficulties, and, relieved of the pressure it had provided, *Oread* now began rolling like a thing demented. There were no lifelines or guardrails of any kind to keep us safely on her decks, for such things were unheard of in small yachts of her day, so we grasped from stark fear the deep sense of the adage 'One hand for yourself, and one for the ship'.

She was still going too fast even when we had finished, so the staysail was lowered as well, and at last her breakneck pace eased and the helm became light enough for us youngsters to manage. No longer did the wavetops clatter aboard as they had done, but the old boat still rolled and lurched heavily. Fatigue from the exertion of our work on deck took its toll, and suddenly half the crew became seasick.

How fortunate it was that the wind that day chose to blow almost exactly in the direction in which we wished to go, for had it done otherwise, we in our inexperienced innocence could soon have been in very serious trouble indeed. Although August, it was bitterly cold. I was drenched to the skin with spray, and rather late in the day I thought of going below for my oilskin coat, but one look down into the dank cabin where greeny-white faces were now grouped in communal misery around an unpleasant bucket on the cabinsole, and I decided to remain wet.

The morning wore on, and now and then those of us in the cockpit discussed our situation. We told each other hopefully that the seas would grow smaller the further we sailed into the Firth of Clyde. Of course they would . . . In fact all that happened was that the wind blew even harder, till it was continually producing a deep howl in the rigging, and the waves became even larger, steeper, and more and more unstable. Thin streaks of foam began trailing long and lacelike downwind over the heaving hills and valleys of churning water, and almost every wavetop broke and was whipped away into a growing mist of driven spume.

Once more, the steering became difficult. Finding that thirteen-year-old Malcolm could no longer hold *Oread* on course during his spell at the tiller, the skipper first helped him for a bit, but seemed restless, and at last asked Peter's father to take over, then began peering into the murk away to port. Nothing had been in sight anywhere since that one faint glimpse of Ailsa Craig had dissolved from view. That had been shortly after sunrise, and it was already long past midday. Peter eventually asked the skipper what he was looking for.

"Holy Island," came the brief reply. "High thing, just this side of Arran. But visibility's . . ." His words were lost in the thunder of a bursting crest, ". . . can't tell how far we've come now, either," he added, glancing astern. Only then did I notice that the log-line, towing its distance-recording rotator behind us, had securely wrapped itself round both of the dinghy painters. We had no other means of checking our progress, for radio-direction-finding sets were not yet available for small yachts, and under such shortened sail and thick visibility, with *Oread* rushing forward one moment and slithering to what seemed like a complete stop the next, any kind of judgement was about as hard as it might be. The empty feeling that we were "lost" suddenly filled me. I was appalled at the ease with which it had happened.

"How about working over to port a bit?" bawled Peter's father, easing the rudder as a sea smashed against the transom to pour white and green over his thighs into the crowded cockpit. The cutter slewed to starboard and all but broached. Gasping, and spitting out a mouthful of seawater, he pulled her back, and shook his head. "She's getting damn hard to control again, Skipper. Going too ruddy fast!"

"We can try reefing the jib," said the skipper doubtfully. He reached for the furling line. "Ease its sheet, somebody." As he tugged on the thin line, the Wykeham-Martin gear began rolling the sail at our bowsprit end smaller and smaller on itself. "Jolly

17

hard on the luff-wire in a wind like this, but that should make her happier", he panted, belaying the line when barely half the sail still showed. "See if she'll now come across a bit, John."

Whether we managed to work anything to the west of our vaguely northerly heading or not I never discovered, but I was as keen as any of us to locate the land – *any* land. The 'open sea' had lost a lot of its romantic appeal – for the moment, anyway! All the same, by the time Peter and I came to share the helm, it was only occasionally possible to swing to port, and that when a sea was passing ahead below the bow, for the next crest had always to be taken exactly stern on. More than once we failed to straighten in time, and she would career round, solid water slamming with the force of an avalanche against her port quarter, to arc high into the air and obscure everything in flying spray. Then she would hang there, heeled over and trembling, for long seconds before we could get her back on course. The jerking tiller flung Peter and me clean across the cockpit on the impact of one such sea. The deafening noise of it all, not to mention the wavering roar and shriek of the wind in the old boat's sparse rigging, was almost overwhelming.

Nowadays, in such conditions, the crew of a small yacht would most probably be wearing both life-jackets and safety harnesses, and truly watertight clothing. This, however, was 1950 and for one thing safety harnesses as such had not been developed for pleasure craft. I remember hitching the end of the mainsheet about my middle, all the same. Forgetting the probably by now soggy kapok lifejackets lurking under one of the cockpit seats, I began wondering how many people could be supported – if necessary – by the ship's single, circular lifebuoy. The motion, chill, wetness and fatigue, and hunger too, at last led not just me, but I think all of us, into imagining that we were in real distress.

By mid-afternoon, Peter's father succumbed to further seasickness, leaving Peter, the skipper and me alone on deck. The seas now appeared to be somehow rolling inside themselves, heaping up and up, with their tops being shredded away in the wind even before they fully broke, so that a white fog of salt was blowing low over the great Firth. Our jib, mostly furled though it was, tugged and jerked at its sheet like a frightened animal, quivering and wavering as though doing all it could to get away from us. We fully thought it would succeed. Again and again it banged across and back, each repeated gybe shaking the whole ship from end to end.

For several hours now my poor little varnished dinghy had been more and more frequently surging right up alongside us, surfing forwards on the steeply overhanging wave-fronts. She would then drop back until her painter and warp snatched her after us on yet another planing rush, down the next advancing sea. Twice already she had hit us a hefty crack on the transom, but there seemed nothing at all we could do about it. Dodges like extending the length of the towing lines, or using another warp trailed over her stern to act as a drogue, did not occur to us. I was only glad I had stowed her tiny CQR anchor right aft under her slatted stern seat. Its weight there seemed to be preventing her from nose-diving. But it was to do more than that before the day was through.

Peter and I had wedged ourselves either side of the tiller, looking astern with our backs against opposite coamings and feet braced across, for we found it easier to co-ordinate our efforts on the helm if we could both watch the oncoming seas. For some time we had ceased trying to steer any kind of compass course; the vital thing now seemed only to prevent *Oread* from swinging broadside on.

As a larger sea reared up and smashed over us, the dinghy's sharp little stem suddenly came cutting through its foaming torrent, riding right into the cockpit and jamming itself firmly between us. For agonising seconds we could do nothing to steer, and it took the added efforts of the skipper to heave the little boat back, stern-first over the yacht's transom. As it went, it filled and capsized.

We must have been shouting a bit, for my father appeared in the hatchway, ducked as a sea broke over him, shook his head like a big and very pale seal, and climbed rapidly out. He took a few deep breaths, sat down and swallowed mightily.

"There's a lot of water inside," he said glumly.

Peter and I looked at each other, and back at the next sea.

"Better pump," said the skipper, and set to himself, strenuously raising and lowering the heavy brass plunger in the corner of the cockpit.

A numbing, blank feeling grasped my stomach.

"Look! A ship!" shouted Peter, briefly lifting a hand from the

'Look! A ship!'

tiller and pointing over my shoulder. I glanced round quickly, and there, faint but unmistakable in the spume-fog, was a small passenger steamer, her black smoke driven down by the storm, low over her dipping, rearing bows. We watched as a huge sea smothered her stern. White cascades poured from her scuppers while she pitched and rolled clear.

"She's having it rougher than we are, by the looks of that," commented my father, and for a moment that put heart in me. But then another thought came to mind.

"Do you think she can see us?" I heard myself asking.

The skipper looked round at each of us in turn, and with a sudden decision reached into a locker and withdrew a small, rust-stained sailcloth bag. From it he hurriedly produced a couple of cylindrical hand-flares. No one said anything, and no one suggested otherwise when he began to strip off the protective tape from one of them. Pulling the tab off its top, he struck one end with it as if lighting a gigantic match, and then held it high. It spat a few short bursts of fire, then popped out a red ball of flame which curved away in the wind, to be followed by a second and third. They didn't go very high; little better than a modest roman candle on bonfire night, I thought. Suddenly it fizzled out and died.

The ship was drawing ahead of us, already almost out of sight as she lurched onwards into the gloom.

"Light another one!" More than one of us said it.

We fired three flares in all, and the skipper got his oilskin and the back of his wrist slightly burned when one didn't work as it should. Someone said an old gardening glove would have been a help, had one been stowed along with the flares in the 'panic bag' – a pointless remark at the time, but one I swore I would remember, if . . .

The ship was gone.

Oread slithered on, swept repeatedly by crests, lonely and forlorn. Astern, the little dinghy had somehow righted itself, but the weight of water in it was making its painters vibrate each time they sprang taut. It wasn't long before one of them parted. Pete and I still had our hands full with that big iron tiller, and my father took over the pumping. It got colder. The afternoon was finished.

Not another thing apart from our own struggling selves and the drifting spume could be seen, though from a long look at the chart before we had set out I knew – we all knew – that ahead somewhere, and surely not very far away now, lay just two small gaps in the unseen coastline through which we could safely pass; those on either side of the Cumbrae Isles, set in the narrow mouth of the Inner Firth. Once beyond them the water would be sheltered, the seas smaller, and there would be places where we could come to an anchor before dark.

But where, exactly, were these Cumbraes? The knowledge that the coast hereabouts was fringed with fangs of rock, and that we could hardly run on much longer before we came upon them, was as chilling as the spray itself. A gap even one mile wide like the better of the two channels was going to be very hard to find in what could now be barely half a mile of visibility.

"There she is again!" Peter, his face tired and white as the foam beyond, was suddenly shouting and pointing. Closer than before, but still indistinct in the flying mist of salt, was what looked indeed very like that same small steamer. She appeared to be stopped, but we could not steer towards her – and I have no idea what help she could have been anyway in those conditions, for one bump against her rolling steel hull would have finished *Oread*. Then we realised she was in fact steadily keeping pace with us. For the best part of twenty minutes she stayed level with us, then very, very slowly drew ahead.

"She's showing us the way!" I shouted, almost before I fully realised the truth of it.

"You're right!" exclaimed the skipper with a grin of relief which changed his thin face completely. He took a rough compass bearing as the ship finally melted from sight. "He's simply got to be heading for the Cumbrae passage – and where he can go, we can. I'll take the helm now, boys. The rest of you keep looking for signs of land ahead there."

We did, and it wasn't long before each one of us in turn had been sure we could 'see' rocks, great black ones stretching in unbroken lines across our bows with seas washing far up over them. Fortunately, all were entirely imaginary.

The day was nearly through, and not one of us had eaten or drunk anything since our supper back in Belfast Lough the evening before. Frozen, soaked, weary beyond measure, unable to think clearly and already experiencing a desperate feeling of hardly caring now anyway, we were all set for one of those classical 'yachting tragedies' so gleefully pounced upon by the popular press. Yet, with that astonishing luck sometimes granted to fools and novices alike, we were permitted to live on, and hopefully thereby to learn from the experience.

In fact, rather than luck alone, it had been the humanity and kindness of a true seaman which was our real saviour, for the steamer's good captain had realised that we were not really in imminent danger, but had simply lost our bearings, and he had indeed shown us the way to safety. All at once there was rock – real, brownish rock with green vegetation – both to port *and* to starboard. We were smack in the middle of the main channel.

Even as the relief flooded over us, a vast sea curled across our stern and crashed down, half filling the cockpit. The dinghy was seen rolling over and over in its frothing crest alongside us, and then, upside-down, it pulled hard back on the warp, dragging astern and slowing us considerably. One; two; maybe four or five such waves broke over us, steepened by the swift ebb pouring southwards under them, out of this narrow sound. We hung on to whatever we could. Again and again *Oread* threatened to broach, but always that dear little waterlogged dinghy of mine tugged her back on course.

And then there were only small waves around us, and it was over.

Oread was in a bad way. There was much more pumping to do, and quickly, for she was sluggish with the weight inside her. Sheets and halyards trailed overboard, and the bigger dinghy, lashed over the skylight, was askew. As the land closed around us, Peter and the skipper went forward to sort things out, and to prepare the anchor. I remember Peter glancing back at me with a grin – then his face lengthened.

"The dinghy's gone!"

We all looked round. For a moment we saw it bobbing on a distant crest, inverted and low – just its bow was flung up before being hidden in a trough. She was my boat, my very own; but even I did not want to go back. I saw my father looking at me, but I shook my head. *Oread* still required careful handling, for the squalls which tore at us here in the lee of the land were incredibly fierce, and even I could see that without a close-reefed mainsail to balance the scrap of jib, she would never beat to windward. The thought of having to make that sort of effort now was too much. We sailed slowly on, closing gradually with the port-hand shore.

A wide bay opened out, and was left astern. And after a while we came to a headland with the pale shapes of houses along its base, and we unrolled the full jib to help the ship reach round it and in towards Rothesay. Off a line of small craft, the skipper rounded *Oread* into the wind and the anchor was soon down and holding. On shore, windows and street-lamps were lighting up in quick yellow gleams, wan in the blustery gloaming, and reflecting on the disturbed, jiggling surface around us.

With our riding light set swinging from the forestay, we followed each other wearily below, peeled off sodden layers of clothes, and tried to find dry ones while we lit the oil-lamps and sorted out the damp, bedraggled mess. Up forward, my father got some tomato soup brewing on one of the twin Primus stoves.

The skipper sat on the companion-steps to take his, with his head in the hatchway – 'to keep anchor-watch', he said. Hungry as we were, not one of us got through a whole bowlful, nor managed to swallow more than a mouthful or two of bread. Our eyelids drooped, and head after head eased forward, nodded and came slowly to rest on chest or table-top.

A faceful of warm soup wakened me, and I jerked upright, wiping it in puzzlement from my cheek and drowsily putting the spoon back in the bowl. The skipper was fast asleep in the companionway, tomato-red liquid dripping spectacularly down his still oilskinned trouserleg. *He's* not keeping much of a watch, I thought. Maybe I said it aloud, for Pete's father looked up suddenly, stared round, yawned, and chuckled.

"Poor young fella! Had all the responsibility, y'know. Must be even more flaked out than the rest of us." He got stiffly to his feet. "Come on, old Skipper! Better all turn in properly. She won't drag now. Didn't you say the tide was falling?"

Next morning, launching the remaining dinghy, we rowed ashore to telephone home, and to report the sad loss of my 8 footer. As we landed, I took just two steps on the firm and solid planking of the low boat-jetty we had chosen, found it apparently heaving like the sea itself under my feet, overbalanced, and went straight over the side – luckily into only a few shallow inches of water. There could be no mistaking it; I had got my sea-legs!

The telephone box was even worse. Its red-painted, iron-framed windows kept lurching about and jostling us while we reassured those at home of our safety, and learned in turn of slates off roofs and damaged chimney-pots and what a dreadful storm there had been, and weren't we lucky not to have been there. . . .

Unsteadily staggering to the Police Station, we furnished the Duty Officer with details of my dinghy, and where we could be contacted should anything be found. The sun was breaking through the already high clouds as we made our way back to the ship, and with barely more than a moderate westerly to blow us out of the bay and give us a fine reach on up the Clyde to the Gareloch, we arrived there still in good time for our week's racing.

And our dinghy was found. Seemingly two young lorry drivers on their way to a building site at Wemyss Bay, on the eastern shore of the Inner Firth, had spotted the upturned boat floating just off the rocks close by the coast road. Stopping for a better look, they were appalled to see what they took to be a hand, waving from under the bow. Without another thought, one of them stripped off and swam out, only to find that the 'hand' was merely the frayed end of a warp, attached down inside the boat. He then tried to pull her ashore, but she wouldn't come, so his mate threw him a rope from the lorry, and together they hove in. The dinghy suddenly came free, and they lifted her up the rocky foreshore, stacked her on top of the building materials, and drove her up to the Police Station – which is where my father went to identify her, in the midst of a lovely rose garden.

Her gear was mostly still in place, apart from the anchor, its warp, and one wooden slat, all missing from the stern. The little CQR must have fallen out during the capsize and, hanging on the end of its warp, which had been secured to the seat-batten, had hooked into the seabed as the boat drifted inshore. It had all broken away only when the lorry drivers had pulled at her, but until that moment it had undoubtedly saved the little boat by keeping her clear of the rocks.

Good luck had been with us – and, like it or not, we had learned quite a bit about 'sea-going'.

2
POCKET SHIPS AND SPRITSAIL BARGES

'A sad old sight . . .'

My initiation into what have been so admirably described as 'the joys of yachting' was fortunately followed by a return passage from the Clyde in very light wind, sunshine and perfect visibility. The cruising bug bit deep, and set me immediately searching out and reading all I could lay hands on about the subject.

In those days, besides a small handful of technical books on navigation and the management of small craft, there was a number of excellent but simple sailing yarns based on the logs of ordinary people who cruised mainly in home waters. True, there were also some very wonderful ocean-goer's tales, but since such long-distance voyaging seemed (rightly, as it turned out) far beyond my reach, it was always the more mundane explorations around our own coasts which fascinated me most of all. The information they contained on pilotage around Britain, on boat-handling and anchoring, tidal waters and so on, was far more relevant to the sort of thing I had in mind, than the no doubt highly romantic and often hair-raising accounts of ocean cross-ings to palm-fringed islands.

I used to save up birthday and Christmas book tokens, to take them to the newly instituted London Boat Show each January, for only there were the latest and best 'boatbooks' to be found. I recall standing one year at Captain O. M. Watt's bookstall, wondering if I really dare spend the combined generosity of several aunts and cousins on that one expensive but so enticing volume called *Uffa Fox's Second Book* (full of logs, designs and yachts' plans), when an unknown voice behind me remarked in a soft, South Coast drawl, "I've read that – it's worth every penny."

My doubts vanished. I handed the book and my fistful of tokens over the counter.

"If you bring it along to my stand," the voice added, "I'll sign it for you." It was Uffa himself!

He did sign it for me, and even spared the time for an intriguing chat into the bargain, which resulted in several often hilarious meetings and even the odd meal together, in later years. I have never regretted that purchase, either, for it is full of knowledge. More importantly still, at just the right moment, it showed me that a young man need not wait to crew in older, richer men's yachts in order to cruise. Uffa Fox made it perfectly clear that there was nothing wrong in putting to sea, with due caution and only *after careful preparation*, in a well-adapted dinghy or small racing craft, if nothing bigger or better was available. As I read, my longing to do just that began to see the light of possibility.

As soon as I left school, I blew all my savings on, well, not *quite* the boat of my dreams, but one which I hoped might be made to do for a year or two anyway. And I converted her just in time to have her shipped over to East Anglia, where I was about to commence training as a flour miller before entering our own family business in that line.

Designer Kenneth Gibb, who drew her clever, attractive lines, would probably have had a seizure had he seen what I had done to his once lovely 15ft (4.6m) Wildcat One-Design racing dinghy. Not that I had altered that pretty hull whose curving upswept stem and long overhanging counter stern made her, in profile, quite unlike any other chine-built plywood craft.

Sporting a tall Bermudian sloop rig, she had started life fully three-quarter decked, with little more than a narrow footwell between sidedecks wide enough to prevent her filling when (not infrequently) capsized. I had raced her like that for most of a summer before deciding that without fairly drastic surgery there

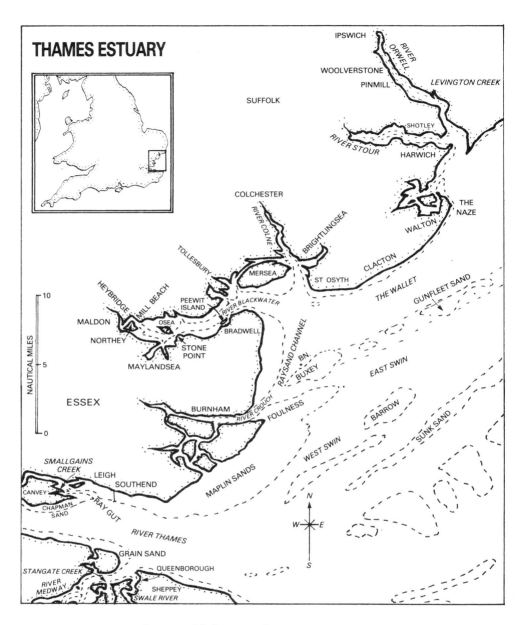

THAMES ESTUARY

was no way she could be used even as a camping cruiser. However, the moment I learned that my milling training was to take place amidst the creeks and rivers of the Thames Estuary, so beguilingly described in books by Arthur Ransome and Maurice Griffiths, I knew I *must* be able to sleep on board, so as to explore at least some of them on my own.

I began by designing a 'hard-top' made of Perspex and wood, with room inside for a canvas bunk to port of the centreboard case, and space for cooking etc to starboard. This of course meant cutting away most of the sidedecking, fitting the hard-top over the resulting area forward, and leaving a short square cockpit which at night could be covered by a hood to make her snug. Sacrilege, no doubt; but that seemed beside the point in the circumstances. (Photo page 33.)

At best, she had never been a stable boat, and having removed her wide protecting decking, the next job was to replace the pivoted wooden centreboard with a galvanised steel dagger-plate, along the foot of which I bolted a streamlined metal blob. This quite heavy assembly could be raised or lowered by a tackle under the hard-top, until only the ballast remained below the hull. When lowered, it made the boat so stiff that I could safely sit inboard under full main and genoa in quite fresh winds.

For the first month or two after my arrival at Ipswich, I spent all free time exploring the sheltered upper reaches of the River Orwell, often sleeping aboard *Sea Cat* at weekends, when I would generally potter down as far as Woolverstone or Pinmill. Then a spell of real 'Indian Summer' set in, and, along with two other young members of the Orwell Yacht Club each sailing their own little boats, I set off downstream with Harwich (and perhaps even a very quick look at the open estuary) in mind.

It was one of those particularly bright, sparkling mornings, typical of Suffolk, and our three very different dinghies seemed to be as keen as we were as they beat in close company down river. A powerful spring ebb was running, urging us along between the shimmering dew-wet fields and copper-tinted woods. Wavelets clopped and chuckled under both the clinker-built bows of my companions' craft as each did their best to keep up with my sleek modern ex-racer. Derek's was a heavy open boat some 13ft (about 4m) overall, and almost three feet longer than Bill's bluff little tub, but with their standing lugsails neither could match my longer Bermudian sloop to windward.

Sea Cat was handling beautifully, slicing out to weather of the others so quickly that I soon had to change down from the genoa to a smaller headsail, despite the gentle breeze; and even then I had frequently to ease sheets to let my friends' more solid, general-purpose dinghies catch up. Needless to say, we could all have piled into Derek's spacious craft, but for each to sail single-handed and have the pleasure of watching the other little vessels creaming along close by, was so much more fun. Besides, there was the added interest (and difficulty) of trying to stay together and 'keep station' on each other – a skill which I found was every bit as demanding as that of racing.

Down past the tattered wartime Nissen huts half-hidden among the trees of Woolverstone Park we tacked, noting the little forest of racing-dinghy masts nestling below the walled-up, painted gable 'window' of the strange old Cat House there. In the past, when it had been a real window, it could be seen from a long way downstream, and, depending on whether or not a large white china cat was placed in its corner, the skippers of certain inward-bound ships would know if the coast was clear of the Revenue men.

The thought added spice to our journey down that same stretch of water.

Close-reaching at Bill's best speed, we found a fresher wind as we came amongst the moored yachts off the long gravel hard at Pin Mill. Several tall spritsail barges were drying out on its firm footing, their slanting spars and tightly furled brown sails huddling together as though trying to see which could get closest to the welcoming walls of the Butt & Oyster. We were not much bothered to be passing the excellent beer on tap behind the old pub's friendly, small-paned windows. For us there was already a far more enticing smell on the breeze – the salty tang of the sea.

Mudflats were already showing widely on either hand by the time we came on the wind again for the last long beat down towards Shotley. The old water-tower and tall, square-rigged flag-mast of the Royal Navy training college capped the skyline over the high ground to port, and far ahead we began to make out large buildings and cranes, and even the upper works of ships berthed in distant Harwich itself.

A couple of sailing barges, no doubt waiting for the flood up the Orwell, had anchored at the spot known as Stone Heaps, close under Shotley's tree-covered heights, and our three tiny craft looked and felt a bit like bath-toys as we spun about close under their flat black topsides, soaring rigging, and those long leaning sprits.

A final tack, and we steered jauntily out across the broad

mouth of the River Stour. Wide waters these, for our little boats, but the sea horizon now lay beckoning before us, and we headed for it, all thoughts of keeping close to each other at last forgotten in our excitement. As I gave *Sea Cat* her head and shifted my weight onto the sidedeck to hold her as upright as possible, she began lifting and slamming over the steepening waves, clearly revelling in the chill, stinging breeze coming in from the sea. All the same, I thought it curious how, after the first few minutes, the others gradually began to drop astern less rapidly. Then I could see they were actually catching up again. Most odd. It was a horrible shock when the reason made itself icily felt around my feet. *Sea Cat* was flooding with water.

Stifling a quick-rising panic, I peered below and wondered with thumping heart what on earth she could have struck without my knowledge to cause so violent a leak. With one white-knuckled hand clutching tiller and mainsheet I jilled her along, bailing hard, in one sense thankful for the heavy ballast keel which kept her on her feet as I crouched to leeward, and in another beginning to worry as to whether the built-in buoyancy at bow and stern would prove sufficient to support it and all the other weight she had on board, if I could not stem the flow.

Then I saw it happen. As we lurched down off a breaker into the trough beyond, a broad jet of water spurted out of the top of the centreboard case, and poured over my bunk into the bilge.

The fault was entirely my own. When designing the various modifications, I had correctly judged that the hull had adequate freeboard to carry all the extra weight, but I had quite forgotten the much lower plate-case, and I realised now that its top was only just above the waterline. Tight-lipped with chagrin and shame, I watched every one of the next six waves slop copiously in. The seventh spouted right up and spattered across the doghouse roof. I pulled the jib to weather, hove to, and bailed out properly. *Sea Cat* lay quietly with her helm free as I worked – I considered it rather generous of her in the circumstances. In my carelessness, I knew I had quite spoiled her as a sea-boat.

With the way off, she no longer plunged so deeply, and only an occasional cupful pulsed high enough to come in. Having made sure I was all right, Bill and Derek had romped away on out to where even their tough little craft at last found the going a bit boisterous. I finished bailing, and reflected that there was more to yacht designing than I had anticipated. By the time the other boats had come charging back to join me, I had temporarily wedged rags into the slot, and worked out a way of reducing the surge within the case itself, so I was a bit happier again as we ran together back homewards, munching our lunchtime sandwiches.

It was going to be a while before the flood tide got going in our favour, and it took us quite a time to recross the mouth of the Stour and enter the Orwell. The sailing barges were still at anchor as we passed Shotley, but with Derek acting as pilot and our centreboards raised, we were able to cheat the last of the ebb along the very edge of the mudbanks over on the opposite bank. Off the tiny gut draining the then deserted marshy area of Levington Creek, he shouted the suggestion that we should all land there and explore, and in seconds we had run our boats up the mud, and waded ashore with our little anchors.

Squelching bare-legged over the saltings, I remember how the sun's heat hit us as we entered that strangely silent, yellow wilderness between the grassy sea walls. Peeling off sweaters and shirts, and wearing only shorts (and mud up to our slim young thighs), we came across the rotting remains of an abandoned Thames Barge lying canted and mastless in an arm of the creek. Her name-boards bore just faded traces of paint, and the holds which once had brimmed with wheat and other cargoes were dark caverns half-filled with muddy water. The trapped tide escaped in burbling spouts from many a gaping seam, and poured down slime-green, disintegrating planks. The wheel and great timber windlass alone spoke to us about her people, for each was worn in places by the countless handling of men and boys from long ago. A sad old sight, as Bill put it, especially when compared with the pair of proud vessels whose vast tanned topsails we could at that same moment clearly see sliding past the mouth of the creek.

"Tide must be making", said Derek, and we splashed muddily back to our dinghies.

The following weekend I was afloat again, this time returning alone from a visit to Woolverstone, and found myself being gradually overtaken by another Ipswich-bound vessel, the Sailing Barge *Kitty*. The wind was light and ahead, and I soon noticed that sometimes she held her course on a much longer tack, passing well beyond the limiting line of the channel buoys,

(*above*) Weekending aboard *Sea Cat* on the River Blackwater, Essex – fifteen feet
of ex-racing-dinghy with keel and cuddy; (*below*) A different proposition – the
view from the wheel of the 82ft Thames spritsail barge *Centaur*

(*above*) Judy decides cruising might be fun; *Ocean Dove,* the Griffiths gaff cutter my father built, at anchor in Strangford Lough; (*below*) *Ocean Dove* again, becalmed off Ailsa Craig in the Firth of Clyde – hardly a fair test for my new ketch rig

and certainly much further over the shallows than I dared to go in *Sea Cat*.

Long after I thought she must run aground, there would at last be a loud clacking rattle of blocks and a slow clumping and thudding of her monstrous sails as she came lumbering round into the wind, her tiny mizzen held aback by the sheet led to the end of her massive rudder. On and on she would glide, and only gradually pay off on the new tack before sliding serenely back across the narrowing river, to do it all again. I remember thinking that her skipper must know the Orwell very intimately indeed, for she wouldn't have had an echo-sounder then, and there was no one standing by the shrouds with a lead line.

I had heard that barge crews were hard to come by – no doubt being a deckhand in a modern motorship was not only better paid and much easier work for a young lad, but a sight more comfortable too. Most spritsail barges had just the skipper and one young boy to handle them anyway; a fact which, considering their ponderous bulk and the weight and size of their gear, was astonishing enough to me. I was utterly amazed when I realised that the *Kitty* was being managed single-handed, for only her old skipper was to be seen on deck as she slowly overhauled me.

She slid enormously past, with her lofty brown canvas catching the air over the trees while I drifted in their shadow, and a smell of tarred cordage, cutched sailcloth and intriguing bilge odours brewed from a variety of long-past cargoes, came wafting around me. The old fellow at the wheel removed a huge hand from his waistcoat pocket, lifted it high and then swiftly dropped it in the time-honoured salute of all East Coast sailormen. Just then both of us were sailing into pretty shoal water, I quite anxiously, for it was after high tide, and the level was already falling. That didn't seem to worry the captain of the *Kitty*. Not one bit, it didn't. The great barge simply stood blithely on, until it seemed she must climb the mud and ram her portly bows hard into the lower branches of the trees.

The incredible thing was that the old man at her wheel hardly looked where he was taking her – he was apparently more interested in something down by the lee rail, at deck level. Only when the huge black leeboard on that side suddenly touched bottom and began to rise, and the chain which led along the rail to its controlling winch therefore fell slack, did he begin fisting

'. . . the *Kitty* was being managed single-handed . . .'

the spokes of his wheel over, and with agonising slowness the barge commenced to answer, turning towards the wind. Locking the wheel with a thing like a massive wing-nut, her master then took a pipe from his pocket and began literally strolling forward along the sidedeck, stuffing tobacco into the bowl with a thumb. I could see everything clearly, for having found a patch of breeze I had been able to tack close by.

The *Kitty* of course carried her way straight up into the wind for tens of yards, leaving *Sea Cat* well astern, while her mighty sails flogged in slow motion. Her colossal mainsheet block suddenly smacked across on its traveller, and flailed back and forth a time or two as she passed the wind's eye, then it settled to leeward.

Up forward, the staysail back-filled with a thump, and only then did the old man give a tug on the line holding its leech to a cleat on the shrouds. The sail thudded across, and walking after it he secured the line on the new lee side and casually wandered aft again, to take the turns out of the wheel and steady her on course with just a single glance up at the long rectangular 'bob' fluttering languidly above the topmast truck. I couldn't say just at what point he had lit his pipe, but by then it was drawing well, and the bitter-sweet blue smoke trailed astern to my nostrils.

As the big vessel pulled away from me, I couldn't help comparing the peacefully relaxed air of her skipper with my own rather frenetic approach to sailing. Here was a man with a complete knowledge of the behaviour of his ship, confidently sailing almost 90ft (27m) of solid timbers and goodness knows what value of cargo up an ever narrowing, ever shoaling river without any help, yet steering her happily over the mudbanks into areas which I treated as infinitely risky. Then and there, I determined to try and acquire that same quiet sureness of control in whatever craft I might later own. I also made up my mind to get myself a sail in a real working spritsail barge.

My chance came the following spring. By now I was working in a small flour mill situated on the quayside at Maldon in Essex (a jolly little business operated by a handful of keen and skilful men, whose rumbling machines were regarded as a collection of good friends), and I had briefly contemplated sailing *Sea Cat* round to the Blackwater from Ipswich. The more I had thought about it, however, the more I knew that, despite the various 'cures' I had attempted on the centreboard case in the meantime, a long open-water passage would not really be sensible the way things were.

My 'weekend cruiser', therefore, arrived ignominiously at Maldon on the back of a lorry, and was lowered into the brown tide to join the other dinghies and small craft snuggling between several ranks of black trading barges alongside the Hythe. Most of the barges came and went frequently, with assorted cargoes, or arrived for repairs or a new suit of sails from the loft behind the pub. Only a few had engines. It was quite common to see one of them perched high on the stout timber 'ways' at low tide, with tar or carpentry being applied, or perhaps lying alongside with mast and gear lowered and stowed along the decks while a new mainsail was bent on.

And that was how one weekend I came across 'Nelson', aboard his trading barge *Centaur*.

She was lying partly aground on the mud below the Hythe, her mast lowered along the deck in an orderly tangle of rigging and what seemed like acres of bright and very dusty red-brown sails – canvas so thick and coarse as to be about as pliable as heavy wire netting. Bringing my little *Sea Cat* upstream, I took in sail so that she glided gently to a stop alongside, and was duly gratified to note that the manoeuvre had not been missed.

"May I come on board?" I asked, my lightly pitched voice no doubt nervously piping higher than my nineteen years might otherwise have dictated, for I was awkwardly timid with strangers.

"Maybe yer can, an' maybe yer carn't," came the skipper's gravelly tones, as he peered down at me. He had only one eye. "Seems to me that if we was to let you up 'ere, you'd 'ave to do some work."

"I don't mind that," I said at once. The thought of working on a real sailing ship, however temporarily, appealed more than anything just then. I was soon clambering aboard over the massive timber rail, and shaking hands with Nelson (a nickname, he explained, due to his missing eye), and nodding to the tubby 'Gearge', who was beyond question the grubbiest human I had ever set eyes on, and very likeable with it. He lost no time in showing me how to make a rope grommet to fit close over the notched top of the 84ft (nearly 25m) sprit and hold up the peak of the newly cutched mainsail.

The colour from that most effective and elaborate proofing concoction came away from everything I touched, and when we retired at lunchtime to the 'local' for beer and a hunk of pie, we were all much the same colour as the sail, decks, rail, hatch-covers and even Gearge himself. The pub too must have retained quite a bit of that cutch, when we left in order to 'raise the gear' with the aid of the great wooden-barrelled foredeck windlass, just as soon as the rising flood had floated *Centaur* on an even keel.

Having, as I thought, shown that I could work hard all that day, I had not too much difficulty in persuading the skipper to let me come for a sail in his ancient engineless ship. My boss at the flour mill agreed that I would probably benefit from the experience, and gave me a few days off.

"It'll broaden your education," he said ominously.

It did, too.

With sleeping-bag and oilskins strapped on the back of my 50cc motorbike, I duly joined *Centaur* at Colchester the following weekend, where I found her alongside the quay just below the bridge, quietly awaiting the top of the tide. There was very little wind, and Nelson and his tubby mate hospitably insisted that once my bike was swung aboard and lashed to the rail aft, I should join them for a quick pint ashore before sailing.

"Where are we bound, Skipper?" I asked, when we were properly ensconced in the dim pub.

"Yer mean, where're we *for*, bor," he grated, and belched confidently in my ear. "'Ave to larn, won't 'e, George? Else we shan't know *wot* 'e's on abart. We're for Ipswich, bor. Cargo of beet sugar to collect there for Tate an' Lyle's at Silvertown, up the London River."

"Can I come all the way?"

"Course yer can, bor! Gearge won't mind a bit of 'elp – lazy young barskit. An' 'e won't mind showin' one o' you yotsmen wot *real* sylin's all abart. Drink up, now. That ol' tide'll 'ave slackened."

I was hungry, and the beer went a little to my head as we returned to the barge. By now there was a light wind, but it was blowing onto *Centaur* across the narrow mud-coloured river. Without setting any sail whatever, and with no motor to help him, Nelson nevertheless proceeded to get his ship under way.

First a long, fine wire was unwound from what I learned to call the 'dolly winch' – a thin-barrelled affair perched above the heavy wooden anchor windlass – and its end was taken away down the quay as far as it would reach. It looked to me too delicate to serve any purpose at all on so heavy a vessel, but Gearge, having cast off our warps, climbed back aboard and began to wind in the slack, while the skipper meantime put his back to the tarred shrouds, and his boots to the quay.

"Don't just stand there, bor!" he bawled at me. "Come an' 'eave!"

I joined him. With what air there was pressing *Centaur* onto the quay, I could not believe that our puny efforts, however much strength he and I could apply, could have even the slightest effect. For a very long time nothing perceptible happened, and I became more and more convinced that my leg was being well and truly pulled.

"She's a-goin' now."

I felt nothing. No movement at all. Then I realised that somehow there was indeed a widening inch or two of clear water showing between the ship's thickly tarred side and the concrete at our feet. And slowly, very slowly, *Centaur* commenced to slide further out and to edge gently forward, as Gearge got another few turns on the dolly winch.

"Na' then, bor," said the skipper, jerking his thumb in the direction of the deck. "Row."

I hesitated. "R-row?"

"Yus. Row. Yer *can* row, carn't yer? Look lively, then. Big sweep there on the main 'atch. 'Ere; let *me* show yer."

He did too. If my memory serves me, *Centaur* was over 80ft (almost 25m) from stem to stern, and beamy at that. Yet before long the steady, slow strokes of that mighty oar, and the mate's careful work on the dolly-winch wire, produced adequate steerage way. As we came abreast of the end of the quay, Gearge hopped ashore again and released his wire, then jumped back as the skipper swung her stern in close, so as to get her bluff bows well out into the river. I worked on at the sweep, feeling incredibly that if I didn't she would stop, and I wondered how long and for how far I would be expected to keep it up.

"Mains'l!" snapped Nelson.

Gearge moved to one of the winches near the mast, an affair rather like an antique cast-iron washing mangle. He released a metal pawl with a loud *clink,* and at once there was a rumble as of thunder, increasing to a roar for all the world like the sound of the avalanche I once experienced as a child in Switzerland. Down from the mast and from its tightly furled position above the slanting sprit, the mainsail came spreading in a cloud of new cutch-dust, to hang solid and still like a rope-festooned brown wall.

"Torps'l!"

Gearge disappeared up the ratlines on the starboard shrouds, and in a moment had loosed the tight, sausage-like bundle at the base of the forward-curving topmast.

"Leave orf a-rowin', bor!" shouted the skipper from the wheel. "You ain't doin' n' good. She's a-sylin' faster 'n you can shove 'er. Leave it on the 'atch, there, an' give Gearge an 'and with the torps'l and stays'l."

I had not realised what big and heavy sails even these smaller ones were, until I discovered just how long it took to hoist them fully. The stays'l was not so bad, since it was simply hauled up on its own block and tackle, but the tops'l took a lot of effort on the windlass for a lot of time, and my arms and back were not tuned to it. I was nearly beaten when Gearge, not even out of breath, said: "Nuff," – the first word I'd heard him speak – and went aft to part-lower one of the huge leeboards.

I looked round to see if the stays'l sheet required trimming, only to discover that the thing was made of chain, and not in any way adjustable. It was permanently set, as though the barge would never be anything other than close-hauled, the chain ending in a wicked-looking iron loop round the curved timber horse – a spar, like that similarly holding the mainsheet, which traversed the entire width of the ship and was almost as thick as a man's body. Going aft, I asked Nelson what he did about the stays'l sheet when the wind was abeam, or even astern.

"Do abart it? Don't do nuffin', bor. Looks arter itself, that do. All in the way them syles is cut, see. 'Int nuffin' as marvellous as a barge's syles, bor. Nuffin'! You'll see!"

I saw a lot of things during the next few hours that I'd never seen before – nor even imagined, come to that. But for the moment we were slipping down the narrow Colne, so close to the banks that it seemed impossible that anything much bigger than a dinghy could be rowed there, far less sailed.

Centaur seemed to fill the gap between the appearing borders of mud more than completely, and that tennis-court-sized mainsail, topped by a further, more triangular area of canvas at least half as big, looked a crazy thing to be spreading aloft when it was already sheeted in tight. There would not be the smallest chance of being able to come about on the other tack should she suddenly be headed, and she was going faster all the time. Even as I watched, the wall of canvas crumpled, rippled in slow, heavy movements, and filled again. Nelson's single eye glanced up at the fluttering 'bob'.

"Can't tack here," I laughed nervously. The river squeezed even narrower at the mouth of a small tributary, and the barge seemed to scrape along the banks.

"Tack? Never do *tack*, bor. Barge's don't tack; they 'wind'. Same thing – through the wind's eye. Yots tack. Barges *wind*." As he spoke, the sails flogged again – and went on flogging. Nelson never moved the wheel, but coolly held her there, shooting her straight towards a slight bend of the river which lay not far ahead. He glanced sideways at me. "Don't fret, bor. Ain't like yor li'l boat, y'know. Got plenty of way on 'er. There now, see that?

41

There's a long ol' reach arter this 'ere bend. We'll get 'er goin' proper in a minute."

At last he spun the wheel, eased it back, and the sails filled and quietened as *Centaur* hastened out over a rather broader stretch of water. The sedge-grass and mud began quickly receding on either hand and, as she heeled slightly, the skipper grinned round at me.

"Had the tide with 'er, see? Couldn't 'elp but come on down, sylin' or not. Better 'ere, though. Bit more depth, too. Leeb'd down, Gearge!"

"What happens when you do tack, er, *wind* a barge? Is there much to do? I once watched one being sailed single-handed up the Orwell, but of course I wasn't on board. I know the stays'l has to be let go where that rope holds it to the shrouds."

"That's the *bowlin'*, bor. 'Ave to make the stays'l go aback, till she's through the wind, like, 'cos bargis don't 'ave no grip on the water, see. Then yer lets that go, and makes it up on the other side, ready for next time."

"What about the vangs? Do you have to control the top of the sprit, or can it be left to look after itself?"

"'Ark at 'im, Gearge! 'Vangs', 'e say. *Wangs*, bor; *wangs*. An' you remember it. Nar, yer simply sets 'em for bein' close-'auled, and they looks arter theirselves. Same as the boards will, *if* she's in quiet water like now. At sea you dursn't leave the weather board down anytime. Do, she'd rip it orf."

I was impressed. "And what about the mizzen? Are we not going to set it?" The smallest sail in the ship, stepped right aft almost on top of the transom and sheeted down to the end of that barn door of a rudder, was still tightly furled about its mast and sprit.

"Ain't no need of it in *Centaur*. That's only to 'elp wind a barge when she's deep laden and not so 'andy. The ol' *Centaur* 'ardly never do need 'ers, anyway. Not with that small torps'l she sets. Balances a treat. Ol' stumpy, they calls 'er. Ruddy cheek! Right though, ain't it, Gearge? Stumpy she is, with that up there."

"You mean the tops'l is smaller than it should be?" I gasped. "Heavens! It seemed more than large enough when we were hoisting it just now."

"Nar," he chuckled. "Li'l tiddler, that is, bor. Reason for it, though. She lorst 'er topm'st in a gyle o' wind coming up past the

Buxey Beacon, one time. Broke it clean orf. For Brittle'sea, we was. An' when we gets in, why there on the jetty was this ol' yacht's mast, left over like, as nobody wants. Been wrecked, they said. So that's it up there. Course, we 'ad to recut the torps'l a bit, but ol' *Centaur* didn't mind. Fast ol' barge, she is. Look, now. There's Brittle'sea opening out ahead. Can just see the 'ouses. We done well. 'Ow abart a cuppa, Gearge?"

Gearge turned and slid out of sight down the companion-hatchway with the swift ease of familiarity. Then his grimy face reappeared – slowly.

"In't got n'tea, Skipper," he said hesitantly. "Well leastways, we got tea, an' wa'er. Clean forgot ter get milk."

The skipper mentioned a few astonishing things concerning his mate's ancestry, added that he hoped I could swallow tea neat, and told Gearge to brew up all the same and bring us something to eat, as he was 'fair to starve'. I wondered why Gearge paused, for he also must have been hungry by now. My own breakfast had been a particularly early one, and I for one was painfully empty. At last he spoke.

"Just remembered," he half mumbled, "we in't got n'grub, either, Skipper."

There was a lengthy silence. Nelson's weather-beaten face went puce.

"You know wot yer bloody done?" he almost shrieked. "Yer bloody made me speechless, that's wot!"

"It's all along of you askin' us ter the pub afore sylin'," complained Gearge, ungratefully. "You *knowed* I was abart to do the vittlin', larst thing!" He looked briefly up at me. "Sorry, bor," he said gruffly, and ducked below.

"That don't 'elp, do it!" Nelson bawled after him. He removed his cloth cap, scratched a surprisingly pale and very pink bald head, replaced his cap, and then swore quietly for the following three minutes. But he never mentioned the matter again for the rest of the trip.

The tide was well down by the time Brightlingsea, with its half-timbered watch-towered houses and crowded creeks and boatyards, had passed astern. We followed the buoyed channel seaward, while to starboard Mersea Island faded rapidly in the south-west and the broad Blackwater River opened out beyond the ever-widening mud-flats. Hot, milkless, sugarless (there wasn't even that) tea sustained us to some extent as we gybed round the Colne Point buoy. The huge wooden sheetblocks clucked and squealed as we hove in that mighty mainsheet and then eased it out on the other side when the towering sprit had swung slowly by overhead and was brought up short by the vangs. Then these too were slackened away, and the great sails squared properly out to starboard.

"Let's 'ave the spinnaker up, Gearge."

I must have looked as surprised as I felt, particularly when the sail which rose, not free and full and balloon-like as I had expected, but flat and hanked to the thin masthead forestay, was what most sailormen would call a jib-topsail. I later discovered its correct 'barge' name was 'topmast staysail', but Nelson repeatedly referred to it as 'the spinnaker'. Even so, this relatively small sail set so high up seemed to catch a good proportion of the fading breeze as we stood on into the evening's hazy, yellowing shades.

We were separated now from the open expanse of the North Sea only by the long shoal of the Gunfleet, whose sands lay beyond the horizon fully five miles off shore on the starboard bow, and, with the St Osyth marshes like a faint mist low to port, *Centaur* responded comfortably to her master's hands as he gentled the wheel a spoke or two this way and that.

"Leeb'ds up, Gearge!" He turned and grinned at me, nodding over his shoulder to the curving wake. "In a li'l ol' swatchway, 'ere," he explained. "Ain't much water, see. Shove 'er a bit much over 'ere, or over there, and we sits there till marnin'. Wouldn't 'urt us, mind; but it'd put Ipswich more'n a tide away." He sucked his teeth noisily. "Yus, real shallow. Look, them seagulls, over to port, bor." A scattering of gulls drifted on the pale, barely ruffled surface, slightly ahead of our position. "They walkin', or swimmin'?"

"Er, swimming, I think," I said. It seemed highly unlikely that they might be doing anything other than swimming so far out from the coast.

"'Ave to be sure, 'cos that do make a difference. 'S all right so long as they ain't a-walkin'. Else we'll 'ave to turn about an' 'ead right back most ways to the Bench 'Ead, there, an' goo the long ways round."

"They are swimming," I assured him, still not sure if he was joking. And the birds really were afloat, paddling out of the path of her bulky bows as the old barge ghosted in amongst them. She was moving surprisingly quickly, despite the fading wind, and I glanced up to see how she managed it. Although her great mainsail hung slack and swinging, above it in the upper wind the topsail held its shape – and so of course did Nelson's 'spinnaker'.

"*They* walkin' or swimmin'?" The skipper nudged my elbow and pointed to another patch of gulls.

I peered at them, and to my astonishment saw that they were, truly, walking. My mouth was opening to say so, but Nelson saw better with his one eye than he liked to pretend, for he was already spinning the wheel.

Steadying the barge on a new course, he looked round for his mate, realised Gearge must have gone below again, and turned to me instead.

"Ever used a leadline, 'ave yer?" He indicated the long grey weight and its coil of braided line which I had already noticed hanging by the rail. It was a very heavy one, but I had handled a lead of that size as a Naval Cadet, and recalled being taught to give it a long swing forwards and back, again and again, and then up and over one's shoulder and away out into the water ahead, so that the vessel's way would bring you over the weight as it hit the bottom, and thus give you a true reading with the line vertical. I nodded.

"Well, give us a soundin' then, bor."

I trotted forward to the main shrouds, marvelling at how far it was to them along the sidedeck, past the main cargo-hatch. Dividing the coil of line in my hands, and with one foot outboard of the bulwark and lodged among the chains and deadeyes of her rigging, I began to swing the lead to and fro, lengthening the line until the weight just cleared the water.

"Git a move on, bor!"

I swung it harder, forwards, back, longer and higher, until at last I got it whirled up clear over my head in true Navy style. Trailing the line, it whizzed out, soaring majestically ahead (though not all that straight) to plunk into the dun-coloured sea; then I was hauling it in hand over hand. There seemed masses of it. Not a moment too soon it tightened, and I dabbed the weight on what I took to be a very hard seabed, probably sand, just as it

45

passed below me. As I brought the rest up I heard hearty guffaws of laughter from back at the wheel. But I had hardly brought any further line in when up came the lead itself on the end of it. Why, it surely couldn't be *that* shallow? I turned to look aft, not knowing whether to call out such an impossibly small depth or not. Nelson was sitting on the companion-hatch, doubled up with mirth and beckoning me over. His good eye and the empty socket were both wet with tears as I approached.

"Cor!" he gasped. "Never did see such a performance! Wot you do all that whirlin' around for, bor? Where'd you ever larn to swing a lead like that? Cor! Gearge should 'ave seen that! You do that again for 'im, when 'e come on deck!" He glanced down at the lead, still dangling from my hand. "Wot yer got, anyway?"

"I, er, I th-think I must have hit a leeboard or something," I stammered, very red-faced. In my youth I was easily embarrassed, and this was quite dreadful. Nelson roared with laughter again, made an effort to stop, and exploded into a choking gurgle. All the time his hand remained on a spoke of the wheel, and the *Centaur* remained on course.

At last he stood up. "Nar, mate. You didn't strike nuffink. That ol' lead goo right out clear of everythin'; that 'ad no hoption, the way you swung it! Nar, I watched yer. Looked a good clean soundin' to me. Wot was it, bor?"

I held up the amount I had judged it to be, there being no markings of any kind on the line. "It – it looks only about four feet, Skipper, so . . ."

"Nar!" He shook his head seriously, eyeing the line. "That ain't four foot. Free foot nine, that is!" (About 1.15m.)

"B-but three foot nine *can't* be right. I mean, surely . . ."

"Wot yer worried abart? That's all right, bor! We ain't got no cargo aboard till we gets to Ipswich; do, we'd be 'ard aground long since. Nar, she's got a good free hinches under 'er, and she'll do nicely at that." His single eye inspected my appalled, disbelieving expression. "Be over the shallow part soon, so don't fret. Know this ol' swatchway well, I do. Got stuck just abart 'ere larst month, didn' I? So I had plenty time to study it. Tide's more of a neap, now." He spat over the rail.

I gazed about at the miles of empty water surrounding us. "But how can you tell just where we are?"

"By that soundin' of yours. Just right that was. Tell you wot, though; ol' Gearge ain't a patch on you when that come to 'eavin' a lead. Ain't 'arf as funny, neither. 'Allo!" Suddenly he glanced astern over his shoulder, and the great sprit above us creaked loudly. "Closish, mind. She's a-smellin' the bottom. Can you feel 'er, bor? All sluggish like. Bit o' sand in 'er wake, too – see that? Ah, now there's it easin'. She'll goo clear all right now. Right, bor. Put that ol' lead away – an' coil it proper! Don't want ol' Gearge to get it tangled next time, when I try an' get 'im to swing it like you did. Dear, oh dear. Right then, now you come an' take 'er for a spell. Reckon Gearge must've turned in, the lazy young barskit. Out on the tiles 'e wos, larst night. Though 'oo the 'ell 'ud go out wiv 'im, Gawd alone knows!"

As I took the wheel, first laying my hands on the spokes between Nelson's before he let go, it seemed that the barge suddenly lengthened to twice or three times her already vast size. Far away ahead of me she stretched, and just visible beyond that distant bow, faint in the haze, I could make out the Martello tower at Walton-on-the-Naze. Clacton-on-Sea was coming up in shore of us, its buildings hard to see under the setting sun. Spread before me, the canvas-coated cargo-hatch seemed almost like a pale-green road, strewn with ladders, huge coils of rope hawser, the mighty rowing sweep and other oddments. Above, over the seaward side of the ship, hung her great tanned cliff of a mainsail, swaying gently and heavily. Over it the topsail tapered ever upwards, blooming bronze and gold now in the reddening sunglow. The little scarlet 'bob' flapped brilliantly but lazily above everything against the fading blue of the sky – but I hardly dared look so far away from our course. Walton was in the weather rigging, and there for the moment I concentrated on keeping it. (Photo page 33.)

There was so little wind, and I imagined the great barge must be sluggish on her helm. Tentatively, by way of experiment, I tried it over a spoke or two. As I had thought; nothing much happened – at first. Then suddenly she was winging round, curving her wake in a wide swathe astern as she swept towards the wind. Nelson grinned evilly at me, as I wound the wheel back again.

"Yo're over-doin' it, bor; an' she don't like that. Twist yer arms orf, she will, if you do that! You steady 'er, bor; and just keep 'er goin' as she was."

47

It grew dusk as we slid darkly on over the now covered sands near the Naze, and Gearge appeared and lit the massive red and green oil navigation lamps in their boxes on the main shrouds. Yellow glints winked on and shimmered from the distant shore lights at Walton, and somewhere ahead a number of small flashing lights began blinking their messages out of the gathering night, dim and low on the water, marking the approaches to Harwich.

When Gearge took over from me, I went straight below, tired out. The vertical ladder into the stern cabin was not easy to manage with cold legs stiffened from standing so long. An oil-lamp with a smoky glass swung slowly from its hook beneath the dark skylight, turned low so as not to destroy night vision if there came a call for 'all hands'. Loud snores from a black rectangle in the panelling to one side told me where the skipper was already asleep. The other black cubbyhole must belong to Gearge. I found my rolled-up sleeping-bag and canvas hold-all by tripping over them, and was soon stretched out on a nine-inch-wide wooden settee along the side of the cabin.

And so I missed probably the most interesting part of the passage, for the first thing that woke me was the distant clanking and clattering of one of the antiquated winches which worked the brails of the huge mainsail. Groggy with a sleep which it seemed had hardly begun, I scrambled out and up on deck. It took me a moment to get my bearings, for the town lights of Harwich and Felixstowe were astern now, and I could only just make out the familiar dark bulk of high land looming nearby to port. We were close in under Shotley Spit, already entering the Orwell River.

Nelson was back at the wheel, and overhead the mainsail was slowly shrinking, bunching itself up and in towards the mast and sprit as Gearge wound home the last of the brails. The little 'spinnaker' and the staysail were gone too, stowed or lowered; only the topsail now remained full and drawing, like a nightmarish black wing hanging above us in the sky, blotting out star after star as we slid on.

Presently the skipper put the wheel hard over, and the sail began to thump as it spilled wind. The night rang with the metallic shrill of a winch when with a deft movement the mate let go the halyard, and the tops'l crumpled to nothing above the crosstrees. Shivering in the cold air, I hurried forward to help him slosh bucketfuls of seawater over the wooden barrel of the windlass, so that the anchor chain could be rapidly veered. At last the call to let go came from the stern, and the vast, rusty anchor was sent plunging on its way. The last rumble of the chain died, and only the quiet *clop* of the tide round the old ship's bows accompanied the repeated and plaintive hoots of an owl hunting among the invisible trees inshore.

With the yellow beams of the riding-light to help us stow the staysail and trice it up like a long thin sausage clear of the foredeck, Gearge became suddenly talkative.

"Just arter 'igh water," he explained, as he belayed its halyard. "Carn't goo n'further, with 'ardly no wind, see. Skipper, 'e say we goo up to Ipswich on the marnin' flood."

And so we did. The strange thing was, although it was something like twenty-eight hours or more since I had last eaten, by the time we were berthed I could hardly finish the delicious fry heaped before me in the waterside canteen there. For one thing, there were no fewer than seven sailing barges made fast just outside the window, and for another, all the chat around me in the smoky atmosphere was of 'wangs' and 'spreets' and 'torps'ls', not to mention the many more feminine matters of which sailormen are wont to talk. No doubt about it; my boss at the Maldon mill had been quite right. It was proving a definite broadening of my education!

3
NEVER TAKE NOTHIN'
FOR GRANTED

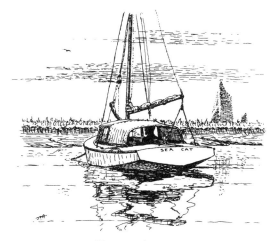

Down river

"Skipper's smashed 'is kneecap," the lad from the half-loaded barge alongside explained. "We could do with a bit of 'elp."

I looked round at Nelson, keenly. His one eye twinkled as he nodded at the youth and jerked a thumb in my direction.

"Can 'ave 'im, if yer don't mind a yotsman," he crackled mischievously. "Knows nuffin' abart bargis, mind; but yer simply *got* ter see 'im 'eavin' the lead, 'cos that 'e *can* 'do, an' no mistake!"

With this unusual recommendation, I became a deck-hand aboard the Sailing Barge *George Smeed*. And half an hour later I was stickily covered in raw beet-sugar from the 200 tons of bagged cargo I was helping to load, while Skipper Hardy directed his sixteen-year-old mate Jim Hale and myself from a beer-crate on which he perched painfully by the wheel. Known as 'Hale and Hardy' they were, or so Nelson had said, and they proved great company in spite of their difficulties. It was quite an

(*above*) Drying out on Medway mud; the expansive foredeck of the 27ft Prout Ranger catamaran, *Paradis*; (*below*) Launching day: *Twintail* emerges into the Canvey Island sunlight from her builder's shed

TWINTAIL

(*above*) 'Where the heck'll I stow the cornflakes?' Provisions come aboard for the 700-mile delivery trip to Ulster; (*below*) The ideal ships for kids to grow up in; an evening anchorage on the West Coast of Scotland

experience, helping them sail that big, engineless ship round to Tate and Lyle's, seventy miles away, and up the winding Thames.

Under our injured skipper's tutoring, us two lads drove the leaky old hull hard to windward through day and dark, in an effort to get him to a London hospital as soon as we could. By the end of that trip I could tack (well, all right, 'wind') a 'spritty' single-handed at night, or scramble aloft in half a gale to clear the remaining ribbons of a blown-out sail from the rigging, while the decks and cargo-hatches 60ft (18m) below were dimly awash with streaming white water.

It was not all 'go', despite our rush. Injuries or no, Gordon Hardy knew that the fastest way to get a sailing boat through the estuary was sometimes to wait out a tide at anchor. And then, with the doors of the coal-burning range wide open before us in the stern cabin, and the roasting glow of its fire glinting merrily on the dark panelling, I was taught a number of astoundingly masculine songs, which quite definitely added further know-ledge to my upbringing.

My own tiny *Sea Cat*, lying peacefully on the mud alongside the Hythe at Maldon, seemed almost too small to set foot in when I looked down at her a couple of weekends later. But the brown, bubbly edge of the flood tide was crawling and swirling in over the muddy depressions made by her resting keel and chines, with such excited little rushes and scurries that its call could not be denied.

Admittedly, it was not a marvellous day, for a brisk April wind shook the sedge-grasses on the far side of the creek, and low clouds marched steadily eastwards overhead – but so what? The barometer in the hall of my 'digs' had been rising at breakfast-time, and besides, I had just been to sea in a real gale, so a mere fresh breeze didn't scare me.

I looked down again at little *Sea Cat*, and watched a frothy finger of water racing towards her along a gully by her stern. The Blackwater, with all its fascinating creeks and anchorages, lay waiting to be explored – and after deserting her for a couple of weeks, I surely owed my own boat a good long sail. A glance at my watch told me it was still barely half past nine. Oilskins I'd need, and something to eat. It would take only a few minutes if I hurried.

On my way back to The Old Coffee House to collect my sleeping-bag, I met young 'Titch' in the main street.

"Not sailin', then?" he asked, looking up at me.

"Just going to," I said. "Hey, do you want to come? I thought of going down river for the rest of the weekend, and it would be nice to have a crew. I reckon you're just about short enough to fit on *Sea Cat's* floor at night. There's an airbed you could . . ."

"Cor!" he squeaked, his small face lighting up with instant enthusiasm. "You bet! Tide'll be lifting your bo't in about twenty minutes, won't it? I'll have to tell me mum, and get me things. See you on board!"

I chuckled as he dashed off, his shock of dark hair bobbing and weaving through the throng of Saturday-morning shoppers. Though without a boat of his own, he knew the details and position of every craft, large or small, berthed at or near Maldon, and could call the precise state of the tide to mind at any moment.

Sea Cat was indeed on the verge of floating as we clambered down the mud-dusted rungs of the ladder and rolled back her hooped canvas cover to stow our bedding and knapsack of provisions. The short-luffed "cruising" mainsail (prized relic of the first boat I had ever sailed in) was already bent on, and could be hoisted in seconds. I had already learned to organise *Sea Cat's* gear with snap-shackles and other quick and easily handled devices in order to avoid wasting precious sailing time, and knew the special joy of being able, more or less, just to step aboard and go, instead of having to spend ages doing up conventional shackle-pins and undoing endless knots and lashings.

"Use your big genoa?" asked Titch expectantly, for he knew every sail I possessed, despite the fact he had never before been on board. "Got to push her over the ol' flood, 'aven't we?"

As I ducked into the cuddy and returned with the bagged sail, the boat gave a small wriggle under us and came suddenly alive, swinging to her tethering warps. We grinned at each other, sharing the thrill of it, and as the strident tones of the old clock in the square church-tower nearby clanged out the hour of ten, we turned her shapely bow downstream, and were soon lowering the heavy drop-keel in the deeper water of the channel. I must say I was glad of its lumpy ballast as we gybed round for the reach past Northey's grassy sea-wall, and sped on towards the masts down at Heybridge. The cold breeze was rather stronger than I think either of us had anticipated.

A fine big bow-wave hissed out from under the forward chines as we rushed through the moorings there, with Titch huddled in the lee of the Perspex-windowed 'cabintop', and myself perched well out on the narrow sidedeck. Thin sunlight momentarily brightened the row of bungalows to port as we freed the sheets again off Mill Beach, to start the long run eastwards. (Page 28.)

Short, steep-faced little seas hurried with us now, tumbling in confusion over the incoming current, and Osea Island, in the distance, seemed to hover across our bow as *Sea Cat* suddenly yawed on a breaking crest. As though looking before she leaped, she hesitated, then all at once lifted her broad flat counter, surfed forward, raised her bow and roared onto a full plane. Spray fanned out on either side from somewhere under her mid-section, and the short tiller went almost rigid in my hand, while a vibrating hum from her keel rose in pitch to a low whine. And she held it, going like a speedboat.

Never before or since have I planed a single-hulled sailing craft so far or at such a breathless, breakneck pace. The dark, bending trees of Osea were quickly brought abeam to port; Maylandsea Bay and Lawling Creek opened out to starboard and equally soon were gone, with only a glimpse of the collection of boats there and the shed roofs of Cardnell's yacht yard. At Stone Point, as we sped by the handful of moorings off the Sailing Club, a momentary wind-shadow from the high end of Osea seemed to clamp around us like a vacuum, and with upflung bow *Sea Cat* fell off the plane and sagged back, so that a wavecrest overtook her and the top of it surged over the aft-decking and into the tiny cockpit. But she was up and off again at once, and in seconds Titch had the little bilge-pump squirting away, its jets scattering into fine spray in the chasing wind.

Inevitably, as we thumped, banged and bounded onwards down the ever widening Blackwater, the seas became longer and larger too, and the little boat swooped and soared on each, overtaking one after the other in her mad rush. I had by now got the cover of her plate-case sufficiently watertight, so that even in these conditions never more than a cupful or two slopped up and inboard, but in my excitement I almost forgot that in making her into a cruising boat I could no longer risk a capsize with impunity. Though undoubtedly self-righting with that ballasted keel, I knew only too well that if we suffered a knock-down now, her cut-away decking and extra weight could well have us in trouble; and there was all our bedding, our stores, and the little cooker to consider, quite apart from us and the boat.

Breaking crests were all about us out here in the open, and as I held her precariously on her course, I began to appreciate the difference between the sort of wind and sea conditions which a sailing barge could happily cope with, and what was safe for a 15ft (4.6m) dinghy. It had been one thing, smashing the bluff and sturdy bows of *George Smeed* into the teeth of a Force 7 a few days previously as we hammered her down the East Swin and along the edge of the Maplin Sands; but while this present Saturday morning breeze was little more than Force 5 at most, the scale of *Sea Cat* was tiny in comparison to the seas being kicked up, even here in the Blackwater.

"Would you rather we turned back, Titch?" I shouted, over the thrumming of the drop-keel. He looked round, his face glistening with blown spray.

"Naw – that's too good, ain't it! Let's hold on for Bradwell. Nearly there, anyway. There's Peewit Island on the lee bow, see? Should pick up the creek at the far end any moment now."

I glanced up at the straining mainsail. There was surely much more wind than when we had set out, and I knew very well that we should have reefed long ago. The trouble was – how? It could not be done with the boat planing like this, yet if we turned into the wind now, both it and the seas would, I realised to my utter consternation, be more than she might safely take.

The lesson that every sailing man learns sooner or later, was being forced upon me in no uncertain manner: a following wind is lessened by one's speed, but when one turns to sail into it, its strength may in effect be doubled.

Suddenly there was no time left for contemplation – the first of the withies marking Bradwell Creek's twisting entrance was already abeam, riding the spray and forcing me to decide.

"Up on the sidedeck, Titch!"

As he wedged himself between my left elbow and the edge of the cuddy, I gingerly eased the helm down. "Jib in flat!" I yelled, and as *Sea Cat* swerved off the plane, I received a wavetop right in the small of my back.

Careering round, the little boat heeled over in a smother of foam, punched through the next crest, and was suddenly head to wind with everything flogging. A sea burst clean over the foredeck and exploded against the cuddy's windows, soaking us with flying spume. It seemed impossible that she should tack successfully, but Titch knew his job, and clung onto that genoa sheet with all his might until the sail back-filled with a thud, and thrust the bow swiftly round to port. At once he let it across and sheeted it in, and with the mainsail flogging, we flew shorewards.

The tops of several withies showed across our course, but neither of us knew the depth over the bank which they marked, for the place was new to both of us. This was long before the days of atomic power stations and marinas, and all that could be seen over the saltings here were the masts of a smack or two, and a handful of houses further in amongst a clutch of windblown trees. It was early in the season for many cruising craft to be about, and there was no one to guide us in.

I wanted badly to risk crossing the bank so as to avoid having to beat, but *Sea Cat* was tearing across the seas, sheering and yawing and roaring among the crests at a great rate, and I did not dare attempt it. Instead I bore away for the tail of the bank, and once more she lifted onto a plane. Coming off it inside the channel was easier than before, for here the water was already smoother; but I had to throw her right up into the wind to help Titch get that big genoa flat enough for the short beat with which we were now inevitably faced.

Of course we would have been better to have dropped the mainsail, but at that time I did not know enough about handling the boat in that wind strength to be sure I could control her under headsail alone. As it was, the drag of the flogging main did nothing to help us, and there was a frightful moment when she missed stays on the inshore end of a tack, and we had to make a second try with the main sheeted home and water pouring in over the lee coaming as she turned. Again it needed the two of us to get the genoa in, and at once *Sea Cat* became unruly, luffing against the helm until we could both hang right out over her side, using our combined weight to bring her more upright. Every time we let her heel more than lee-rail down, she got so hard-mouthed that the rudder could do nothing to hold her. But we made it, somehow.

At last the sheltering banks, though only a few feet above what was now high water, closed around us, and we were able to bear off on a reach within the creek itself. A violent gust hissed off the grass-topped bank to windward, filling the mainsail with a bang, and this time she griped round so far that we must have been within inches of ramming the mud. But still I had insufficient wit to get the sail off her – and nearly paid for this omission dearly.

An aged smack-yacht was lying peacefully at anchor across our course, the smoke from her cabin chimney swirling past her old owner, who stood pipe in mouth, watching us with his back against the boom. Fearing her long bowsprit, I bore away slightly, intending to pass cleanly astern of her; but the blustering wind had not completed its lesson.

At the crucial moment, a squall angled unexpectedly over Peewit Island and no amount of eased sheet could prevent the mainsail from taking charge. *Sea Cat* heeled, luffed, and I hove on the tiller. The rudder stalled with a gurgling rumble, and round she came against it in a swirl of foam, heading right for the smack's sharply raked transom. I remember seeing the old skipper above me bite clean through his pipe-stem as our bow swept round below that overhanging stern. How our forestay cleared it and the end of the heavy boom, I shall never be sure.

'The rudder stalled with a gurgling rumble . . .'

The squall died or something, and we found ourselves sailing on round the next bend, to anchor rather breathlessly and safely out of sight of the smack, off the rotting remains of the ancient jetty.

Neither of us mentioned the incident as we tidied the sodden sails, rigged the cockpit-cover and then crawled in to the cramped confines of the cuddy for a well-earned lunch – to discover that it was by no means yet lunchtime. After peering at my watch in disbelief, Titch looked up in amazement.

"You sure that thing's right, bor? If that is, we just done almost nine miles in not much over an hour! Why, that must be all of eight knots we average! More, I reckon, 'cos we 'ad the tide floodin' most of the way. Cor! She can goo, your lil' ol' bo't. Real flier! Reckon she's a bit of a joker too, mind. Gave me quite a start, comin' in under that ol' smack!"

Our simple lunch, despite being early, tasted very good indeed, but all through the gusty afternoon which followed, my mind kept playing back over the way the boat had kept rounding into the wind each time her rail went down. She had never done that in her standard trim as a racing dinghy, and I concluded that although her hull shape had been perfectly all right for that, now that I had added so much weight, her new deeper waterlines were ill-balanced when heeled to any great extent. Fascinated, I spent an hour or two sketching her lines on a page from Titch's school exercise book, and working out the certainly curious-looking shapes presented as she was progressively pressed over. Ever since that day, different hull forms and their various effects at sea have constantly intrigued me.

It was some time before I realised that Titch was becoming anxious about something. He kept wiping the condensation from the cuddy's windows and peering out at the windy creek. The tide had gone, and the banks of Peewit Island afforded perfect shelter, but every so often a squall would still shake the top of our metal mast, and remind us that it was even yet blowing hard outside.

"I gotta be back to school Monday mornin'," said Titch at last. "Got exams, see. You reckon she'll go to wind'ard all right if that's still blowin' like this tomorrow?"

I shrugged. "The glass was rising when we left, so I think the wind could come more out of the west, and maybe drop a bit, don't you?"

He shook his head. "Old westerly tends to hang on, bor. Wouldn't count on that changing much. Tell you what, though; that'll drop calmer come sunset, leastways for an hour or so. We could work upriver a bit then."

"How can you be sure it will?"

"Why, that always do drop with the sun, after the glass has been low. Don't you know that? 'Course that do! Flood'll be makin' by then, too. Reckon we should sail back up towards Osea or Maylandsea. Be a bit nearer home." He grinned sheepishly for a moment. "Not sayin' but what I *want* not to get 'eld up, mind. Never was no good at French verbs."

Tea was followed by supper, and between the two I prepared the boat as best I could for her first night sail. Titch was sure he could pilot us safely enough once we got to the upper part of the river, which he knew well, and my good night vision should come in handy. *Sea Cat*, however, carried no lights other than a torch and a tiny paraffin 'storm lantern' which passed as a riding-light when at anchor.

Titch at least was proved right about the sunset calm. As we put away the supper things, a brilliant orange gleam gradually spread from under a blue-black band of cloud over Tollesbury way, glaring over the saltings and warmly lighting the drunken posts of the tumbledown jetty on the village side of our creek.

"Be windy tomorrow all right," announced Titch as we scrambled out to have a better look.

"It's dropping now though, just like you said," I remarked, and began rolling the cover out of the way. "We'd best get away now,if we're going at all. Working jib, though; I'm none too keen on scaring that smack skipper again as we sail out."

"Owe 'im a new pipe, you do," giggled Titch. "Chumped 'is old one clean in two, he did, thinkin' we was about to board 'im."

Once safely clear of the entrance channel, we rounded the final tall withy, and gratefully found the seas much quieter than before. After one short tack out towards the middle, we were able almost to lay straight up the Blackwater, but what wind there was kept fading more and more as the sun sank and finally vanished. At last, in order to keep her going, I went forward and changed the jib for the genoa.

Not another craft was moving, and as blue dusk closed in it got very cold. *Sea Cat* seemed content enough, rustling softly through the dark water so upright that the two of us could sit down on the floorboards, in the shelter of the little cuddy. We sang to keep warm, but soon we had other problems. Heavy clouds had again covered the moonless sky, leaving only a few distant farm lights as virtually our only points of reference. It was hard to make out where water stopped and saltings began, so dark did that night become.

The compass, an ex-RAF wartime affair in a grey wooden box, was placed on the floor between us and its dimly luminous grid helped somewhat, though its accuracy so close to our steel drop-keel was as much in doubt as the course we chose to set on it, for I had only an Esso road map by way of a chart. In those narrow, muddy waters, it had always seemed good enough – for daytime pottering.

An hour passed, and one by one the yellow glints from farmhouse windows blinked out as the occupants went to bed, and we felt lonely and disorientated in their absence. I became gradually more uneasy, for the tide was now turning, and I imagined us being swept back downstream, and maybe having to spend the whole night blundering about. Titch was just saying he thought we must be close to the moorings off Stone Point, when he suddenly jerked round and stared back over the quarter.

"Wasn't that a mooring buoy? Where's that torch?"

He flicked its beam on, and sure enough picked out the dark outline of a small barrel such as many a mooring was buoyed with, receding in our wake. He kept the light trained on it as I gybed round, and in moments he was on his tummy on the foredeck with an outstretched arm either side of the forestay, one still holding the torch.

"Got it!" he called back a moment later, and with a surge of relief, I let go the halyards and began stowing sail. Titch seemed to be taking his time getting the mooring on board.

"You all right?" I enquired eventually.

"That ain't got no strop on it!" his puzzled tones came back. "Hey – you know what? That ain't a mooring at all, just an old floatin' barrel!"

Quick as I was at getting the sails up again, it took a further half hour of steady cajoling *Sea Cat* through the faint air before we once more picked up something ahead in the now waning beam of the torch. This time it was the squarish stern of a motorboat, and there could be no doubting that.

"We're up off Stone Point this time, all right," said Titch. "There'll be lots of spare buoys here, this time o' year."

I wasn't keen on any more blind hunting, however. In these conditions the motorboat's mooring could easily hold the both of us.

"Get a line on her," I said, luffing towards her quarter. "We can drop back astern of her for the rest of the night."

As Titch grappled with a large cleat, I heard him mumble something.

"What's that?" I asked.

"Just checking she really is moored," he said solemnly. Then his bright laugh rang suddenly out of the darkness. "When that comes to sailin', you can't never take nothin' for granted, can yer!"

4
THE KEEL'S FALLEN OFF!

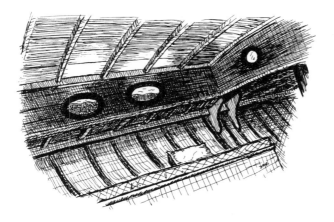

'Up the glass of her little portholes it rose . . .'

Not even people can put you in your place with quite the same deftness as the sea. It demands a respect it will never return. Now, I was not a precocious lad – quite the reverse. I usually kept myself in the background of almost any conversation, unless it was about sailing, in which case I invariably became animated and spoke out keenly. Somehow, one day, I must thus have given *Merry Maid*'s owner the impression that I was competent enough to skipper that long, lean and elegant old yacht of his. I wasn't, of course. What happened next served me right, and cut me firmly down to size.

I had sailed with Dave only two or three times when he mooted the idea of racing her in the Cruiser Class during the forthcoming 'Burnham Week'. In asking if I would crew for him, in the same breath and to my considerable surprise, he proposed that I should sail the old ship round to the Crouch for him. He would then join me there the next day. (Map page 28.)

"I – I'd love to," I stammered, "but I don't know the waters, and . . ." Vague things I'd read concerning the 'Buxey Beacon' and 'iron-hard sands' skittered through my mind.

"H'mm. Well; shouldn't worry about that," he said, puffing contentedly at his pipe in his favourite corner of the tunnel-like cabin. "Sam's going, in his little Blackwater Sloop. He'll show you the way. You can sail this old girl under easy canvas, so's to keep pace with him. I'll ask young Jack to go as your crew. Thing is, I simply can't get away next Saturday, and it's then or never. With the weather the way it's been, I hardly dare leave it till Sunday. How about it?"

He knew very well I had never been in sole charge of anything bigger than an International Dragon, but that seemed not to bother him, and besides, *Merry Maid* was also rigged as a Bermudian sloop and was basically the same shape as a Dragon, despite her age.

Designed and built by the famous Sibbick of Cowes way back in 1906, her overall length was in the order of 35ft (10.6m), but long overhangs at bow and stern reduced her waterline to a mere 24ft (7.3m). Her beam was incredibly narrow, at just 6ft 3in (1.9m), and her draught to the heel of her short ballast-keel was barely 4ft 8in (1.4m). On this was stepped a towering 40ft (12.2m) wooden mast, which had once been even longer.

Originally she had a huge gaff rig, and I used to think how wise it was of her designer to have provided her with a cabintop extending right out to the sides of the hull, instead of one which stopped short to leave sidedecks between coachroof and rail, in the more usual manner. As it was, old *Merry Maid* habitually heeled so far over that the whole side of this raised extension would immerse completely, thus presenting a much-needed reserve of buoyancy. What I did not know was that I was about to require its extra lift most earnestly, the very day I set out in her, for Burnham.

Sam and I had planned a rendezvous off the entrance to Lawling Creek at 1030, and a pleasant westerly was rippling the fawny-grey water as Jack and I rowed out to *Merry Maid* from Cardnell's yard. We soon had the big mainsail set, with a small headsail added, and reached out into Maylandsea Bay just as Sam's jolly little white sloop came running down past Osea Island, a short way ahead of us.

The need to stay close to Sam for pilotage reasons was foremost in my mind, and I therefore steered slightly more diagonally downwind across the river so as to close with him. *Merry Maid*, as usual already rail-down, lifted a little more upright as I bore away, and picked up speed. Then to my surprise she heeled again – but went on and on over. After a moment of dumb-founded astonishment I heard Jack yelling at me.

"My *God*!" he almost shrieked. "The bloody keel's fallen off!"

We could only cling to the cockpit coaming as *Merry Maid* fell even further onto her side – then very slowly and smoothly, stopped dead. The dinghy, on its long sea-going painter astern, slammed into her crazily tilted counter with a bang – and I was more relieved than words can say to hear it do so.

"It's not the keel, Jack! I've sailed her up a ruddy mudbank, that's all. She's hard aground." The understatement of the sailing season. I glanced across to where Sam was gybing round towards us, and could hardly bear the thought of the grin on his craggy face.

"You're there for the tide, boy!" he called brightly. "It's ebbing hard, and you'll never shift her at that angle. Always did say if you're going to do something, do it good and proper!"

I didn't like to ask what we should do next, but he had already worked that out for me.

"I'm going on, or I'll miss my tide through the Raysand Channel. You'll have to wait till she floats, then put her back on her mooring. I'll 'phone Dave when I get to Burnham."

Jack looked round at me. "I say, d'you think you could manage without me? See, I'd been planning to go to a dance in Burnham tonight. Made a date with this girl, and, well, I could still get there with Sam, if he'll have me."

It seemed extremely odd just to leave the old ship lying on her side like that with all sail set, and row Jack and his kitbag over to where Sam had hove to, waiting. It felt even stranger rowing back on my own, and watching them head off down river without me, while I clambered about on the motionless and slanting deck. As they finally disappeared behind Stone Point, I tried desperately to shake off the dreadful knowledge that I had made a spectacular fool of myself, and in front of a seasoned seaman like Sam, of all people. Why, he actually *lived* afloat.

Out of interest, I dabbed over the side with the boathook in the hope that perhaps . . . But her bilge was already firmly down in the mud below me. The water was barely two feet deep and falling fast, as Sam himself had said. Placing the boathook where it wouldn't roll overboard, I busied myself in lowering *Merry Maid*'s sails and stowing them as neatly as I knew how. Then I sat down to wait.

It took quite a time to remember that I should have laid out an anchor towards the channel, away on our port quarter, and it was as well I got on with doing so right away, for the dinghy itself went aground on the way back, and I only just managed to slide it over the mud by poling strenuously with the butt of an oar, to within reach of the careened yacht. The shore, the real shore bordered by its grass-covered sea-wall, looked so very far away.

Working things out, I realised that *Merry Maid* should begin to lift again in the late afternoon, and as one or two other craft were by now sailing about over where I *ought* to have steered to meet Sam, I perched myself in what I hoped looked like a comfortable and relaxed attitude on the long afterdeck, and pretended as casually as I could, to read a paperback novel I had found. It was

'. . . trying to look nonchalant . . .'

66

no good. I couldn't concentrate, gave up trying to look non-chalant, and retired to the keeled over chaos of the dark little saloon, and ate a miserable and very half-hearted lunch.

By mid-afternoon all the little mud-creatures around the curving bilge planks had begun to bubble and hiss to each other. I could hear them quite plainly, even though the wind had increased a good deal and was now moaning rather eerily in the rigging. Tiny crabs gave me an awful fright (a moment of fearful panic which I recall vividly even now) by scuttling against the planking, their clicking legs and carapaces reproducing exactly the sound of water trickling in through a bad leak. Springing to my feet, I searched under bunks and floorboards for what I felt sure was at least a badly started plank or two – but there was no more than the usual cupful or so of rusty water in the well-built old yacht's bilge, and none was coming in.

I soon thought it would, though – over the cockpit coaming. With astonishing speed, the muddy brown flood crept up and up, levelled with her rail, and climbed on steadily across the narrow bit of sidedecking abreast of her cockpit. Up the glass of the little portholes in her wide cabintop sides it rose, until finally wavelets reached and disappeared beyond the tops of the glass, and a dun-coloured gloom dimmed the steeply heeled cabin. I scrambled out, and to my horror saw the moving tide brimming towards the top of the curved cockpit coaming.

"Surely she must lift!"

I gasped the words aloud, as panic gripped my throat. Wide-eyed, mesmerised, I watched a wavelet lip over the capping rail and trickle down inside. I stared wildly round, but not a boat was in sight now, just when I could do with help. For a moment I clawed my way right up onto the weather sidedeck, but even there my weight was not far enough outboard to have the slightest effect in helping her to lift. This was one of many 'give-up-boating-for-ever' moments which have beset me, and most yachtsmen, from time to time.

In seconds, water was pouring over in little rushes, carrying with it flecks of grubby froth which swirled round and round as they found their way through gaps in the cockpit floor. I could hear it (and no mistake this time) trickling into the bilge below me. Leaping down, I hastily manned the small brass bilge-pump, but it took only seconds to see that it would be nothing like quick enough to beat the flood coming in.

Leaving the pump, I jumped into the dinghy alongside – not to abandon ship, for I was still convinced that somehow this could not really be happening and that she would surely lift. She had to. After all, I thought, as I grasped *Merry Maid*'s shrouds and tried to lift her by holding the dinghy close and leaning back, she always took the ground at her moorings in Lawling Creek quite safely, coming up each time without any of this nonsense. I had seen her doing it, dammit!

And then of course it struck me that because of her keel normally pressing into soft creek-mud, she never ordinarily heeled over as much. Out here the bottom was relatively hard and more glutinous, and her keel had hardly sunk more than a few inches. Another half minute like this, and . . . Almost numb with the thought of it, I jumped back aboard with the idea of thrusting downwards with the big whisker-pole stowed on her long foredeck. As I bent to loosen it, the sloping deck trembled, and she lurched upwards with water pouring off the sidedeck.

My sudden movement near the bow had apparently broken the mud's hold, and my relief was indescribable. A few lusty minutes at the little bilge-pump cleared all that had come in, and it was seemingly no time at all before she began slowly and jerkily to turn round, upright and lively, to face her anchor. At least I now understood the full meaning of the term 'stuck in the mud'.

The next problem was to get my charge back to her mooring, but I was badly unnerved by having put her aground and could barely recall the lie of the channel back into the creek. Besides, how ever would I put this engineless yacht, with all her miles of elongated foredeck, back on a mooring single-handed? To make matters worse, evening was approaching, and before long it would be dark.

I funked it, and setting the big mainsail, got the anchor and found she had paid off in the direction of Osea Island. Well, if that was the way she wanted to go, why not? She would lie safely afloat over there. Reaching over to the island's tree-lined shore was easy; then I put the helm down, ran forward, and soon had her anchored.

I never feel at my best at dusk, but I lay worrying long into the night. I fretted about the tide sluicing past the anchor chain, and about the wind clapping the unfrapped halyards on that huge pole of a mast. Was it strengthening? What if she started to drag? And, whatever would her owner think when he got Sam's message and arrived at Lawling Creek to find her mooring still vacant . . .?

Going to sleep took ages.

And nothing awful did happen.

By morning I had regained enough confidence to attempt putting her back in the creek, and was already sailing gently towards it when a large motor-yacht came creaming down from the direction of Maldon. Dave's unmistakably bulky figure was on her foredeck. He said not a word as I shot *Merry Maid* head to wind alongside, nor when he climbed aboard with another lad of about my own age, and indeed never ever mentioned the incident, beyond asking if everything was all right. Thanking the motor-yacht's owner for his trouble, he took the helm and off we cruised down the Blackwater and out into the Thames Estuary as though this was what he had planned in the first place.

That taught me much about what makes a skipper popular with his crew.

Past the Buxey Beacon, we threaded our way down the Raysand Channel until Foulness Sand and the low grey entrance to the Crouch opened up on the starboard bow. By then the weather really was threatening, and the wind decidedly fresher. A fine rain began falling as we tore up river on our side (I thought of the water lipping over that coaming again and again, but kept it to myself), and by the time we had rounded into the wind beyond the large clubhouse at Burnham a gale was quite obviously brewing. Had it come twenty-four hours earlier, things might have been very different indeed.

Merry Maid won no prizes during Burnham Week that year, though we certainly had some fast and exciting sailing. I remember seeing the big ocean-racer *Jocasta* chasing down to the river-mouth astern of us, setting up a rhythmic roll of such gigantic proportions that not only was her main boom end gouging deep into the water on one side, but her much higher spinnaker boom was also dipping as she swung away over onto the other. Behind her, *Maid of Pligh*, one of the first hard-chine plywood cruiser-racers, was flying a colossal pale-blue spin-naker, and while we watched *Jocasta*'s antics as she roared past us, a wisp of something tickled my ear. Brushing at it, I found myself with a handful of pale-blue nylon, and glanced over our counter to see *Maid of Pligh*'s kite in tatters, flags of its gossamer cloth ripping from the leech-lines, and nothing, nothing at all, in the middle.

But the sight which made its most lasting mark on me came just after the final race. We were back at anchor above the clubhouse, and busy stowing *Merry Maid*'s mainsail preparatory to going ashore, when a small craft of some kind shot out from the club slipway. Sailing bolt upright, it rocketed across the river at what seemed a completely impossible pace, gybed without the slightest suggestion of a roll or any sort of difficulty despite the extremely fresh breeze, and then tore off downstream. And all the while it remained as upright as a church, but with a couple of speedboat-like 'rooster-tails' rising from behind what at first sight seemed a most unusually broad stern.

"What in blazes was that?" enquired Dave.

"Some new-fangled design the Prout boys are playing with," said Tony, the other member of our crew. "They call it a 'catamaran', or something. Doesn't half go!"

I stared after it, wondering how any sailboat could go so fast – and so upright. "Just imagine a cruising boat that didn't heel," I said without thinking, and got a very stony look from Dave.

5
BUILDING ON A DREAM

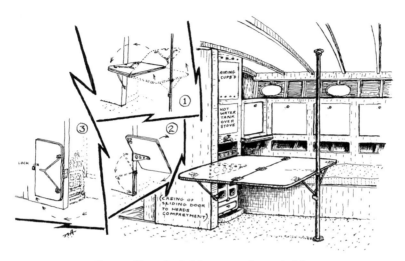

Ocean Dove's foldaway saloon table

By now I had read such yachting classics as McMullen's *Down Channel*, Eric Hiscock's *Wandering Under Sail*, and of course Slocum's *Sailing Alone Round the World*, and though ocean-going did not greatly appeal, I nevertheless began longing for a more ambitious kind of coastal cruising than could reasonably be accomplished in tiny *Sea Cat*. With my training over, I put her up for sale, returned to the business in Ulster, and once more took up evening racing on Belfast Lough. But there was something now really worth looking forward to: a partnership with my father in the 28ft 6in (8.7m) gaff cutter *Ocean Dove*, which he then had commenced to build in our own back garden.

Now, of all the traps which lie in wait for the would-be cruising man, one of the worst and most common is this romantic desire to start by building one's own first boat. Lurking too in the 'small print' of one's mind is often the delightful fantasy of - someday – sailing her across the oceans of the world. There would be dolphins under the bow, a steady tradewind, and nought but a swimsuit or less to impede a golden tan; then perhaps a warp ashore to the leaning stem of a stout palm tree, whose waving fronds rustled beneath the pinnacled peaks of a tropical isle. Grass skirts, even . . .

The result of such bewitching, if one then goes ahead and builds the vessel with one's own hands, is a natural tendency to add extra strength to the construction, so as to be sure she will 'withstand anything'. (A letter to the designer should bring forth either advice on how to do this properly, or the firm assurance that she is already arranged to be quite strong enough for such purposes, thus saving you much extra work and expense, not to mention your spoiling a good ship with excess weight.)

One thing is certain: the job of building (even of finishing a fibreglass hull) will take *much* longer than one imagines. That is why there are always a number of sad advertisements in the yachting magazines for 'part finished' or 'almost completed' craft. (And some of them might well be worth a cautious glance, if you are thinking along such lines.) But the job *can* be done, and sometimes expertly, by amateurs. The main benefit is ending up knowing exactly what holds the boat together, and the only snag *may* be that she will fetch a slightly lower price than a professionally built sistership, if you ever came to sell her. But then of course, you never would.

The only advice worth offering to someone afflicted with this urge to build his very first cruising yacht – apart from that disheartening word 'don't' – is that he should first of all sail in as many different sorts of craft as he can get invited aboard, and read all he can about the kind of cruising he (honestly) has in mind. That is the only way to end up with anything like the 'right' boat. Coastal sailing in north European waters, for example, demands one type of vessel; island-hopping in sunnier climes quite another. And any sort of prolonged ocean-cruising favours something else again, as does family sailing, as opposed to purely single-handed stuff – or passage racing.

It is undoubtedly wiser to start by buying, second-hand, something *like* your dreamship, and then to sail her for a year or two, before selling her and building in the light of that experience – *if* you can bear to wait that long. But well, once the building idea has taken root . . .

We already knew, my father and I, that what makes any boat suitable or unsuitable for an individual, or a given purpose, is not the number of bunks nor the engine nor the rig, nor even the external appearance of her as she lies afloat; it is always the bit you cannot normally see: the profile and entire set of sections of her underwater body, keel and rudder. Careful study of other people's cruising yarns, with that in mind, will help one choose the right design features to satisfy one's own special needs correctly.

Even so, like many beginners, we were certain that by building the boat ourselves we would end up with our 'ideal' craft, first time off. But we did read, and we did manage to sail in a number of very different boats belonging to understanding and very tolerant friends, before finalising our ideas.

Gradually we reached the conclusion that, for us, the most perfect yacht would be beamy and stiff, with powerful, full-sectioned bows and a long keel to provide steadiness on the helm. A sheltered cockpit seemed a good idea too, for we planned mainly to cruise off the West Coast of Scotland, our nearest and unquestionably most beautiful explorable area. Beautiful, that is, when the sun shone. Whenever it didn't it could be very chilly even in the height of summer, and we figured a spacious, cosy saloon lit and warmed by oil-lamps and a real, slow-combustion bogey stove would be just the thing.

Other folk could have their fast, furious, sail-on-your-ear type of semi-racing yachts if they liked, but, enfolded for good now in the cruising bug's dreamlike wings, we reasoned that it would always be nicer to arrive in a slow but steady ship that hadn't exhausted us *en route*, than to come into an anchorage soaked, cold and tired out, with only cramped, cheerless accommodation in which to try and recuperate.

There seemed no designer more completely at one with our feelings than Maurice Griffiths, whose evocative East Coast cruising yarns and wonderful books contained, it appeared to us, the very essence of sensible, seamanlike cruising. Nothing spectacular – just comfortable, homely pottering under sail.

Thus, during the next few years, there steadily grew in the covered yard at the back of our home a modified Griffiths Maplin Class gaff cutter, carvel-built of tough African mahogany planking on, quite literally as it happened, home-grown Irish oak ribs.

We cut her keel and bilge-stringers by hand from massive pitch-pine beams rescued from a dismantled warehouse. And so excellent were those three-hundred-year-old timbers that as I adzed them into shape in the garden one winter weekend, the golden resin oozed from the shavings as though from fresh-cut branches, unbelievably tangy and sharp-smelling in the crisp, frosty air. They had, however, occasional hidden snags in the form of long-forgotten iron nails, often invisibly embedded where they had rusted away during the centuries of the wood's commercial life.

I had just resharpened the great curved-handled adze and standing astride what was to be the port bilge-stringer, I was chipping away manfully when the blade leapt slightly sideways towards my right ankle.

Thinking I had better be more careful, I bent to look at the wood for the tell-tale shine of one of those ancient nails – and felt my foot slip and seem to squirm wetly. From beneath a darkening stain on my trouserleg I was astonished to see blood come welling over the edge of my shoe to spread rapidly in a scarlet pool among the yellow shavings. Yelling to my father, I managed to slow the spurting by pressing with my thumbs above my split shin, and within half an hour we were back from the doctor's, coldly comforted by that worthy's comment that it would have been worse if the blade had not been good and sharp. He made the necessary stitches with strong black Irish linen thread, instead of gut, and it worked every bit as well.

Only one other major accident occurred during the building, but this time, alas, to our lovely ship. It was during the planking up stage, when her ribs and stringers were being held to the designed shape in the traditional manner by stout but temporary 'frames', cut to the required sections and screwed down to the keel so that they could later be removed when planking was complete. Normally a boatyard would build such a boat in a tall shed, and brace these frames downwards from the roof beams in order to counteract the immense upward squeeze as successive planks (in *Ocean Dove*'s case admittedly of much tougher wood than specified) were added below her bilges. We, unfortunately, had no adequate means of doing this, and one night the whole household was awoken by a sudden loud report.

A hasty torchlight search revealed nothing other than repeated rips in our night-clothes as we clambered among the rough timbers – but daylight presented us with the full and awful truth. Every one of those temporary frames had burst off the keel and sprung up, by varying amounts, allowing the hull to become noticeably more 'V'eed below the waterline than its good designer would ever have thought typical of his work. There was absolutely nothing we could do to force them back down.

In due course, therefore, when *Ocean Dove* (the 'Dove of Peace' being our family crest from a previous era) was launched and moored in Belfast Lough, complete with black hull, white rails, tall Dutch-type gaff rig and tanned sails – yes, and the oil-lamps and bogey stove – she floated several inches below her marks. And still did after all our friends and well-wishers had had their drinks on board, and been ferried ashore again.

The altered shape and slacker bilges caused by that regrettable breaking-away of the frames was, we saw now, in fact only half the culprit. The other half had been our own excessive determination to 'make her good and strong'. In our innocence, we had not only used heavier woods than those prescribed on the plans, but had unnecessarily increased most of the rigging and fitting sizes as well. It was a stiff lesson, and did much to teach me about yacht design.

All the same, the newly launched *Ocean Dove* to our eyes looked absolutely magnificent, and fortunately she proved in due course to have first-rate sea-going qualities, which was just as well, since her very first sail was to last sixteen hours and take us across to Scottish waters. This was not quite as unplanned as it may sound, but our holiday was restricted to a particular fortnight in July, and bad weather prevented any earlier excursions other than those essential for engine trials and compass adjusting.

Knowing that our own navigational abilities were still somewhat doubtful, we managed to persuade Herbert, a previous shipmate of mine, to pilot us out of Belfast Lough, fifty miles diagonally across the strong tides of the North Channel to Campbeltown on the Kintyre peninsula, into the furthest reaches of the Firth of Clyde, and then home again. We remained prepared to turn back at any stage of that initial passage, but the conditions on the evening we let go our mooring at Cultra were little short of perfect for sail-stretching – virtually flat calm.

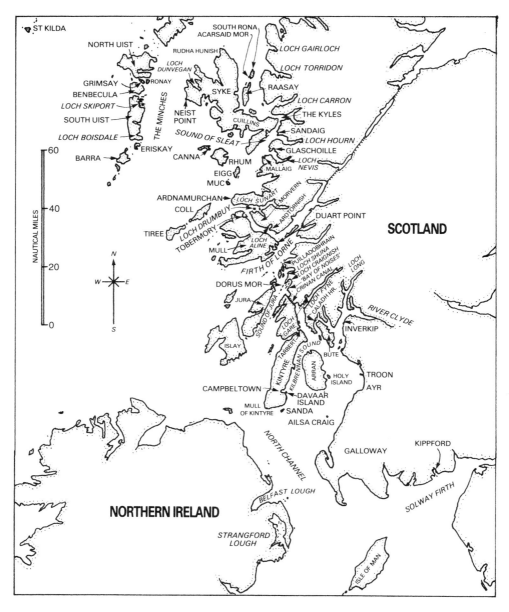

After an hour and a half of help from the diesel installed beneath the cockpit floor, we picked up a Force 2 sou'easterly at the mouth of the big lough and, leaving the Ulster coast astern in its sunset shadows, we sailed out over a smoothly undulating sea. Supper somehow tasted especially good, and the passing of big ships as dusk folded over the horizon ahead seemed

76

companionable, rather than menacing. Friendly too were first one and then other lighthouses as they flickered and sparked into life around us, to send their reassuring, swirling beams of light arching over the darkening sea.

Too soon it was time for my watch below. I lit one of the gimballed oil-lamps on the aft saloon bulkhead, where its low-trimmed flame would not shine into the helmsman's eyes, and spent a while restowing various errant items which I found were making irregular small thuds and clinks on the many shelves, and in the panel-fronted lockers. We still had a lot to learn about 'stowing for sea'!

At last I went forward, and turned into one of the cosy fo'c'sle bunks. Snuggling down, and feeling myself moving to the vessel's slow roll, I thought how similar it was to the last night passage I had experienced in a boat of this size. That had been the trip on which I had first met Herbert, and had learned what a very skilful navigator this quiet and friendly fellow was. Like a vivid film, almost, it all came back to me . . .

There was a long, smooth Atlantic swell sturdily lifting and lowering *Maid of York*'s pale-blue hull as she lay hove to for supper-time on the edge of the ocean, her red sails blushing

'. . . hove to on the edge of the ocean . . .'

golden in the yellowing glow of a spectacular sunset. Somewhere out there, two thousand miles beyond the lonely, gleaming line of the horizon, Americans were about to enjoy mid-afternoon, and the feeling that there was nothing but water between us and them added a certain zest to our meal.

By now I had become used to the peculiarly slow, surging sensation of these waters. When I had first joined the fine Giles Brittany 9-tonner (once the property of no less an ocean wanderer than Humphrey Barton) at Killybegs in County Donegal, this same unusual sluggish motion had made me seasick; but that seemed to have cured me, and now, several days later, we were well down off the south-west coast of Ireland. In fact the bleak bluish outline of the stony Aran Islands, astern of us, was the only land in sight.

I found myself hurrying through the delicious meal which our cheery skipper had cooked in preparation for a night passage, for we were bound across the wide Shannon Estuary, down to the Dingle Peninsula, more than eighty miles away to the sou'-sou'west. Finishing his coffee, and donning his oilskins for warmth, he climbed out on deck to get the ship properly under way again, while I began the washing up. Herbert, our normally silent navigator, followed him out with the hand-bearing compass, then returned and settled to his work at the chart-table behind me.

The sloop had now become more lively as she gathered speed, and as I carefully wedged each dried item in its slotted place I realised I could hear Herbert muttering away to himself, above the noise of the hissing seas outside. Must be facing a bit of a challenge, I thought, though I had no conception of its magnitude until he told me. Of navigation, or indeed of inshore pilotage amongst rocks, I had no practical experience at all, though I did know the vital importance of always keeping a regular and accurate record of one's progress. Herbert, however, was a navigator of considerable talent, and it was just as well.

"Lovely lot of charts, this," he said suddenly.

"What way, lovely?" I asked, hooking up the tea-towel and grabbing at the handrail overhead as I turned to look over his shoulder. It was unusual of him to be so conversational.

"Three of them – all large scale. And not one covering the whole of our course in one go," he chuckled. "At least, they do

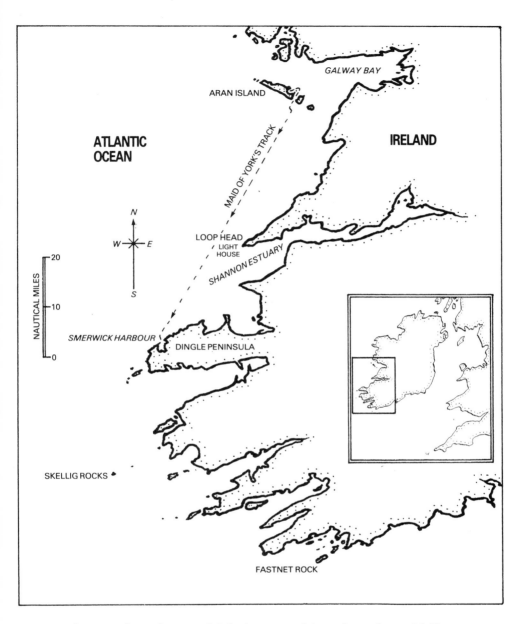

overlap at the edges, which is something, but the middle one doesn't come anything like far enough west. Look – only its top-left corner is on the direct course-line. The skipper did tell me he'd got charts for every inch of the coast, and so he has. Trouble is, now he's decided to leave the coast and do this long hop, there is no one chart we can plot the correct course on. That part's a huge gap, where we've nothing at all."

"So what do we do?" The discovery would have stumped me completely, and seemed unkind when we were already well off shore and settling into the night-sailing routine.

"Just have to make a chart to suit," said Herbert, as though there was nothing to it. A glint in his eyes told me he was in his element. "Look," he said, lightly touching the northernmost chart with the point of the dividers, "Here are the Aran Isles, which we've just left, on Chart 2173. I've marked where we were hove to for supper; you saw me take the bearings a moment ago." Then he pulled the next chart out from under it and spread it on top. "Number 2254 overlaps here, see? But it doesn't extend as far west. The next one does, though, and *it*'s the one we'll want on arrival down there at the tip of the Dingle Peninsula. I can use a spare bit of paper, mark the lines of Latitude and Longitude covering the entire passage, and plot our present position and then that of Smerwick Harbour, where we're going. Luckily I know it's clear water all the way, as the course takes us miles off shore. The Shannon's away in there to the east of us, you see."

And so, while *Maid of York* set up her particular brand of rolling as the skipper took us downwind into the dusk, Herbert created his new chart. A glance through the doghouse window above me showed the remains of the sun's afterglow being rapidly extinguished by low cloud, and the full mainsail and jib seemed soon to be hurling us along at near maximum hull speed.

With the course worked out, and the result confidently passed up to the skipper in exchange for a reading from the Patent Log's whirring dial on the taffrail, the chart-table was at last folded away and I was able to turn into my snug quarter-berth for the rest of my watch below. Hardly, I swear, had I closed my eyes, than the skipper's torchlit face appeared out of the darkness by my head, saying with demon-like jollity: "It's your watch, Jim!" I was sure he was joking – but he wasn't.

I had slept heavily, for it had been a very long day, starting with a brisk, damp walk along ancient walled paths, getting a glimpse of the bleak life style of the tough Aran islanders and their barren, rain-swept habitat. Then we had watched their stout but creaking black *curraghs* being rowed out to sea for the evening's fishing as we ourselves made sail, feeling somewhat guilty at the obvious affluence portrayed by our immaculately kept modern cruising yacht, as compared to those small open boats. Built of driftwood with tarred canvas skins, they looked such hard-working and almost prehistoric little craft, and I wondered at the hardiness of their poorly clad crews of weather-beaten men who apparently owned not even a small outboard motor to take them onto the ocean in their hunt for food. No wonder they had stared with such blank expressions at us pleasure-bound people, from so different a world, when we swept by in our gleaming yacht.

Fighting my way out of the bewildering depths of sleep, I pulled on oilskins and climbed clumsily into the cold blackness of the cockpit. I saw the skipper make way for me in the glow of the binnacle, and shuddered at his far-too-cheerful greeting.

"Morning, boy!"

Morning? Never. This couldn't be more middle-of-the-nightish.

"Come on, come on! Grand wind, and we're making a steady seven. Have a good look round, and then take the helm; it's glorious sailing!"

That 'good look round' was, I knew, as important a part of the routine of watch-keeping as was accurately steering the course ordered, or writing up the deck-log every hour. But everything was so pitchy dark that at first I could make out little beyond the compass light's dim glow, or the pools of red and blue-green sidedecking where our electric navigation lamps glittered on fittings and varnish-work.

Gradually, the foam erupting from under the hurrying hull became visible in the yellowish stern-light, and deep in the swirling depths below, a faint-green snake writhed and twisted in spooky luminescence, where the turbulence from the free-spinning propeller spun a rope of excited plankton into a phosphorescent frenzy.

As soon as I got the feel of the tiller and the way each successively overtaking sea would try to swing her this way or that, the skipper went below and pulled the sliding hatch over, to keep out the damp night air. Alone, with my eyes becoming more and more accustomed to the night, I began to react more easily and automatically to the wavering card in the binnacle, and was at last able to turn down the intensity of its lamp and still see it clearly. Crests broke alongside as *Maid of York* hissed sibilantly on her way, and I felt this must be what it would be like in the tradewinds. Warmer, of course . . .

On and on; with the yellow-green flecks fizzing past beyond the rail, and only a faint-blue paleness in the northern sky astern to suggest that there was anything, anywhere, but sea and the night and this small vessel, and me. No sign of ships, people or land was even hinted at in the cloud-laden blackness. Now and then a smudgy gap would materialise briefly in the cloud coverage overhead, so that a star or two would appear, circle uncertainly about the black masthead, then mist over and return to their dark homes in the windy, invisible heavens.

I kept glancing to port, because somewhere not many miles that way lay the low coastline of County Clare, terminating at its southern end with the powerful lighthouse on Loop Head at the Mouth of the Shannon. Whether there was rain or something between me and it, I couldn't tell, but it never showed up. My imagination, often accursedly active, began to play on what might happen if for some reason the light had gone out, and if some current or a quite understandable error of Herbert's in the drafting of his own chart was taking us close in shore (may I be forgiven).

Even as that ridiculous thought blossomed, the sea just ahead of our plunging, racing bows suddenly lit up in a wide area of boiling phosphorescence. Rocks! I opened my mouth to scream a warning, and leapt to my feet, every nerve tingling with fright. I shoved the helm down too, but it was too late – we were into the patch, and – and – and – it wasn't there any more. Nothing. Only the dark sea, heaving blackly, surging us onwards as before. Wildly, with my heart thumping like a berserk steam-hammer, I swung round and peered at the receding wake, but there was no sign of anything unusual. Yet it had all been so *real*! I had *seen* the disturbed water.

I sat down again and steadied the *Maid* back on course. Should I call Herbert? Or the skipper? We had no echo-sounder, for such things were still uncommon in yachts, or I would immediately have checked the depth. With only a hand lead-line and the ship tearing along at full speed, using that was out of the question. Besides, the seas *felt* just as they had before, and the two recent years in Thames Estuary waters had taught me to know instinctively when I was sailing into shallows, and this didn't seem like that. Anyway, Herbert himself was due on watch in less then half an hour.

I remember wondering if perhaps the compass light had been having some strange effect on me, making me 'see' things. I fiddled with the dimmer-switch, and sailed on, puzzled by the still certain feeling that we were in fact in deep water. Deep enough at least for whatever it had been to be far enough down (even though it had seemed to be on the surface), or else just so much in my own imagination that it would not harm us anyway. After all, Herbert had said there would be no 'nasties' on our course.

I wasn't tired, particularly. That two-and-a-half-hour trick when standing solo watches on deck was just about right, I decided. The first half-hour or so after coming on deck to take over, one is trying to get the feel of the steering and the way the boat is behaving. During the following hour one fully enjoys it all, weather permitting, of course. After that the cold starts to get through, eyes try to shut, and one begins a little at first and then more so, to think of the warm bunk waiting below. The completion of a third hour or more at the helm is always increasingly tiring, brewing the attendant risk of making a wrong decision. Much better to change watches after just two and a half hours. Indeed I was still very much enjoying myself when I realised that Herbert should be woken. Even as I reached forward to call down the slot in the companion doorway, he slid the hatch back from within, and poked his head and shoulders out into the cold dimness.

"Morning, Jim." (The words sounded much nicer this time.) "What have we on the log?"

I groped for the rubber torch, and turned its beam on the dial at the taffrail. "Thirty-eight point – er – four," I said, flicking it off again lest it should blind him. He bobbed down out of sight, and I saw the red glow of the chart-table lamp, and his shadow from it moving over parts of the cabin. How warm that rosy light looked.

In a moment he was climbing out, and I could just make out his dark form standing before me as he turned and stared slowly round in a full circle.

"Anything of interest?" he asked quietly. "Loop Head should be in sight, just abaft the port beam."

"Haven't seen it," I replied. "Must be misty or something.

About what depth of water should we be in?"

"Depth?" I felt his hand on mine as he took the tiller. "Masses. Why? OK, I've got her now."

"Course one-five-eight," I said automatically. "I just wondered."

"One-five-eight," he intoned. "Wow, she's going like a train! Right, Jim. Your watch below."

"I'll just go forward for a moment. I might be able to see Loop Head from up there," I told him, and felt my way cautiously out of the cockpit and along the sidedeck past the upturned dinghy on the cabintop. I'm sure he realised that I was in fact being coy and actually going forward for a more physical reason. I got to the bow, and had just taken a firm grip of the stainless-steel tubing of the pulpit rail when to my horror the sea again lit up in a rushing explosion of green foam, only a yard or two ahead of us. I heard Herbert's startled shout from the stern, but kept my eyes on that flashing swathe of agitated phosphorescence as it swept under us, for this time I had seen what had caused it. Indeed I was still chuckling to myself when a few moments later I made my way aft again, but in the light of the binnacle Herbert's wide-eyed look had me laughing properly.

"What in blazes was *that*?" he gasped.

"A shoal of sleeping fish," I explained. "We just woke them up. You'd have thought we were a whale about to pounce on them, the way they scattered."

"H'mmm . . .," said Herbert's voice from the rear of the cockpit as I reversed down the companion-ladder. But there was more than a touch of seriousness in his tone. "You didn't see the whale which passed us just before dark, did you? It was shortly after you turned in. We didn't like to wake you."

I remembered shutting the hatch rather pensively. Tired, and otherwise very contented as I was, the remark had hardly been calculated to induce sleep – not for a minute or two, anyway.

I was awoken again by the sudden blast of *Maid of York*'s great plunger-type foghorn, blaring like an enraged donkey from the cockpit. What a journey of surprises this was! I wriggled out of my sleeping-bag and peered out. No, it had not been just another means of waking Andrews from his slumbers. The yellowish morning light held a strange brilliance and blankness, and as I scrambled into my clothes and up to the cockpit, I knew now why

Loop Head Light had not been visible during the night. We were engulfed in fog, now very thick indeed.

I could only admire Herbert's confidence when, in the middle of his bowl of cereal during breakfast, he looked up at the cabin clock and said that with any luck we ought to be closing the coast in another forty minutes or so. It was then 0510, and since leaving the Aran Islands fading in the twilight we had seen no other sign of land. All around us now there was even less sign of it – nothing indeed other than a close little circle of lumpy grey waves, which kept looming up and vanishing again like roving phantoms in the moist air.

"What should the coast look like, when – if – we do see it?" I asked.

"Should be low cliffs and probably rocks," said Herbert, taking a sip at his coffee. "Never been there, but the chart shows something of the kind. Smerwick Harbour's just an open bay, bit like a horseshoe. There's no real harbour in the built sense. Could be we'll only see the top of the mountain behind it at first, as the fog's pretty low and thick." Raising his voice, he called up to the skipper. "What's the log reading now, please?"

"Sixty-two, almost," came the reply.

"How almost?" asked Herbert, downing his mug and going to the chart-table.

"You're pernickety, Herbert," said his captain. "Sixty-one point eight."

"H'mmm. I think we could safely alter course to port, now. Try steering one-nine-oh, Skipper."

A pause; then: "One-nine-oh it is, Herbert. We'll gybe if we aren't careful. Lucky the wind's come so much lighter."

"Probably because we're near the land," muttered Herbert, fiddling with the dividers.

"How ever do you know to turn now?" I got up and peered over his shoulder.

He looked round at me and grinned. "I don't, really," he admitted sheepishly. "Sort of instinct, I suppose. You develop a kind of feeling inside if you navigate a lot. I don't know what it's based on. Changes in wave formation that you don't consciously register, maybe – I don't know. It's like plotting a course in the first place. I lay off all the allowances one naturally calculates for leeway, tide and so on; surface-drift too, if it's been blowing at all freshly. We had some of that, last night. But then just sometimes I add in a little – or subtract it perhaps – for, oh, just the *feel* of it all, too. A bit unscientific, but . . . Come on," he added, and climbed out into the cockpit. "Must be nearly there, and there's no sense in hitting the cliffs full tilt, even if our speed has slackened."

"Cliffs, Herbert?"

"Either side of the entrance, Skipper."

"I think I'll start the engine."

"I'd really rather be able to hear," said Herbert quickly. "You bring in the main sheet, Jim, as I let the halyard go."

We were stowing the sail along the boom when Herbert suddenly lifted his head and stood stock still. "Time we blew that foghorn again," he said softly.

The skipper withdrew the long brass plunger, and rammed it firmly down, so that the horn blasted its reedy note into the dank mist around us. Herbert allowed himself the smallest of smiles as its muffled echo came reverberating back to us from somewhere on the port side.

"Land!" I exclaimed a minute later, pointing to starboard. "Something, anyway. Look, there it is again!"

Very indistinctly, a dark angular bulk seemed to be slowly sliding by, and a dim burst of white at its base could only be the breaking of a wavetop. Then Herbert nudged me, and pointed to port before passing another sail-tie around the bunt of damp red canvas. Sure enough, a grey something was forming out of the fog, and coming gradually abeam. We were creeping gently in between the very arms of the still invisible bay.

"Better take a sounding, just to be sure," said Herbert.

A few seconds later, standing by the lee shrouds and recoiling the dripping lead-line, I was able to report six fathoms.

"Haven't seen it swung Navy style in a long while," said Herbert, and looked at his watch. His little smile broadened into a definite grin. I glanced at my own watch. Herbert's Dead Reckoning, after some eighty miles without any kind of check, was less than two minutes out.

And now, almost incredibly, here I was in a bunk in the forecabin of our very own *Ocean Dove*. That thump would be Herbert coming below to check something at the little chart-table I had designed, opposite the galley. I heard him mutter something to my father out in the cockpit, before turning in on the port settee-berth in the panelled saloon. A wave gurgled as the bow-wave surged beyond the planking by my ear, and I lay listening, contentedly drowsy. It seemed almost too good. Perhaps – perhaps it *was* just a dream we had built . . .

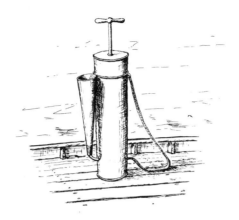

6
CUTTERS, CATS AND KETCHES

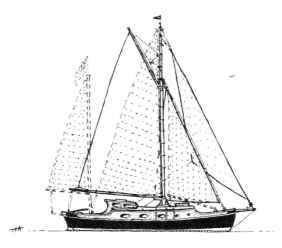

Ocean Dove 28ft 6in, 8.6 tons; original Griffiths gaff cutter rig, with Andrews' Bermudian ketch rig dotted in

Ocean Dove's first sea-dawn found her almost becalmed well off the shipping routes, roughly four miles west-nor'west of Ailsa Craig, which could faintly be seen like a dirty grey bun on the flat plate of the horizon astern. After an hour or so of daylight, I began to develop the impression that it was in tow, and not coming along too well.

At 0500, my father came on deck, stared at it for a moment, said an emphatic "H'mm!" and started the engine. Two hours later we were sliding past the clifftop lighthouse on Davaar Island and heading in towards what was to be our new ship's very first anchorage, at the head of Campbeltown's hill-bordered loch. We wasted little time ashore, just buying milk and telephoning home, for sailing was the thing, and we were soon discovering *Ocean Dove*'s modest but adequate windward ability as we beat out again, and then settled down to a swift and comfortable run up Kilbrennan Sound between the Isle of Arran's lofty peaks and the lower, more humpy Kintyre shore. (Map page 76.)

During the next ten varied and fascinating days, we managed to explore most of the quite breathtaking, yet all very different mountain-girt lochs around the Firth of Clyde. And that clinched it, as far as I was concerned. How could there ever be any holiday to equal that of sailing in one's own homely boat amidst such beautiful scenery? There were exciting moments, of course, when *Ocean Dove* flew before curling seas up the Inner Firth with the speedometer's needle wavering near the 7 knot mark; and others when squalls in the narrow Kyles of Bute hove her down until the oval portholes in her raised topsides looked from inside like the windows in a row of washing machines, with greeny-white bubbles tearing past while the wind shrieked overhead in the taut and slanting rigging. Then there were the silver hours, as we trundled smoothly along under power down the straight fjord of Loch Long, with the steep-sided hills on either hand reflecting as though on sheets of polished steel.

This blend of sheltered seawater and tree-clad hillsides was like some ever changing miracle, but there were other pleasant surprises. One day we came upon old *Oread*, who started us cruising, now rolling her way up Loch Fyne under new

'. . . squalls in the narrow Kyles of Bute hove her down . . .'

ownership. Later on, we found ourselves anchored next to her in East Loch Tarbert's attractive and superbly land-locked natural harbour. Floating a trifle tiredly there on a wavering reflection of Tarbert's sixteenth-century castle ruins, that elderly cutter brought back many memories as we rowed around her in our dinghy.

Tarbert itself, with its shops and chandlery, was a great find, being clearly the sort of place we would visit again and again. It was what we like to call an "all-round" anchorage – the sort where one could be sure of a sheltered berth no matter what wind might blow. I had no idea then that eventually I would come to live for some years there, in one of the quaint stone houses overlooking the harbour approaches.

The clearness of the Loch Fyne seawater, as we turned back for home, allowed us to watch crabs scuttling about on the seabed while our echo-sounder faithfully read 35ft (10.6m), close under the steep-to edge of the Kintyre hills, and the two large basking sharks for whom we altered course later that same day in Kilbrennan Sound were but another part of the new, exciting and wonderful world we had discovered. Filled with the spicy smells of sea-salt, wet bracken, and sweet heather-honey, we returned to Ulster, our eyes glazed with remembered images of sea-greens and mountain-purples.

It hadn't all been marvellous, of course, for there had been nights when the wind and rain had fought for which could make the loudest din overhead, as we lay wakeful in our bunks and felt our ship tug restlessly at her anchor chain, heeling suddenly this way and that as she yawed to the gusts, but with 281 nautical miles proudly put astern, at an average speed of 3.3 knots over the entire distance, we had nevertheless achieved a modest but happy maiden cruise. It was tainted however – just slightly – by an uncomfortable awareness that we might have gone a little faster and certainly more comfortably to windward on many occasions, had our new vessel not proved quite so tender. Again and again that lee rail of hers had been submerged and dragging through the water, while other yachts around us had been carrying comparatively greater amounts of sail, and at noticeably smaller angles of heel.

This was of course in no way the fault of *Ocean Dove*'s designer, for had it not been for the mishap that night during her construction, she would have retained the broad flatness with which her bilges should have been endowed, and would have stood up to her powerful gaff rig without the slightest difficulty.

It was in thinking about this problem that I found myself belatedly wishing that, instead of training as a miller, I had followed my heart and studied yacht design as a profession. After all, naval architecture was also in the family's blood, for had not a first cousin of my grandfather, one Thomas Andrews, designed the long successful *Oceanic*, amongst other famous and highly popular ocean liners? Had he not developed watertight bulkheads for such ships, and alas felt obliged to drown, when in his ill-managed *Titanic*'s final hours he knew he had not taken his idea high enough? Perhaps it was not so strange that my mind kept mulling over various ways of improving *Ocean Dove*, the ship which already bore some of my own small ideas.

In the years to come, when we repeatedly extended our cruises northwards up Scotland's rugged but unbeatable Hebridean coasts, we came fully to appreciate the long, straight keel below her beamy hull, and to love the steadiness of helm and ability to hold a course unattended, which, typical of the design work of Maurice Griffiths, was everything we had hoped for.

I learned too how different was this boat's motion compared to that of narrower, more deeply keeled yachts of her size, and how her full-sectioned bow and stern kept her drier than most in a short sea. We came to understand the flexible usefulness of the gaff-cutter rig too, as well as its limitation and drawbacks, such as the inability to point high on the wind, and the time-consuming and laborious coiling down of halyard falls each time we got under way, reefed, or changed sail. But all along I felt certain she could somehow be made to sail more uprightly, and to have far less need for sail to be shortened every time the wind freshened a bit.

It took a 650 mile cruise to the Isle of Skye in unrelenting and quite unnecessarily strong headwinds (there *and* back) during the violent 'summer' of 1961, to convince me that a change to Bermudian ketch rig might be the answer.

I knew enough by then from my collection of books on yacht design to see that with the recent advent of lightweight alloy spars, we could at last lower the centre of gravity to an effective degree, and that the centre of effort of a carefully worked-out ketch rig would also be significantly lower. Combined calculation indicated that *Ocean Dove*, with these modifications, should carry her canvas much more powerfully, in spite of her accidentally altered hull shape.

Had it not been for the keenness I had recently developed for evening and Saturday Class racing at the Royal North of Ireland Yacht Club, I would have set up my drawing-board immediately on our return from Skye, instead of waiting until that exciting season's points-racing was over. The consequences of that delay, as it turned out, dramatically affected not just *Ocean Dove*, but my own life as well.

Having graduated from the club's own three-quarter-decked 'Lake' Class, and raced regularly in the International Dragons, I had gone one thrilling stage further and bought myself what was then arguably the fastest sailing craft of all – a 16ft (4.9m) Shearwater III catamaran, direct descendant of the Prout brothers' prototype double-canoe, which I had watched sprinting down the River Crouch in a smoke of spray from the decks of old *Merry Maid* a few years earlier.

In this superbly exhilarating development of the sailing machine, my crew and I on one occasion hurtled clean across the three and a half miles from Carrickfergus, on one side of Belfast Lough, to Cultra on the other, at a timed average speed of 16.2 knots – a record under sail which I believe still stands at the time of writing. So much solid water was flung over us on that crazy dash, that we had to face aft to breathe, and the small speedometer at my toe-strapped feet was frequently jammed hard against the stop at the 20 knot mark, while the roar of the twin rudders rose to a wavering whine and the cat seemed to bang from one concrete wavetop to the next in a series of swooping, crashing leaps – an unforgettable ride!

It was on a much quieter evening, however, when I was sailing that same little catamaran single-handed just for the fun of it after our own race had ended and my crew had hitched a lift ashore to celebrate, that I found myself watching a real neck-and-neck ding-dong battle for first place going on between two of the old Lake Class boats. Sixteen footers also, they could hardly have been more different to my light-flying cat, but I knew only too well from my own happy days in their beamy, short-ended, and heavily ballasted hulls, that slow though they were, the very closest and most fiercely contested racing was to be had in that particularly enthusiastic little fleet.

The two leaders on that golden evening were both sailing single-handed. Tack for tack, each watching the other's every twitch or finger-movement on the long, straight tillers, they came bustling up towards the line. In the lead was the then Class Champion, but the boat which had kept pace with his was owned by a girl – I wasn't sure of her name, though I knew she had been sailing there for the last couple of years. Without warning, one boat suddenly came about, and as though in tow, so did the other, flinging round in a quickly stilled rattle of canvas, and the two stood out once more from the shore, preparatory to making the final, decisive tack for the finish.

Watching the second boat, I saw the girl's hand suddenly start pushing her tiller down – a trifle too soon, surely? But her opponent saw the movement too, and fairly threw his boat round in a swirl of water – only to find that the girl had been bluffing and was back on the old tack, still sailing fast. He hesitated, then tacked back to cover her again, but it was too late; his boat had lost speed, and in that moment the girl tacked smoothly round for the line. The finishing cannon puffed smoke, its thin *bang* racketing triumphantly across the anchorage. The girl's mainsail came fluttering down, and she stowed it while steering for her mooring with a foot, under jib only. It had been beautifully done, I thought.

Later on, at supper in the clubhouse, I managed to find myself sitting opposite this quietly capable female. Never till that second had I made approaches to a girl, but . . .

"Nice bit of bluff-tacking," I heard myself saying. "You deserved your win." Then, to my amazement, my voice continued: "It's a long time since I had a race in one of those boats."

Dead silence. I saw she had remarkable eyes; sort of flecked with an ocean-blue, and smiling at the edges. And she had ruffled, brownish hair.

"There's Thursday evening," she said at last. A low-toned voice. The eyes twinkled now. "I haven't arranged for a crew."

I felt my breath catch in a funny way.

"It'll be rather dull after that cat-thing of yours," she added with a sudden grin, "but you're welcome to come out in *Corrib* if you'd like to."

She won that race too, in a very strong breeze, and said afterwards she had been glad of my extra weight as ballast.

Two weekends later, I had little difficulty in persuading Judy to come for an exchange sail in *Ocean Dove*, so that she could try her hand for the first time at the helm of a sea-going yacht, on the attractively islanded inlet of Strangford Lough, where 'O.D.' was now kept. We landed, just the two of us, on a stony islet shore, and rambled over its rounded, grassy slopes, then sat watching the cutter lying peacefully below us at her anchor. And in Judy, the fascination of cruising took root, gently but surely. (Page 34.)

Our courtship progressed throughout the winter, and she showed much interest in my efforts to balance the sail plan of the new Bermudian ketch rig for *Ocean Dove*. It took a lone journey far away from Judy to a firm of alloy spar-makers in the south of England for me to realise that I heartily wished she was with me, and that life would never be the same unless I could share it and all its comings and goings with my girl with the ocean-blue eyes.

In the midst of buying a house and furniture, and making preparations for (I have to admit) the only wedding I have ever truly enjoyed, the new masts and spars arrived. A week's honeymoon by car around the Solway Firth and Lake District (with a bit of sailing thrown in), preceded a subsequent three-week cruise to introduce my new wife to Scottish waters. It also introduced both of us to the peculiar ways of ketch rig.

Stepping the new masts and living aboard for a day or two while everything was sorted out was as much a part of home-building for us as was the fortnight spent turning our house ashore into some semblance of order and snugness before we set out for Scotland. It set a pattern of life which has continued to oscillate between our various boats and homes ever since.

Judy's initiation might easily have put her off cruising for good, had she not been so strong-minded. For a start, although that first cruise together was in a sense an extension of our honeymoon, she was not alone with her husband, for my father (who after all owned the boat) and our young friend Dave, had also come along.

Battered and bruised by the vicious rolling during a windy overnight crossing of the North Channel, Judy greeted the dawnlit outlines of Sanda and the Mull of Kintyre with some gratitude, not least because they formed a lee from the steadily rising westerly gale. During the night, a lockerful of biscuit-tins containing heavy objects had opened, cascading its contents painfully down her shins, adding to the abrasions sustained earlier when spilled oil on the foredeck had caused her sudden downfall onto the anchor windlass. Yet here she was, hair blowing around her knitted cap, bright-eyed and affecting us all with her obvious enthusiasm.

Our new ketch rig had proved its worth at the outset, for we had been able to stow the mainsail and continue nicely balanced under mizzen and headsail for most of the passage. This was pleasing in itself; but now, as we came swooping in under the reddish-brown cliffs of green-capped Kintyre, and turned into a white-flecked Campbeltown Loch, the morning sun and my wife's excitement at seeing the heather-clad hills gave me a completely new and thrilling sense of enjoyment.

Drifting northwards in the relative calm of the following day, she discovered that other, more relaxing kind of cruising. The faint chuckle of the bow-wave as an air filled our biggest sails and drew the ship forward over a limpid waterland cobbled here and there with mauve-ringed jellyfish, while nearby mountains reflected amongst them, were things to savour and soak up, slowly and deliciously. As she put it herself, the great advantage was that one needn't be for ever worrying about 'being back home in time for tea', as one would in a dayboat. (Page 34.)

But if Campbeltown Loch had looked to her like heaven, that gem of all natural harbours, Tarbert, lay hidden and waiting even more appealingly between its headlands a few miles up wide Loch Fyne. It was not until well after teatime that our CQR anchor splashed down into the still water below its ancient castle, and the impression which Tarbert made that evening, and next morning when we rowed ashore to shop and water ship, was to stay in Judy's mind, just as it had in mine, ever since my own first visit.

The Crinan Canal too, which we entered at Ardrishaig further up Loch Fyne that afternoon, was to implant an equally pleasant set of memories. The old Telford-designed locks; the banks of wildly blooming rhododendrons cascading to the waterside; pine trees crowding the slopes above us, or the low fields over the foxglove-covered bank to starboard, from where grazing cows looked up at our passing masts; and a glimpse across the flat flood-plain of the Moine Mor to intriguing archaeological sites (another hobby we shared), were only rivalled for my new shipmate by the sudden views of the western seas and distant isles, as successive lock gates creaked open on to each new vista. I had been through before, and was yet to make the transit many, many times, yet always the sense of anticipation and magic prevailed.

We made the descent to the winding, rock-cut reaches leading to Crinan itself, meeting a fresh sea-wind as we stowed the fenders away and motored out into Loch Crinan to catch the first of the flood tide through the Dorus Mor, which is Gaelic for, literally, 'Big Door'. This narrow gap between the mainland and a tight-wrought line of slanted rocky islands at the northern end of the Sound of Jura often presents a veritable maelstrom of fast-swirling tides, and I recalled hotly how two years earlier, after my very first journey through the canal, I had nearly sunk *Ocean Dove* right here in this most unfavourable spot. (She would have been in good company at that, for Bell's *Comet*, the world's very first sea-going steamboat, had ended her days in exactly the same place.)

There had been some delay in the sea-lock, I remembered, during which we had started to pump *Ocean Dove*'s bilges. In those days she was fitted with a Vortex pump, the base and main works of which stood permanently in the bilge-water, and consisted of an impeller driven by a cranked, vertical handle, which forced the water up to a skin-fitting in the topsides, above the waterline. Normally one closed the sea-cock there after using the pump, but the lock gates had unexpectedly opened, there had been a scramble to take in warps, and as we spilled out into salt water again, my mind was taken up with trying to identify from the chart which gap was what between the sprinkling of islands and headlands spread suddenly before us. At last we had sufficiently sorted ourselves out to cut the motor and make sail, and with the old cutter rig were soon well heeled to a fine sou'wester.

We were charging towards the Dorus Mor in grand style, and relaxing at last, when someone had fortunately suggested a celebratory cup of tea (that first canal trip having been a nerve-wracking business for all of us). Going below, my crew had stepped into several inches of cold seawater.

The half-heard yell about 'sinking' had me momentarily but desperately looking for the nearest spot to beach, and there were some awful moments before I realised the cause of the trouble. We had simply heeled far enough to put the pump's outlet under water, and the forgotten, still open sea-cock had worked in reverse! It was days before we got the carpets dried.

This time all went well, and now, turning to starboard into the peaceful loveliness of Loch Shuna, I sat on the foredeck with Judy, and told her about the fun my father and I had, when the ship was almost completed. We had gone to one of the main furnishing houses in Belfast, and my father had informed the young salesman who came forward that we wished to purchase carpets for 'the yacht'. That last magical word lit up a senior salesman's beady eyes and, elbowing the younger lad aside and rubbing his hands gleefully, he had bowed us towards vast rolls of magnificent patterns. Finally, we had selected a lush-looking rubber-backed red mottle which seemed suitable, and my innocent mention of how well this would go with the other furnishings in 'the saloon' had the poor man almost rolling his eyes at the thought of the opulent gin-palace he clearly envisaged.

"And how many yards will you require, gentlemen?" he had whispered at last, washing his hands in mid-air even more vigorously than before.

My father never batted an eyelid. "Um – about six feet by three," he said pleasantly.

I have never seen anyone's expression, or attitude, change so abruptly!

Ahead now, as the afternoon waned, a small group of rocky islets ringed closely around a tiny bay on the mainland shore to starboard. With sail stowed and the engine rumbling slowly underfoot, I steered us between the high, seaweedy points, and after a tour round watching the echo-sounder, anchored at last on the island side.

The engine thumped to a halt, and the deep quietness of that utterly deserted place wrapped itself around us. A pungent smell of damp bracken drifted out, and from the far side of this perfect, unspoiled place came the faint tinkle of some unseen burn, as it poured its silver way downwards amid the dark trees and ferns. Later that night, after an excellent dinner, we returned quietly on deck, and going forward, reached over the bow to tap the anchor chain with a foot and watch enchanted as the cable lit up in a pale-green cord of phosphorescence, deep down through the black water below.

Alas, this once unsullied natural harbour is now a busy marina dotted with pontoons and clanking masts and dinky little chalets on the islands – totally altered by its own popularity, excellent and all as it is. The contrast between that peaceful night and what happened to us just forty-eight hours later demonstrates dramatically the almost unbelievable changeability of West Highland weather. We had headed northwards up the swift-flowing Sound of Luing, and crossed the Firth of Lorn into the seaway dividing the spectacularly mountained Isle of Mull from the Morvern mainland. Good shelter from the strong headwind which met us there had been readily sought and found under the magnificent 600ft (183m) cliffs surrounding Ardtornish Bay, and we had anchored with the BBC's assurance of a steady nor'-westerly ringing in our ears.

Granted that this was in the days before meteorological satellites, but a 180° windshift had seemed a most unlikely event – we thought. Sure enough, a rapidly strengthening south-easterly woke us next morning, putting us on a lee shore with the bowsprit plunging into cream-topped seas under a lowering sky. Not bothering with breakfast, we left at once, and ran before it under staysail alone, up the long Sound of Mull.

Deciding (quite rightly) that the town anchorage in Tobermory Bay would be badly exposed, and that the one at the opposite end of that inlet would doubtless be crowded with other yachts, we bore away to starboard instead, rounding Auliston Head into Loch Sunart. So thick was the weather now, that in the driving rain we had to lay a compass course to locate the north end of Oronsay, a humpy island spread across the centre of the loch, two miles further up.

As we progressed, the wind westered, funnelling into the long sea-loch astern of us, and we tore on with all sail lowered, making over 4 knots under masts only. Round the ends of Oronsay and steep-sided Charna we blew, finally to start the engine in order to negotiate the reef guarding the entrance to Salen's narrow inlet, which nestled into the hills about half-way up on the northern shore.

Securely anchored at last in this rocky but pretty gut, with the wind whistling overhead across the enclosing mountain tops, we rowed ashore through torrential downpour to seek hot baths in the local hotel, splashing along a flooded road to get there.

"Sorry," the then owner told us without much feeling. "We're short of water." (It is now under new management, I'm glad to say, but at the time we reckoned they must recently have had some very uncouth yachtsmen in who had caused some kind of trouble. It only takes one rotten apple to spoil the barrel for everyone.)

Back on board after telephoning home, we spent a pleasant enough night, and the following day saw us drifting back down this exceptionally beautiful and interesting loch, in hardly a breath of wind. What air there was came down between the high surrounding crags from the east, so, having rounded Oronsay once more, we made a series of very short tacks behind that island, through the almost canal-like channel cutting it off from Morvern, into Loch Drumbuy – 'Loch of the Yellow Hill'.

By this time, though the evening was innocently still, a warning of severe gales from the south-west was being forecast, and the best spot in such conditions, under the steeply rising trees just inside the entrance to starboard, was already chock-full of anchored yachts that had fled from Tobermory, so we had to find ourselves another, rather more exposed bay further in. Had we known it then, we would have gone to very much better shelter round on the north side of Oronsay – but that was a pleasure we were not to discover for some years.

By morning it was blowing Force 8, but fortunately coming off the high land which rose directly south-west of us, so all seemed well enough. As the day wore on, however, the squalls increased, until by nightfall it was fully up to Force 10, with gusts far beyond the scope of our '80 mph' anemometer. Between these most violent blasts, a sort of uneasy silence would fall, leaving the swishing of the breaking seas in the entrance and the pounding of smaller waves sounding loudly from the shores around us. *Ocean Dove* would then ride innocently forward over her anchor cable, to which we had already added a heavy weight for extra security.

A distant, growing roar like the coming of a jet aircraft would be heard, howling down over the flat-topped mountain to windward, and in seconds it would scream around us out of the night in an ear-splitting avalanche of tearing, buffeting wind, to fling the ship hard over on her side. With vibrating masts and squealing rigging, she would sheer away, bringing up with a nerve-jarring jolt as her chain, weight and all, sprang bar taut. Then, once more, that eerie calm would fall . . .

Again and again this happened, until we were all extremely tense and jittery, and although one or other of us sat in the hatch by the engine's starter button throughout that hellish night, no one off watch was able to get much sleep. After one particularly shrill squall had exploded about us, young Dave suddenly leapt out into the wild cockpit yelling: "There's lights going by! *Lights going by!*"

I was out of my bunk and up the ladder not three seconds behind him, sure that our cable must at last have snapped, and that we would be blown ashore in moments. But then we saw that the lights were those of a car, disappearing amongst the trees close to us.

A car?

We looked at each other in the wailing, hissing darkness – for neither of us had noticed any kind of a road there, and when we checked on the large-scale chart, none was shown within miles, for this is one of the most lonely and inaccessible parts of the Scottish mainland. We suffered several heart-thumping seconds wondering just how far we could have dragged or drifted to have come near a road, until the ship lay back in yet another staggering gust, and yet again, but most reassuringly, snubbed to the very firmest of halts at the end of her chain. We were not, and could not be, dragging.

Edgy and shaken, and very puzzled indeed (had we been 'seeing things'?) we went below and sat together where we could watch the blackness from the shelter of the doghouse windows. Judy saved the next few minutes by lighting a lamp and the stove, and making us all steaming hot mugs of chocolate.

By daybreak, the little steep-sided loch was a sheet of driving white, but the barometer had at last begun to rise. With that change, the wind naturally swung round and was soon forcing huge seas in through the narrow mouth, setting up a fiercely uneven motion. By the time full daylight was with us, the wind had once or twice shown signs of longer pauses between squalls

(*above*) 'Like a sullen duck . . .' The Colin Archer ketch we didn't sail to Scotland, moored at Risör, South Norway; (*below*) Happy with the new steering wheel, the author takes *Twintail* round Duart Point, Isle of Mull

(*above*) *Aku-Aku*, at home in Highland waters, ghosting out of Tarbert, Loch Fyne; (*below*) *Aku-Aku*'s saloon had a fine all-round view – a popular place at anchor and underway

as though the power of the storm was breaking up. It knew we had withstood it, and beaten it.

We were still and somewhat to our surprise just where we had anchored, and – why, yes; there was indeed a grassy track among the scrawny trees. Dave and I felt dreadfully sheepish about our panic in the night. After breakfast, a detailed inspection of things on deck showed all the same that we were not entirely unscathed. There was a fair bit of chafe here and there, where ropes had rubbed or vibrated against things, but it was not until we commenced winching in the anchor cable to get under way at midday, that we discovered one of the chain's links had been bent through quite an angle, apparently where it had led through the bow fairlead.

How pleased we were with the 35lb (16kg) CQR anchor though! It took two of us on the long winch handle and the engine going full ahead over it to break it out, so well dug in it must have become in the incredible violence of that memorable night. If we had known (but how?) that it was so firmly entrenched, we might have saved ourselves a very great deal of near terror. Even so, that bent chain-link certainly made us think.

When at last we clawed our way into the final gusty remains of the blow across the north end of the Sound of Mull, and into the now sheltered anchorage at Tobermory, we were told of all sorts of chaos which had occurred there. Something like ten yachts had gone adrift during the storm, causing collisions and even a few fortunately none-too-serious strandings. Later that evening, a friend came sailing in from what is generally reckoned to be one of the finest, most secure anchorages on the whole of the West Coast, with a horrifying tale of several small yachts being washed up clear above the High Water mark, after some larger craft had dragged into them and tripped out their anchors.

In the mercifully better spell of weather which followed, we continued northward, taking Judy round mainland Britain's most westerly headland, the bluff and impressive Ardnamurchan Point, in flat calm. As evening fell, we found ourselves surrounded by vast flocks of resting guillemots and razorbills, drifting with us between the flat-topped island of Eigg and the jagged extinct volcano of Rhum. A pink sunset blushed on the Cuillin mountains over on Skye as we rounded to our anchor in Rhum's east-facing Loch Scresort, and next day we explored a little of this most spectacular island on foot, with the intention of spending a further night in its tranquil but open bay, the forecasts being predominantly for westerlies.

That year, however, the radio seemed merely to taunt the wind-gods into changing their already too fickle minds, and a strong breeze came funnelling straight in from the open sea as dusk fell, raising a nasty sea right out of the *east*, dammit. We had no option but to clear out and, under engine and staysail, hammer our way into the teeth of yet another black and windy night, across thirteen miles of troubled, leaping water towards the mainland shelter of Mallaig's fish harbour. On through the small hours the ship lurched and plunged, while unseen spray rattled aft like hailstones. Once again Judy kept us cheerful and almost enjoying it all, by providing us with a constant stream of hot mugs of soup or coffee and lots of things to nibble.

Slowly but steadily, the Point of Sleat light crept by to port, and the seas gradually grew less as we picked out the rain-blurred lights of Mallaig in the blackness ahead. After a while, the green leading lights became clear, and cautiously we edged between the sucking rocks and into the pool behind the fish quays. From my single previous visit, the year before, I vaguely remembered anchoring off a large, white-painted, rectangular building on the eastern shore. Plugging in the Aldis lamp, and holding it well outboard so that it did not reflect back into our eyes off the deck-fittings, we picked up the big building in its beam, rounded to and let go, and, with one last warming cup of cocoa inside us, gratefully climbed into our bunks.

In the morning we looked out to find not one white-painted block, but four identical buildings of that description. By luck alone, we had chosen the right one – all of which goes to show that, when cruising, it is not sensible ever to rely on faint memories. Only the chart and pilot book, compass and echo-sounder are fit friends, and even they, as we all learn eventually, can sometimes mislead.

I still shudder at the narrow escape some fellow club members once had when coasting in their newly acquired and very handsome motor-yacht. During lunch, a dense fog had un-expectedly closed about them, but they knew enough of navi-gation to have fixed rapidly their position by taking immediate shore bearings before all was lost to view. They then laid a compass course to the nearest harbour, and within minutes had piled her up on the rocks so thoroughly that they just had time to jump off her bows before she slid backward and sank in deep water. Their compass had been professionally swung, and they had used the deviation card when plotting that course. It was several days before one of them recalled the metal beer can which had complemented his lunch at the wheel, and which had still been standing within four inches of the compass when they struck. Judging by where they found themselves to be later, the compass must have been deflected something like twenty-five degrees out of true.

From Mallaig, we in *Ocean Dove* now entered the Sound of Sleat, and headed up through the 7 knot tide-rips in what is virtually the flooded mountain pass called Kyle Rhea. For once the weather seemed to have improved, and two mornings later in the lightest of following winds, we were standing gently towards the broad Sound of Raasay, out of Loch Carron. Now we felt to be truly up in the wilds of the north, for this was new ground to all of us. Here the scenery was more grand, more barren; the rocks more rounded, worn and ancient, and the very daylight itself seemed to have a strangely primitive clarity and brilliance.

The wildlife was amazingly tame – barely bothered at all by our presence. For hours we slid silently amongst great 'rafts' of razorbills, which croaked and chatted to each other on all sides, and away to starboard, close under the steep, cliffy coastline, the only boat in sight – a small open motor-launch – was gradually overtaking us on a parallel course. The lone woman at its controls obviously felt as we did about that perfect sunlit morning, and was lifting her voice in fine, open-throated song over the droning thrum of her engine. From her very soul she poured out the loveliest string of Gaelic melodies any of us had heard, the tunes lilting across the pale water one after another, gradually fading as we were slowly left behind. On the warm planking of our decks, my father and young Dave stretched out to sunbathe, and Judy and I sat together, young lovers in the stern. Now *that* is what cruising should be like!

We had to resort to the racket of mechanical propulsion ourselves in the end, in order to get the ship even further north, to our target anchorage of Acarsaid Mor on the isle of South Rona, before darkness made the tricky entrance impossible.

Off the northern tip of Raasay, which stretches like a spine up the broad sound between Skye and the Torridon mountains, South Rona has but one good anchorage. It could hardly be better. A mere rock-studded gap, often hard to see against the bare pink granite of which most of the island consists, its entrance would have been risky to attempt without the cautious description in the Clyde Cruising Club's excellent *Sailing Directions for the West Coast of Scotland*, since no available chart showed the dangers adequately.

We had made the mistake, however, of arriving at the very top of high water springs, and exceptionally big springs they were, too. Thus when the said *Sailing Directions* warned of a 'dangerous rock' to port on the way in, and stressed that one should 'hold the starboard shore close aboard' to avoid it, we could see no sign of any such rock and had no idea how close was 'close'.

As the evening-tinted granite arms of the island closed about us, we slowed to a crawl, and Dave went forward to prepare the anchor – and suddenly saw a great spur of rock sliding in under our starboard bilge. His shout came just in time, and we sheered off, and so came onto the correct leading line towards the white cottage (deserted since the island was evacuated many years ago) at the head of the inlet.

After a peaceful night, totally landlocked behind a heather-covered islet, Judy and I set out in the dinghy first thing next morning, taking a lead-line to find that 'dangerous rock' spoken of, on the port hand when entering. We also took along a length of line attached to an empty plastic bottle, with a stone from the nearby branch as an anchor for it, the idea being to buoy the rock's position as we did not want further frights on the way out again. To our astonishment and amusement, far from having to use the lead-line to find it, we had to climb up eight feet of the great slimy pinnacle of a thing in order to attach our 'marker buoy' to a point where its anchoring stone would not roll off.

In the afternoon (another damp one, alas) we explored ashore. Leaving the others on board, we climbed together to the island's highest point, some 400 feet (122m) up. All around us were rocky gorges and flat boggy plains, bordered by massive ice-worn humps of that gleaming, softly rosy rock, up here very crumbly and weathered. Strangely, the bare crowns of this and indeed all of Rona's highest hills are as it were 'iced' with a thin crust of white quartz, like a small cap of somehow petrified frosted glass, through which the clean pink stone beneath faintly glows.

"They say that's among the oldest known rock in the world," said my mate, fingering the sugary surface as we rested out of the wind near the summit. It certainly seemed timeless, as did the whole atmosphere of the place, and for the two of us just then, it was all ours. Definitely a moment to cherish, as we looked down to the speck on the silver inlet far below that was the fine little ship in which we had sailed here.

7
THE SORT OF CRUISING WE WANTED

Acarsaid Mor, South Rona

The Island of Rona, and that hill upon which Judy and I had rested, was to be our 'furthest north' that year, but although we enjoyed every moment of the subsequent journey home, even it was a succession of calms and gales. Never since have we known the West Coast weather to be quite so unpredictable and bad. We were forced to find shelter many, many times.

One such place of refuge we chose was a tiny bay on the southern side of Loch Nevis, just north of Mallaig. While the wind howled past overhead, young Dave sat all day in the cockpit, happily fishing. Earlier in the cruise his first catches had made such a mess of the galley that the rest of us had rebelled, and had banned the bringing of fish below decks. That didn't worry him in the least, for he at once borrowed the little camping stove we carried, and continued to catch his fish (mostly little ones, luckily), keeping them in the ship's bucket until he judged he had enough to fry on the stove, down out of the wind on the cockpit floor. On this occasion, the rest of us were still in the cabin, listening to the activity on the short-wave radio, when a sudden yell brought us to our feet.

"It's a BIG one! I've hooked a *big* one!"

Similar cries had come from him before, but some extra wildness in his tones suggested that for once there might be some truth in it, and we arrived in the cockpit just as he reeled in a very angry, bright orange octopus. As astonished as ourselves, it blew two fat jets of filthy ink into the air, which spattered on the dinghy lying astern, but fortunately missed our teak decks.

"What'll I do with it?" shrieked Dave hysterically.

"Stick it in the bucket, of course," I said, grabbing for my camera bag. "We've got to have a photograph of *that*!"

At first its wiggly, squirming tentacles seemed reluctant to stay in the bucket along with the five shining fish already there, but gradually, while assorted cameras clicked or whirred, it seemed to settle to the idea and rather enjoy the publicity. Its large droopy eyes meantime regarded us with deep suspicion and (could it be?) a touch of cunning.

Sure enough, when having carefully unhooked it we finally dropped it back into the loch and watched it inject itself downwards in a series of slanting jerks to more secluded depths, we discovered its revenge on Dave had indeed been sweet. Of the five fat little fishes in the bottom of the bucket, there remained one and a half and a few mushy bits. Our octopus had had a meal on the house!

My father and Dave departed a couple of days later via the railhead at Mallaig, and Judy and I were thus left cruising on our own, for the very first time, and eventually, in a gap between gales, the two of us worked *Ocean Dove* round Ardnamurchan.

While storm-bound, we had spent a while changing the powerful working staysail (which slightly overlapped the mast and therefore required a pair of sheets, as did the jib) for a smaller, ex-Dragon Class No 1 foresail which happened to be on board. Though quite a bit less in area, the low-cut foot of this sail had the merit of being short enough to be set on a small boom operated by a single sheet, and it was therefore self-tacking. It still pulled very well, as we discovered when beating tediously down the Sound of Mull in relenting weather, which became sunnier and altogether nicer as we stood out across the Firth of Lorn, for a night at Puilladobhrain (pronounced 'Puldoran', meaning the Otter's Pool).

Due to the Crinan Canal always closing on the Sabbath, we found we now had perforce a day in hand, until it reopened on Monday, so we took the opportunity to explore the nearby and utterly beautiful Loch Craignish. It was to be the first of many happy visits, and here we made a new and very good friend – and found a kind of paradise.

It was the last day of August, yet as we crept round the northern tip of a final tiny islet on the port hand, near the head of the narrow loch, and silently anchored off the dreamy village of Ardfern, there were just two other yachts in the lovely natural pool formed behind it. (Nowadays, there would be dozens at that time of year, on permanent moorings and at pontoons.) One was a small deserted sloop, and the other a longer but very old-fashioned motor-yacht, with a rounded, forward-leaning 'cruiser' stern, and a straight, upright stem. Her name, *Pandora*, simply must have been inspired by the tall, decoratively panelled box of a deckhouse which stood amidships like a gigantic wardrobe.

As we finished stowing sail, a red-capped lad, slight of build, stepped down into the big clinker dinghy at her varnished companion-ladder, and began rowing towards us. We watched his approach with mixed feelings, for in those days there was even more of a social rift between people with sailing yachts and those who owned motorboats than there is now. I began to think he was about to row into us, for having as it were set course from his parent craft, the oarsman had not once looked round, and was now within a few yards of our transom. I was on the point of shouting a warning when, with smartly backed oar, the boat was turned and stopped, and from under the faded knitted hat smiled not the face of a callow youth, but that of a small and astonishingly weather-beaten old lady.

"I do hope you won't mind my asking," she said, in no way out of breath, "but did you by any chance design that rig youself?"

"Y-yes, as a matter of fact I did," I stammered in surprise. "However did you know?"

"I just thought perhaps you had, because it is so very like the rig that I designed for my own ship." She must have seen our startled glances towards the ancient *Pandora*, for she laughed merrily. "Oh, *Pan* isn't mine," she explained. "I'm just helping out for an old friend. My ship's *Sybil of Cumae*, a 52ft (15.9m) blue

"Did you by any chance design that rig yourself?"

ketch. You may have seen her about."

We hadn't, but that did not stop us inviting this incredible little lady on board for a cup of tea and bite of fruit-cake. A fascinating series of sea-going yarns came forth, which lasted to our great delight for the rest of the afternoon. Then, having told us where to find drinking-water and milk and a telephone box, she bid us goodbye, stepped into her dinghy, and rowed away in the most relaxed and seamanlike manner one could imagine. As before, she took just the one look over her shoulder to settle the boat on course, and with a cheery grin on her sun-browned, wrinkled face, and a nod of the red cap, sped away leaving a wake of bubbles as straight as a ruler.

After a quick expedition ashore to avail ourselves of her kindly offered information, we got under way again as the sun yellowed and sank, aiming to try another anchorage which she had recommended, behind the string of islands on the eastern side of the loch.

Setting both working headsails, we determined to sail out just as quietly as we had managed to sail in, now that we knew a real sailor was watching us. And although well within speaking range, she politely said not a word as I very foolishly hoisted the mizzen and *then* tried to turn *Ocean Dove* downwind in the light wind – which was how I learned some more about the handling of a ketch.

Had I left her under headsails only, we would have had full control as we ran out past *Pandora*, to gybe round that odd stern of hers. We could then profitably have added all our after-canvas. Unfortunately, having set the mizzen too early, each time I tried to swing our own stern into the wind, that quite large sail put the headsails into its lee, took charge, and forced us back onto a reach. The old motor-yacht loomed close across our bows, and Judy glanced questioningly in my direction as I held the tiller hard over – with not the slightest effect.

At the last, panic-filled moment, I jumped to my feet and reaching up behind me grabbed the mizzen boom, forced it across and held it there desperately. We gybed with a great crash and swept past *Pandora*'s tall white bow in a long, foaming curve. In the orange-gold glow of the sunset, my face must have appeared very red indeed, and I was relieved to notice that our elderly friend had most considerately been attending to the securing of something on the deck, and had at least pretended not to be watching. Another lesson about sail balancing and boat-handling was well and truly rammed home!

I grew quickly calmer as we drifted serenely round the head of that glorious loch, lost the wind altogether in the lee of the line of islands on the far side, and finally motored down the very narrow sound behind them, along the steep eastern shore. Precipitous mountains of tumbled rock rose almost vertically from within a few yards of our port side, while on the other hand the long island shores were covered in tangled oak-scrub, like the remains of some long-forgotten, primeval forest, green with hanging mosses and lichens.

At last the channel widened slightly, and here a smaller island, sheer and stony, filled the gap between the two longer ones. Off a low whale-back of ice-worn rock we dropped anchor, and as the last rumble of the diesel died, an absolute peace enfolded us. Not another soul, not another boat nor a house, nor indeed any sign of man's existence was in sight. A low-gliding seagull was the only other living creature we could see. Slowly, contendedly, we tidied up on deck and went below for supper.

Sitting at the cabin table, we were discussing our charming and extremely unusual visitor of the afternoon, when our chat was abruptly halted by what sounded like a nearby round of rather thin applause.

Climbing into the cockpit to see what yacht had come in, we found everything as before. No other boat; no people; nothing. Just the darkening tree-covered islands, and the rocks, and the fabulous glory of the mountain of barren stone which soared up from the opposite shore, a few hundred yards away. Every facet of it was bathed in the rosy-pink afterglow of the sunset, with an intensity of colour that took the mysterious 'hand-clapping' from our minds – until it occurred again just behind us.

Spinning round, we still saw nothing whatever to account for it. Then one of the trees on the island astern shook its leaves momentarily, as a large grey bird took flight from its branches.

"Heron," said Judy quietly. We watched it fly off up the narrow sound with characteristic long slow flaps of its huge wings, just as another swooped in from over the long island on our right, and emitted a soft yet harsh squawk as it came near to the trees. Immediately a noise of vigorous applause clattered out over the stillness from the same patch of trees, and the answer was presented. The young heron nestlings had heard the announcement of approaching supper, and in excited anticipation were busily snapping their beaks.

Grinning at each other rather foolishly, we went quietly below to our own meal.

Night grew around *Ocean Dove* in a total and oddly unreal silence. We got ready for bed, whispering even in the cabin. Then suddenly the very hull seemed to vibrate to a terrifying, reverberating roar that bellowed over the deserted anchorage as though some vast prehistoric monster was at large.

We scrambled on deck into the blackness, shining a shaking torch in all directions, but nothing – absolutely nothing – was to be seen, and as the echoes died, stillness reigned again.

"Turn the torch off, and listen a moment," said my mate.

As our eyes and ears became accustomed to the starlit darkness of the space around us, after the lamplit confines of the saloon, we began to make out the intense black outlines of the hills, and to hear the faint chatter of some very distant waterfall.

"Look," whispered Judy. "Each star has its own reflection;

unmoving, like a dot of light in the water."

We gazed speechless at the miracle of it, two honeymooners lost in a soundless bliss – then that roar curdled the air again, louder and even more blood-freezing than before. The hair prickled the back of my neck, and fighting a pounding heart, I flicked on the torch. As its beam lanced across the sound, finding the far shore, that enraged bellow shattered the night yet again – and was followed by a bubbling snort.

Panning the beam quickly back over a dark, slanting rock which its yellow circle of light had just passed, we saw something move. Like long black sausages, lying on its sloping face, were a handful of what for all our wild imaginings could only be a harem of seals, hauled out for the night. And in their midst could dimly be seen the thicker, rearing figure of their bull. Even as we watched, he threw back his head and bawled forth his fury once more, and at that moment the reflected light silhouetted the cause of his wrath – the head and squat neck of a younger male seal in the water below him.

A clear case of "Keep off, boy! These ones are mine!"

And so this anchorage, which has another name, came to be for us the 'Bay of Noises'. Indeed, when some years later we returned, and found ourselves sharing it with an English yacht exploring Scottish waters for the first time, we told the crew of those incidents, over drinks in our cockpit. By chance it was again a fairly still sort of evening, and just as before the sun had begun to set and cast its spectacular flood of colour over the bare, towering mountain of Craig à Bhannan across the narrow water. Our guests were remarking how extremely peaceful it was, and that this night anyway seemed to offer no odd noises or occurrences, when conversation was interrupted by a loud, extenuated '*whooOOFF!*' from further up the loch.

Not a moving thing could be seen amongst the islands, or on the water – just the darkening trees and the long shadows on the hills. Then came another '*whooOOFF*', louder this time and a trifle more clipped. And into our sight from over the top of Eilean Righ floated a large, gaily striped hot-air balloon, complete with hanging gondola, in which the pilot at that moment reached up and gave his gas-burner yet another hissing 'huff' of flame. In open-mouthed astonishment, we watched as it drifted across the sound and slowly, gently, vanished into a hidden glen.

That place remains, for us anyway, the Bay of Noises.

From there, we took *Ocean Dove* next day on down the loch and round to Crinan. Locking into the canal basin, we rather wondered how the two of us were going to work the ship through on our own, for her 9ft 6in (2.9m) beam would mean both gates would need to be opened at each lock, and the by-laws of the canal would require one of us to be ashore to help the lock-keepers. Although in those happy days there was a keeper on duty at every lock, he was only expected to operate one gate, not both. (Nowadays, apart from the bridges and the big sea-locks at each end, you do it *all* yourself − in the name of 'modern-isation'.)

So there we were, standing by the first lock in a state of considerable doubt, when who should arrive but *Pandora*. Berthing next to us, the little red-capped lady soon came across for another chat, and asked would we like her to help us 'up to the top of the ladder'.

And what a marvellous lesson she gave us in canal-work! No hurry. No fuss. Warps thrown just so; and never allowed to go slack in the up-locks. They were always hardened in just enough to keep *Ocean Dove* lying quietly parallel to the wall as the water boiled into the lock around her. And all the while our friend carried on a lively, chirpy conversation with the various keepers, all of whom knew her well and would smile and make some comment about her having taken to 'small' boats for a change, and "when will you be bringing *Sybil* through again, Miss Edwards?"

We were very sad when we came at last to Summit Reach, and 'Jimmy', as she insisted all her friends called her, tucked her bundle of well-worn oilskins under her arm and strode off back along the road towards Crinan. "Don't worry," she called with a cheerful wave. "Someone's *bound* to give me a lift."

Much later, after a really pleasant North Channel crossing from Campbeltown, we discovered she had left her oilskin hat on board. Having posted it to her (her address was in our visitor's book), we got a delightful letter in return, scattered with nautical terms, and assuring us that she had in fact walked less than a hundred yards on the Crinan road before "an acquaintance happened to come past" and had driven her the rest of the way. And so 'Jimmy' became a firm friend indeed, with whom we swapped many a visit, both afloat and ashore, over the years that followed.

On that first cruise together, Judy and I had learned that the two of us could manage pretty well on our own. *Ocean Dove*, for her part, despite all the calms and gales, had taken us some 563 nautical miles at an overall average speed (for time underway) of 3.4 knots. Not fast – but very comfortable. The interesting thing was that much of this had been to windward, whereas her cruise under gaff-cutter rig of the previous year, just thirty miles longer, had had a much greater percentage of downwind sailing, also in strong winds, yet at no higher an average speed. There was therefore clear indication that the new Bermudian ketch rig was a noticeable improvement at least to windward, and it was certainly easier to handle. The prime object of the change, however, namely to reduce weight aloft and make the boat stiffer, was undoubtedly achieved, for now she stood up to her canvas magnificently, and so behaved at last as her good designer had intended.

The following summer, though, Judy and I stayed at home, for the daughter we produced in August gave us all the joy we wanted. And we named her Rona, to remind us of that first cruise together, and of the beautiful rose-coloured rock of our furthest-north island anchorage.

8
TWO FOR THE PRICE OF ONE?

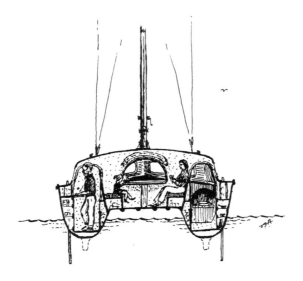

Section through *Twintail*'s accommodation (not to scale); keels which replaced centreboards dotted in

At the sensible age of five weeks, Rona had her first mini-cruise; a leisurely, five-day affair aboard *Ocean Dove* on the relatively still and sheltered waters of Strangford Lough. Apart from the cruelly awakening business of 'night feeds', Judy and I found that boating with a baby was no real problem, and it seemed that during the carrycot stage at any rate an infant at sea was unlikely to be much trouble. Indeed, our tiny daughter seemed to enjoy whatever motion there was, just so long as her cot was securely wedged in place.

However, as further weekends afloat soon demonstrated, a major difficulty faced us – the added amount of personal paraphernalia needed for the baby. Carting everything there and back by dinghy and car each time we wanted a night or two afloat was both cumbersome and wearing, and while sharing *Ocean*

Dove with my father was in many ways marvellous, it became increasingly obvious that we could not go on expecting him to put up with packages of disposable nappies stacked around his bunk, potties in the cockpit, inflatable baby-baths in the heads, or the rest of Rona's clutter.

During the early spring of 1964, a back injury laid me out flat for six weeks, and gave me plenty of time to think. We would clearly be better with a boat of our own, once I recovered. The question was, what type of boat?

Together, we went carefully over our exact requirements and ideals. Standing headroom, for a start. And five or even six berths, so that we could ask friends to join us – and later on perhaps increase our family. A separate toilet compartment was deemed essential, *and* a layout below suitable for mixed parties in general. Shoal draught, we both felt strongly, was especially desirable, and, above all, we wished for maximum comfort at sea, and great stability. Lastly, recalling *Ocean Dove's* ladylike performance, we agreed that we would not object to something just a trifle faster, though this would not be vital, provided we had a vessel that could stand up well to her canvas.

Grand ideas, and on the face of it, a very tall order, since any conventional yacht with such attributes would in those days have been much larger than we could possibly afford, to buy or to run. And then, the more we thought about it, the more we realised we were probably discussing a cruising catamaran. My 16ft (4.9m) Shearwater III racing cat had already taught us what level, rapid sailing could be like on a smaller scale, and, where a family with small children were concerned, a cruiser which stayed firmly upright even when beating into a fresh breeze seemed almost unbelievably sensible.

A nautical friend once described me as being 'a staunch traditionalist', and I suppose I am that at heart, for I do love the look of gaff rig and bowsprits and all the old nonsense of flag etiquette. It was therefore natural that even though I understood some of the good and bad points about lightweight catamarans, I hesitated at the idea of taking my family to sea in a totally unballasted cruising yacht of this revolutionary concept. Supposing she capsized, for goodness sake? And how likely was that to happen? There were many, many questions we kept asking each other. But the only way to find any of the answers at that

(*above*) Reefed down off the Sgurr of Eigg, on passage from Mallaig to Ardnamurchan with the spray-hood suffering; (*below*) *Aku Mor*, with fixed helmsman's shelter, twin inboards and other refinements – superb for chartering and family cruises

(*above*) The added staysail gave our 19ft van de Stadt-designed Mirror Offshore *Farthing* an extra half knot at times; (*below*) Judy in *Farthing*'s tiny galley, sharing the joy of yet another kind of cruising

time, when no one had yet written much about multihulled craft, would be to locate and borrow a cruising cat, and try her out for ourselves.

With the strictly limited sum available to us, we could only contemplate something relatively small, and there were then very few suitable catamarans other than the 26ft (8m) plywood Bobcat and much smaller Shamrock motor-sailer, both designed by Bill O'Brien, and the Prout brothers' new 27ft (8.2m) Ranger, built of fibreglass. With the permanent damage to my spine, DIY maintenance of a wooden yacht was likely to be a problem, so the matter was to a goodly extent decided for us in favour of at least going to see the fibreglass boat. Thus we arranged to charter a 27ft (8.2m) Prout Ranger for four days in August 1964.

With my backbone supported in a kind of mediaeval torture-corset, I borrowed a motor caravan, and with Judy, one-year-old Rona and friend Patrick, set off on the ferry across to Stranraer. Our route took us down through England in one go, so that we arrived more than a little travel-weary at Canvey Island in Essex, on the north side of the Thames' mouth, in the late evening.

Almost before we could stretch our limbs, we were greeted enthusiastically by the Prout brothers, and hustled at once aboard the almost rectangular little craft waiting for us at the end of the ricketty jetty. Her pale-blue moulded resin upperworks felt strangely smooth to our fingers as we passed things down, but seemed to give adequate grip for our feet, despite the angle at which her two lean and canoe-like white hulls lay on the slanting bed of the entirely empty and very muddy creek.

Trying to settle ourselves in while Roland and Francis kindly explained the gear, the drop-keels and the workings of engine and heads was quite a business, and we ended up with a very late supper. Indeed it had long gone dark before we were sufficiently sorted to get to bed. Rona's carrycot was parked in the tunnel-like but spacious starboard quarter-bunk, which extended under the cockpit side-bench. We put Patrick into the port one, and Judy and I snuggled exhausted into our sleeping-bags on the athwartships double bunk in the forecabin.

The very idea of a double bunk in a sailing boat was then rather novel, but one placed across the ship instead of fore-and-aft, to us looked even stranger. We soon realised the advantage, however, for with the catamaran slightly heeled on the sloped mud of the creek, we were able to lie comfortably 'head up' instead of rolling into one another, as we might with a more conventional set-up, and were soon soundly asleep.

By morning, although the boat had floated unnoticed during the night, quite naturally the tide was falling again, and by the time breakfast was over there was not a drop of water in the creek. *Paradis*, as we found she was named, was once more lying in comfort on the mud, and this allowed us now to study her at our leisure. We liked what we saw.

On deck, the amount of space was extraordinary for such a relatively small boat. Her huge cockpit measured roughly 6ft by 5ft (1.8m × 1.5m). Its floor was self-draining through holes in the bridgedeck, allowing any water to drop straight into the sea beneath, between the two slim hulls. Over the back of the cockpit was a neat sliding bracket for the 9½hp outboard motor, which could therefore be raised and tilted well clear of the water when the yacht was under sail, and in each of the sterns projecting aft on either side of the engine was a large storage locker, above a buoyancy compartment. Lifting rudders, with their tillers connected by a stout crossbar, completed the picture.

Working towards the bows, we found sensibly wide sidedecks only slightly obstructed by the tackles, slots and top-arms of the big plywood drop-keels, but the cabintop and the 11ft (3.4m) wide foredeck presented truly magnificent working areas. A pulpit rail as long as a garden fence, it seemed, ran protectively round the entire forward part of the ship, and her fine-ended bows peeped beyond it like narrow noses on either side, each fitted with a bollard and a fairlead for the rope/chain anchor cable.

On asking one of the Prouts why there was no central fairlead for the cable, I learned that by mooring the boat to one bow or the other, rather than centrally, one could give her a sheer to one side, and this kept her from swinging about at anchor. With such extremely light draft, only 14in (0.36m) or so when the plates and rudders were raised, she otherwise tended to yaw to and fro when moored in anything of a breeze, as would any really shallow craft.

The one odd feature of her rig which caused us all to look slightly doubtful, was a cigar-shaped float, sitting like a small airship right on the top of the 34ft (10.4m) mast. One could not help feeling that whatever insurance properties it might have, its presence was much like the sword of Damocles, in that it formed a constant reminder of what just conceivably could happen.

It is worth mentioning out of fairness to the type, that whereas the first forty or so of these Prout Ranger catamarans were all fitted with these masthead floats, the only ones to have gone over were the prototype, purposely capsized with great difficulty in a strong gale during the testing period, and – to my knowledge – one other, which got caught by rather freak conditions in the mouth of the River Elbe in a storm. She, incidentally, righted herself within four minutes, and there was no loss of life or limb. The designers eventually decided that however light, the inevitable weight and windage of such a float so high above the water was perhaps more of a danger than a benefit, and few of the later Rangers were so fitted. The class as a whole proved both safe and stable, in spite of what in later times would be thought to be a very narrow beam/length ratio for a cruising cat – only 12¼ft (3.8m) beam on her 25ft (7.6m) waterline length.

Below decks, entering from the cockpit via the large companion-doorway and big sliding hatch, one finds a small dining or lounging area with seating for two or three people either side of a central table. This could be lowered if need be, to form a spare double berth. Headroom here over the raised bridgedeck amidships was barely 4¼ft (1.3m); enough for sitting in comfort. If one wanted to stand upright, a couple of steps led down into either of the two hulls.

Down there on the starboard side was a neat little galley with cooker, sink and draining board, and looking aft, the way into the quarter-bunk. Forward, a door in the main 'thwartships bulkhead opened into the double-berth forecabin. The port hull was similar aft, but with a hanging space in place of where the galley was on the other side. (I felt at once I would prefer to have a proper chart-table at this point.) Then instead of a sleeping cabin forward, there was a large washroom and toilet compartment with full standing headroom. In all, she seemed adequately equipped (or so we thought) with built-in lockers, and though the accommodation was rather odd, it could easily match our listed requirements. It only remained to see how she would handle.

123

At last the tide showed up in the distance, its dun-coloured fingers feeling their way up the bed of the creek, swelling and filling it astonishingly quickly, and as soon as lunch was cleared away, we cast off with Roland Prout at the helm for a demonstration trip.

Under mainsail and working jib, the catamaran behaved just like any conventional yacht in the lightish wind off Leigh-on-Sea, with the exception that she required us to let her headsail backwind fully each time we tacked. Roland explained that her very light weight was insufficient to carry her through the wind's eye reliably unless this was done, and if she lost steerage-way, she tended to weathercock and drift astern. New ships, new tricks; we thought. But I was not altogether unfamiliar with this technique, since the same procedure was usually necessary aboard my little Prout racing cat. Indeed, in a number of respects, the Ranger was just an enlarged version of the same basic concept, with hulls of almost identical, if rather bigger, sections and profile.

Once he was satisfied that we could handle his boat, we motored Roland back up the creek where he jumped ashore at the Prout's jetty. On our own, we silenced the engine and ran back down towards open water, feeling not a little adventurous now in the sparkling sunshine. It was high water, and the creek full to the brim, so it was as well we had taken good note of the route round its various shoal spits when the tide had been lower.

Safely clearing Canvey Point, we headed off down what I hoped was the middle of the Ray Channel. The wind was getting still lighter, and very soon I was up forward on that great rectangular foredeck, helping Patrick set the big masthead genoa in place of the working headsail. No problems with sails falling into the water here; the deck was too wide for that. Our speed at once increased as we trimmed the larger sail, and, turning to starboard over the tail of the Chapman Sands, we headed for the West Nore Buoy, way across the buff-coloured estuary near the entrance to the River Medway, on the distant Kentish shore.

Several large ocean-going cargo vessels were busily crossing our course in either direction, and when the wind fell away and we began to drift on the already powerful beginnings of the ebb, we started the outboard again. With 5 knots showing on the speedometer in the cabin bulkhead, by teatime we had rounded

Grain Sand, and were bursting over the brown tide sluicing out of the Medway, carefully studying our copy of Jack Coote's *East Coast Rivers*. (Map page 28.)

Nothing would do but that I took us to one of those wild, deserted creeks among the saltings, to let Judy and Patrick sample the typical East Anglian skyline of waving sedge-grass, and the long glistening curves of down-sweeping mudbanks as the water ebbed away to the sea. Though the Medway itself was as new to me as to them, I felt certain it would be just like the other Thames Estuary backwaters I remembered from my years in Essex. A Roman writer almost two thousand years earlier had described this very area in a report to his Emperor as 'the lung of the sea', poetically capturing the weirdness and romance that thousands of others since have felt among these strange come-and-go waters.

Slowly we passed Queenborough on the eastern end of the Isle of Sheppey, and then the entrance to the Swale, and a mile further up were rewarded by the broad opening of Stangate Creek, stretching away to port among the saltings. It was just as Jack Coote had described, and exactly what I sought.

Anchored in 'the lung of the sea'

125

Marshes, unaltered by man, closed around us as I headed in, and in a little while the only other boat to be seen was a bit of a wreck showing above the half-tide mark near the muddy shore of Burnwick Island. A winding gut opened to starboard now, and round we went, following its tight curve right round a horseshoe bend. And there, with nothing but a ramshackle hut on the deserted saltings around us, we anchored. There was not a lot of swinging-room, but the tide held us centrally in the gully, and we happily commenced putting Rona to bed and getting our supper on the stove.

Next day we pottered about in a virtual calm, and eventually decided to try a night dried out on the mudflat at Queenborough, before returning to Canvey. Here, below the old town, having sounded all round with the spinnaker pole to check the bottom was both even and free from obstructions, we waited at anchor while the tide left us, and *Paradis* settled herself gently upright on the mud. It proved a most pleasant way to spend the night, and there was only one disturbance. In the small hours before dawn, a tug passed in the nearby channel just as we were on the point of floating off again. The steep wash from the vessel's stern caught us exactly beam on, and rocked the catamaran violently, thumping the alternate hulls on the ground with considerable force. We did not have time to panic, before it was all over, and no harm was done. (Photo page 51.)

Next morning Rona had her first birthday and, by way of adding to the range of presents, produced her twelfth tooth with, for a short time, the usual accompanying sound-effects. She soon settled, and was enjoying her birthday tea when we refloated to a light wind in the early afternoon.

Setting main and genoa, we were delighted to find the catamaran easily capable of short-tacking out over the strong flood tide. Indeed, and to our mutual surprise, she most satisfactorily overtook a racing dinghy which was going the same way. So much for all the derogatory gossip we had heard about catamarans being poor to windward!

From the point of view of pure cruising, we had already decided that living in this type of boat was in most respects superior to being down in the deep hull of a monohulled craft, for one could always 'see out' whether sitting or standing, quite apart from the space provided by the comparatively wide beam.

For the moment, however, it was really her shallow draught which came to the fore, enabling us to cut safely over the banks in relatively slack water, while the one or two other yachts under way that afternoon had to sail much greater distances in order to keep to the deep channels.

Out in the Thames itself, we found a slightly stronger breeze ruffling the fawn tideway; quite enough to push the little catamaran effortlessly along at 4 to 6 knots all the way across. And that was a whole knot or more faster than *Ocean Dove* could possibly have managed in those same conditions, had she been there beside us.

We located Leigh Buoy and bore away up the Ray Gut with our speed at once soaring to 7 knots as soon as we eased the sheets. Riding utterly level and steady, *Paradis* rushed on into Smallgains Creek in ample time to get alongside the Prouts' drying jetty before the tide got too low. So, in light conditions she had proved all that we had hoped and far more. But in a strong wind, what then? I knew I had to be completely satisfied about the cat's stability in those conditions too, before ordering such a 'way out' craft for my family.

Our luck was in. Next day the fresh wind we had wished for arrived lustily, and as soon as we floated, we motored out into the teeth of it, a grand stiff breeze from the east. Some of the gusts we met were obviously in the region of Force 6, rather than 5, and I tried to reef the mainsail as we set it, but for some reason the roller gear had seized, so that we could not rotate the boom. It therefore had to be whole main or none at all, and rightly or wrongly, we thought that the tiny storm jib might be too little to balance it properly, so we hoisted the full working headsail.

With hands on sheets, dinghy-style, and very conscious of our total lack of any kind of ballast and of that big float waiting ominously at the masthead, we cut the engine and bore away. *Paradis* accelerated as though some huge animal had given her twin sterns an almighty shove, and she went tearing off among the white breakers like a startled colt. At 7½, 8 and even 8½ knots she sprinted, hard on the wind, bouncing noisily along from crest to crest, banging and thumping her low bridgedeck on every other wave with considerable force. This seemed to slow her not at all, and she still sailed virtually dead upright all the time, even in the squalls. A weird experience. I noticed Judy sitting with Rona in the saloon, watching through the big archway in the middle of the main bulkhead as occasional seas splashed aboard forward and washed the forecabin windows. They remained completely comfortable in the safety and dryness of the accommodation, out of the blustering wind, yet on the same level as Patrick and myself, who were equally delighted to find that hardly any spray even got to us. How ideal could a family cruiser be!

Though the helm remained light, I have no doubt at all that her balance would have been that much better with at least a couple of rolls in the mains'l. As it was, the Ranger seemed a bit slow to tack when we tried, and in fact we once got her into irons, so that she shot briefly backwards before we reversed the rudders. She then fell off onto the correct tack without further hesitation, and had soon resumed her galloping rush to windward. We held off trying her on a beam reach until we had achieved a number of successful tacks, but at last we eased the sheets and headed back towards the creek.

Watching in delighted awe as the Sumlog's needle quivered round the dial to hover just beyond the 10 knot mark, we held our breaths. *Paradis* heeled maybe eight degrees at times when wavetops passed under her weather hull, but there was not the slightest sign of it lifting anything like enough to 'fly'.

With the end of the island and the mouth of the creek apparently charging towards us, I considered it best to motor in, so as to be able to turn and stop at Prouts' jetty in a civilised fashion. Do what we would, neither Patrick nor I could get the outboard to fire, and all of a sudden we were right in the creek, still doing a good 9 knots, and with the flooding tide adding to that. In a flurry of activity we clawed down all sail into heaps of billowing Terylene, and blew untidily on under mast windage – at 4 knots. The creek was far too narrow for us to try and turn amongst all the moored craft. Our jetty was close ahead. I thought of lassoing it with a warp but luckily, before I could, we had swept past and were careering on up the creek, dodging boats as best we could.

Too late, I realised what I should have done, but dashed forward and let the anchor go all the same. Had I done this earlier, we could have stopped abreast the jetty, and sheered in on the cable by applying a bit of helm to the current, recovering the anchor after we had made fast; but tide and wind together had hustled us well past. As the anchor bit and spun us round on the end of its warp, we set about getting sorted out. Relieved at having hit nothing, I realised with dismay that there would not be a hope of towing the cat back to her berth with the folding dinghy she carried – not in that wind-plus-tide situation. Yet neither could we stay where we were, for we were completely blocking the narrow fairway for other craft.

"What about 'walking' her up?" suggested Judy. "We've got two anchors, after all, and one of you can surely row the spare one away upwind and drop it?"

Within minutes we had the little kedge on deck and, heaving as short as we dared on the main anchor without breaking it out, we rowed the kedge back down the creek as far as its warp would let us, let go, returned to the ship, and hove in. As we passed over the main anchor we broke it out, hauled further up to the kedge, then rowed the bower anchor to windward to the extent of *its* cable, and let that go. This process was repeated once more, and we were then easily able to reach the jetty itself with the end of a rope. As we pulled ourselves in, we lifted the main anchor for the last time, and warped *Paradis* alongside the staging without the slightest difficulty. Someone on the sea-wall applauded! I must say we were rather pleased at the ease with which the business of 'walking with anchors' had worked, and have since used the same manoeuvre on several occasions, in even bigger boats, and with just the same ease.

As to the catamaran, whatever shortcomings her particular design might have when it came to tacking in a breeze, we felt now, at any rate as a temporary measure for the next few years, she offered so much more than a conventional yacht that she would do us very nicely. Her performance under sail compared impressively with *Ocean Dove*; she remained blissfully level and seemingly stable in a blow; had lifted over the short estuary seas both buoyantly, dryly and safely, and had stayed comfortable – if rather noisy at times – below decks. The accommodation was certainly what we required. Above all, the price was just within our means. By nightfall, we had placed our order for a Ranger 27 to be built for us during the winter.

And that is how *Twintail* came to be launched over the Canvey Island seawall, on 14 May 1965. (Photo page 51.)

9
THE FAMILY CAT

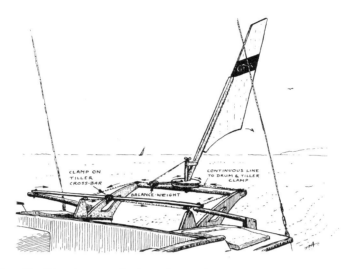

Twintail's Henderson-designed wind-vane gear (not to scale)

The twin-hulled culmination of nine months of planning and list-making slid westwards under my feet through the darkly overcast night, with a most peculiar surging motion. To starboard the seafront lights of Hastings came steadily abeam and passed astern, creating a reflected glow off the low clouds bright enough to let me read the otherwise unlit compass. Not that there was much need. The lines of its dim card and grid-wires remained uncannily parallel, despite the short quartering seas, because even though I was quite alone on deck, *Twintail* was being steered by a far steadier hand than mine.

This way and that, the stout wooden tillers wavered behind me in the darkness, always correcting, always keeping the little catamaran's stern on the preset angle to the wind, as the tall plywood wind-vane to which they were connected swung gently on its axis, a black shape tapering upwards over the wake which rushed pale and pulsing from under the bridgedeck. Compressed between the two sledging hulls, that wake was like a mountain torrent at times, filling the blackness with excited tumult, hissing out the continuing news of our speed.

Inklike seas alongside threw dim yellow reflections up at me from the distant promenade's hanging chains of bulbs, while away to port nothing other than the tiny rows of lit-up portholes and powerful navigation lights of big ships could be seen. Our shallow draught allowed us to stay safely inshore of their busy lanes.

For the first time since the frenetic day in early May when I had arrived at Canvey Island to help launch and name our new ship, I felt at last that I could relax. Delayed first by various fittings which had failed to turn up in time, and then by strong unfavourable winds, the last few days had been hectic, worrying and exhausting. Engineless till the very last minute, in desperation I had eventually bought second-hand the engine we had used aboard *Paradis* the previous summer. The lovely grid compass, mounted under the armoured glass lid of a locker running across the front of the cockpit, had also been installed at the last moment, which was why we still had only a torch to light it at night. (Photo page 52.)

Twintail had been given a marvellous send-off from Canvey, not just from the men who had built her, but from three generations of the Prout family as well. Clear of the creek, a brisk southerly had bustled us out of the Thames Estuary at a most promising pace, until it headed us and began failing as we rounded the North Foreland. My crew, Roland Prout and Nicco, a friend from Ulster, agreed that it was wiser not to try beating through the unfamiliar Downs after dark, and in the last of the daylight we had put into Ramsgate Harbour.

The early start next morning taught me forcibly just how the Ranger's low bridgedeck could slam, as laden with stores for the entire journey down-Channel and up the Irish Sea, she bumped and banged southwards into the steep, wind-over-tide popple. Gaunt, sad masts of various wrecks projected at forlorn angles from the brown-grey water on the edge of the Goodwin Sands to port, as we tacked, stood in towards Deal, and tacked again. Then South Foreland, and a final hitch which took us close past Dover – only to find the wind departing yet again and the strong flood stream beginning to sweep nor'eastwards against us. We motored on as far as Folkestone, and refuelled while we waited for the ebb.

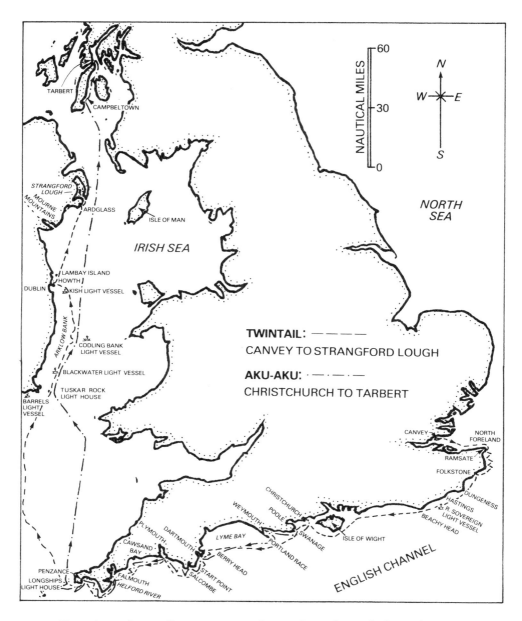

Buzzing dreamily on over the pale calm of the afternoon, captive in a yellow haze, a compass course produced Dungeness magically ahead at the appointed hour. The slim, elegant line of its still new black-and-white-banded lighthouse contrasted starkly with the squarish bulk of the noisy, blue-sparking, steel erection behind it. For several years they had been building that massive nuclear power station, but despite its long-to-be-unfinished ugliness, it nevertheless recalls happy memories for me – a setting sun, and the first of a light air which in its coming grew to a perfect sailing breeze from over our port quarter, as we bore away under sail into the gathering dusk, on course for Beachy Head.

That had been two and a half hours ago. Up forward, the jib swung loosely for a moment in the lee of the bigger sail, then filled with a clap and a thud as the wind caught it again. I checked the compass with the rubber torch. Still perfectly on course. What a wonderful thing this vane steering gear was! And how marvellous for me not to be chained to the tiller for the next couple of hours.

To prove it all to myself, I clipped the hook of my safety harness into the eye of the slide in one of the long tracks we had had fitted onto the cabintop handrails, climbed out over the snug, high-backed cockpit coaming and, dragging the slide after me, felt my way cautiously forward. Out on the wide foredeck, the odd motion of the little cat made itself even more apparent, and I crossed to the broad pulpit rail to watch and enjoy it for a few seconds, before booming out the headsail on its long wooden whisker-pole.

Twintail was running onwards in a series of small swoops between each of which she would briefly hesitate, before dashing on again, rocking slightly from side to side as she did so. It was just like sledging down a long, undulating, and unending slope. And how strange to turn round and face aft into the wind as I struggled with the long spar, and to know that no one was in the cockpit, that no one other than an invisible physical relationship between the wind and the boat and the sea was holding her on course.

With everything clipped in place, and the clew of the jib brought across, I made my way aft and pulled in on the weather sheet. The sail filled, pulling vigorously as the whisker-pole poked it further out to windward, and at once I felt *Twintail* respond. The swish of water from between her sterns rumbled into a muted roar, and I staggered a little as she launched herself forward with a surprising acceleration down the overtaking face of a sea.

The torch beam showed me the Sumlog's needle moving up

from 5 to 7 knots and back, and I sat down just in time to have to get up again as I realised she was bearing away for a gybe. Booming out the jib had of course upset the previous balance between rig and wind-vane, and I had to release the gear's little clamp, settle *Twintail* back on course by hand, and then lock it in again, before I could regain my comfortable seat. Then there was the deck-log to write up. How could I so nearly forget that?

'*Wind: E, 2-3. Course: 254°Mag. Speed: 6kts. Position: Roughly on line between Hastings and . . .*' – I checked the flash of that light to seaward – '. . . *the Royal Sovereign Light Vessel.*'

The Royal Sovereign . . . so often I had heard its weather reports relayed on the BBC shipping forecasts. Now here it was. Famous names! There had been Deal and the Downs, the Goodwins, Dover. And more to come, what with Beachy Head, the Owers, St Albans and the dreaded Portland Race. I was thinking of that, and whether we would go round outside it or take the inside passage, when the hatch suddenly slid back, and the oilskinned shape of Nicco emerged into the cold cockpit.

"Morning," he said quietly.

Why, so it was! But very early. I told him the course, heard him repeat it, showed him where the torch and the deck-log could be found in the darkness, and wished him, in spite of myself, 'Goodnight'. Then I ducked into the saloon.

A shaded candle stood on the cabin table, its flame wavering in a draught as I slid the hatch shut and closed the twin doors behind me. The light steadied, warming the varnished mahogany arch of the main bulkhead, beyond which was my double-berth forecabin. Going down the steps into the starboard hull and forward past the galley, I felt again that slight rocking as *Twintail* accelerated down a wave and rumbled softly, swiftly, on into the night.

Just a minute or two (it seemed) after I had climbed onto that big athwartships bunk, I was suddenly aware of bright-blue sky above my head. Opening my eyes fully, I realised it truly was morning, and found I could look straight up through the sloping pane of the wide forward window to the sunlit burgee lazily flapping above our pale-blue masthead float. All the brilliance of that fresh new day shone on the yellow genoa, which Roland had apparently set in place of the boomed-out working jib during the small hours.

The Family Cat

I lay there on my back, head cradled in my hands, feeling the boat lifting along under me, and wishing with all my heart that Judy was there to share it all. She, poor girl, was all those hundreds of miles away at home, looking after not just Rona, but now our latest model too, the three-month-old Susan, named after an ocean-voyaging friend.

The sizzle and spicy tang of frying bacon quickly got me up, and I remember glancing at the carved scroll on the main bulkhead as I took my place at the table. It bore our ship's motto, the words of the telegram received by the Walker children in Arthur Ransome's delightful book, *Swallows and Amazons*: 'IF NOT DUFFERS, WON'T DROWN.' Well, hopefully we weren't, and wouldn't. I had chosen the month of May for this delivery trip with the utmost care, for the pilot books all stated clearly that we would then have the best chance of easterly winds. For most of our way down-Channel, this in fact proved correct, the drawback (which they hadn't mentioned) being a succession of calms and fogs.

We also got held up by contrary tides south of the Isle of Wight, when in teeming rain and the pitch blackness of night it soon became obvious from the changing bearings of the Needles Light that we were being set rapidly into Poole Bay. Starting the outboard and lowering sail, we altered course for Swanage Bay, where one or two shore lights occasionally showed, faint and out of focus through the downpour.

We found a vacant mooring in the light of the black rubber waterproof torch, which I then laid on deck with its beam pointing forward, and gaffed the illuminated pick-up buoy with the boathook. Not unnaturally, in struggling to lift the thing on deck, I then kicked the torch overboard, and the darn thing stopped lens uppermost on the seabed, some 10ft (3m) down. Its wan, accusing beam glared back up at us all night, but we had no way of retrieving it.

A good fresh wind sprang up in the early hours, and we made a quick start under working jib and a few rolls in the mainsail, to catch the first of the west-going ebb. Thumping our way to windward over a tidal jobble to skirt the Peveril Ledge reef, we came about for what proved one of the finest sails of the trip, passing Portland Bill at slack water, and easing sheets to reach away westwards, rocking rapidly and irregularly to the short

135

beam seas at a most impressive speed.

Visibility in Lyme Bay was poor, to say the least, but I was initially more interested in the catamaran's behaviour. Breaking tops came curling across from France before the ever freshening breeze, and at first I fully expected every other crest to catch her wrong and perhaps throw her up on one hull. But no; the weather hull never once came unstuck, and my interest in a very short time changed to an admiring confidence.

By lunchtime the wind was up to Force 6 or so, just ahead of the beam, and our speed was often around 8 knots, so that the motion became uncomfortably jerky and fierce. A further roll or two in the mainsail acted like magic, however, slowing the little boat just slightly, but producing a more buoyant, bouncing motion, something like that of a car being driven rather quickly over a bumpy road.

I tried to recall and imagine how any of the conventional craft I had sailed in would have felt, even in considerably easier beam-on conditions, and concluded that not only had I bought myself a good sea-boat, but an amazingly untiring one into the bargain.

Although the little cat's movements were decidedly staccato in the circumstances, they were always small in actual extent, and we did not seem to be exerting ourselves in coping with them, which seemed a considerable bonus. Another was that throughout the entire seventy-mile passage to Dartmouth, an open glass milk bottle stood forgotten in the middle of the cabin table, along with the Tilley lamp and other unsecured items. The only thing that slid around a little bit was an empty plastic water-can, which, being light, found its way unaided across the painted surface of the wooden flooring in one hull. 'Stowing for sea' looked like being a thing of the past in this boat!

The amount of noise that went on inside the fibreglass hull was, however, more than a bit overwhelming at times. Intermittent slams as waves broke under the centre-sections of the flat bridgedeck forward made sleeping in the forecabin out of the question now, though I managed a peaceful enough snooze in one of the quarter-bunks. In the cockpit the din of the meeting 'inner' bow-waves as they streaked aft and churned out between the twin sterns, just beyond the helmsman's elbow, proved literally deafening over a period, especially when our speed rose beyond 7 knots.

Visibility remained bad all day, and at last I began to wonder if I had made enough allowance for leeway when setting the course. Some instinct told me I had not, and fortunately we were able to verify this, for I had installed a tiny Radio-Direction-Finding set. A good bearing on Berry Head showed we were indeed much deeper into the huge bight of Lyme Bay than planned. Hauling up hard on the wind to correct matters, we were more than ever glad of the reefed mainsail. I learned in due course that there is often a considerable tidal set into most of the big bays along the south coast of England, which accounted for the fact that the land which eventually appeared through the murk fine on our starboard bow was Berry Head itself, in spite of our course alteration. So we were still several miles to leeward of our target of Dartmouth.

A tough beat into the teeth of a vicious hailstorm took us down the iron-hard Devon shore, towards the sinister sloping fang of the 125ft (38m) Mewstone. We shot inshore of it, and at last a gap materialised in the wall of land to leeward, forming a rough 'V' in the skyline, and our speed rocketed to 10 knots as we turned towards it. Close under Kingswear Castle, we handed sail to motor into the wonderful calm of Dartmouth Harbour. The rain had stopped, and a little clear sky appeared, flushed with the first pale colours of sunset. Steep piles of houses clung almost miraculously to the close hillsides on either hand, and we could see people enjoying evening drinks in their gardens above us. Up past the ancient seafaring town we buzzed, taking in the sights and sounds of the famous old seaport before rounding up alongside a vacant pontoon at the marina.

We had averaged 5.6 knots from Swanage, and were delighted with our little 'double canoe'. She had given us a fine and relatively easy sail in what had been uncompromisingly brisk conditions.

Our next hold-up was a day of light headwinds which dissolved into dense fog as soon as we had worked south, rounded Start Point and cleared Bolt Head. Motoring on, we reluctantly decided it was too risky to continue into the night, for fog with darkness is not at all a happy combination.

The most suitable anchorage mentioned in the pilot book lay somewhere ahead, in Cawsand Bay off Plymouth, and in a while we heard the uneasy mooing grunt of Penlee fog signal blending with the foghorns of a number of assorted unseen vessels. Like ourselves, most of them seemed to be seeking a way in out of the cold, now that daylight had deserted us all. Alone, and without seeing a thing, we began to sense the invisible muffling blankness of high land somewhere close to port, and with the echo-sounder's neon light flickering and only the red and blue-green glare of our navigation lamps now lighting the moist air ahead, we crept gingerly in.

Suddenly there was the hint of a yellow glow in the fog upwind of us, and a whiff of coalsmoke from house chimneys wafted around us on the heavily saturated atmosphere. The beam of our second torch, an unwieldy but powerful battery lantern, nevertheless lost itself in a mere cottonwool column of light, no matter which way we pointed it. We crawled on for a yard or two with the engine in neutral, found good anchorable depth, turned into the last of the breeze and let go. The dark, dripping silence closed in on us as we lit the paraffin riding-lamp and hung it on the glistening forestay. In its gently swinging gleams, we stowed the soaked mainsail and retired below.

The last dregs of dawnlit fog were just tearing themselves slowly out of the tree-lined cliffs above us as we came on deck to make sail, early next morning. The village of Cawsand, perched upon its rocks in the angle of the bay, slept on – apart from some observant dog who barked distantly as we got our anchor. And the wind was again in the west, dammit!

Under a blanket of cloud, we slowly coasted past our first bit of Cornwall, and I was beginning to feel that my home and family in Ulster were a very, very long way off, when quite suddenly the air fell away, the clouds pulled back, the sun came out, and all at once from the north-west a bright new breeze came glittering over the water. *Twintail*, with her sheets eased, went flying off on a broad reach, twin white wakes roaring out astern, and the drop-keels vibrating as she topped 8 knots.

The wind gathered strength, and soon we felt the big yellow genoa was a bit much, and changed it for the more sensibly sized working sail. Just as we sheeted the latter home, however, an empty sail-bag, drying on the lifelines, blew loose and before anyone could grab it, was a soggy bundle fast dropping astern in our wake.

It took only a second to trip out the self-steering system and then gybe round, but by the time we had everything close-hauled and were crossing our track, the bag was already hard to see, for it disappeared regularly between the waves. If the tall Nicco had not carefully kept his eye on its position from the outset, we might well have lost it. Even then, as we drew alongside to gaff it with the boathook, we agreed that the difficulty of getting it on board had it been one of us in a heavy, waterlogged and maybe shocked condition would have been considerable.

We all wore safety harnesses on deck after that.

The succession of delays had thus run us into a period of strong northerlies, which really freshened up as we crossed Mounts Bay. Deciding against trying to beat into them up the Irish Sea, I now deemed it better to wait for a fairer slant in Penzance. Here Roland had to leave us anyway, and, off his own bat, Nicco generously took it upon himself to telephone his wife and ask her to look after the two Andrews infants, so that Judy could be free to join us and her new ship by air and rail, and so share the fun of the final passage home. Friends of that order are precious indeed.

Wednesday 2 June had dawned miraculously calm, with just a faltering hint of the remaining northerlies as we buzzed out of Penzance dock under power. There were now four of us on board, for at the last moment our 'old' shipmate Dave had also managed to take time off, and, typically, his particular sense of humour was greatly tickled by the thought of us sailing our 'cat' down past the tiny fishing village of Mousehole, that pale and sunny morning. *Twintail* had her main and genoa goosewinged, and was making just sufficient speed to give her new crew the feel of the weird 'sledging' motion which her double hulls somehow produced.

The Runnelstone buoy came abeam just after midday, the wind by then getting fickle (heralding a shift perhaps?), but off Land's End's black lines of rock we were suddenly confronted by a nasty-looking tide-rip which erupted out of nowhere and in seconds had extended right across our bows, all white-capped and jumping. We were hardly making enough way to keep out of it so, lowering the outboard, we motored rather ignominiously round its rustling, leaping tail. Land's End itself and the Longships' evil reefs slid finally astern, and at last we could stop the engine, tip and lift it clear of the water, and come round close-hauled on starboard tack. Slowly and rather tentatively, *Twintail* stole softly out towards the empty, sunlit horizon.

Now, the cruises I had so far accomplished had either been purely coastal, or ones in which the land was seldom hidden for more than a few brief hours. And the truth of the matter, as I got down to my work at the chart-table in the port hull, was that I honestly had no idea if I were capable of the necessary navigation. I knew the principles and theory from books and all that Herbert had taught me, of course – and also that doing it in practice might be quite another matter. My feelings of uncertainty were heightened by the fact that the light but still more or less northerly wind kept shifting. Never once would it let us sail the direct course, and *Twintail*, joining in the fun of making my Dead Reckoning even more tricky, was generally steered by her vane. Faithfully, she followed every whim of the vagrant air.

After worrying unnecessarily for the first two or three hours, I suddenly realised that so long as we were able to make careful notes in the deck-log as to each of the new headings she settled on, and the times and distances recorded between course alterations, all this, allowing for the leeway involved, could easily be plotted on the chart later, or whenever the wind had changed sufficiently to allow us to steer more nearly northwards on the desired track. I put the chart away, and discovered it was supper-time, and that Judy had neatly laid the cabin table. Out here, already far from land, there was something very luxurious and homely about that.

At sunset we lit the navigation lamps, and wandered on, making approximately north-westwards at 2–3 knots. The evening shipping forecast suggested now that with luck we might get a lift sometime next morning, but even as we switched the radio off, we were severely headed yet again. Trying hard to keep up with our ever changing compass headings, we blundered on into the encroaching night. It would not have helped had we steered by hand; the object just then was to sail as close to our direct course as we could, and the vane had already proved it could do that far more effectively than any of us.

Perhaps the greatest advantage of the vane gear (designed specially for *Twintail* by Mike Henderson of Cowes) was that the person on watch could move about freely, and so keep an all-round lookout instead of having to sit for two and a half hours in more or less a fixed position at the helm. I remember dozens of times when, seated at a tiller or wheel thinking I had been keeping a constant watch for shipping, someone had come on deck to glance wide-eyed over my shoulder and say: "Do you *know* he's as close as that?" I would then twist round in horror to find some vast vessel bearing down upon us in the one sector I had been unable comfortably to observe. But with this 'hands off' kind of steering there was never any such problem, for we each developed a habit of standing up every few minutes and turning slowly round in the middle of the cockpit, to scan all parts of the horizon in turn. Modern electronic autopilots of course offer the same benefit.

For Judy and me, settling into our sleeping-bags in the cosy forecabin, that first watch below together in our very own ship proved happy and peaceful. The wind remained light enough that even here, with all the open Atlantic Ocean off our port bow, none of its waves were sufficient to slap the underside of the bridgedeck below us, and only the quiet trickling sounds of the starboard bow-waves and the occasional muffled comments of our crew, back in the cockpit, came to our ears.

It was well after midnight when we took over again. The clouds had vanished, and we gazed up in wonder at the sparkling miracle of this, our first totally unbroken and full view of the whole marvellous canopy of starlit heavens. It looked slightly more than a complete hemisphere, curving over us like an inverted deep blue bowl whose 'rim' rested on the black horizon, and whose convex sides and dome were pin-pricked with myriads of tiny holes, through which silver and blue lights continually winked and gleamed. There was no moon, and the illusion of being centred beneath that upturned bowl was quite unforgettable. We both had the impression that as little *Twintail* slid steadily on, it all moved along with her, invisibly attached to her masthead.

'0600 Thursday. Utterly becalmed.' Until now our erratic course had taken us on average in the general direction of Ireland's south-western extremity, not at all where we wished, but as the catamaran slowed to a stop and lay gently swaying and bobbing, wakeless on the glassy surface, I felt sure that the commencement of the long forecast westerly windshift was imminent.

We breakfasted, and waited.

It took two more hours before we felt another breath, but it came, and to our relief, from the north-west. The moment we had steerage-way, we came round on port tack, and for the first time *Twintail* could lay comfortably just east of north, directly for the Tuskar Rock. Off the sou'eastern corner of Ireland, that counted as the gatepost of the Irish Sea itself.

Having carefully worked out the previous fourteen hours' Dead Reckoning since losing sight of the Cornish coast (a job lasting barely twenty minutes), I now estimated the Tuskar to be some 105 nautical miles away. One thing was certain; catamaran or no catamaran, we were *not* about to break any speed records.

It was midday before I had the fun of fulfilling an old and entirely romantic ambition, in that for the first time I was able to calculate a 'Noon Run' on board my own little ship out at sea. It was a pitiful sixty-two miles!

Sunset came again, and the 'wind', still a faint Force 2, finally enabled us to get our first non-stop 100 miles onto the Patent Log, just half an hour before midnight. Slowly, however, throughout the small hours the breeze began backing round, and though still weak it steadied in the sou'west around breakfast-time on Friday morning.

At last I managed to get a Radio Fix, which surprisingly indicated that we were six miles north of my DR position, though I could not imagine why this might be. At least my reckoning was wrong by only a little; pleasing enough after all those hours of drifting aimlessly. Months later, I was told that a set northwards into the Irish Sea is quite commonly experienced.

By Friday noon the haze had intensified into a definite fog. We would otherwise have had Ireland well in sight by then, but there was nothing other than our own somewhat diminishing circle of empty water, moving with us. I was down below rooting in one of the forward lockers for a heavier sweater to keep out the clammy coldness, when I heard, quite distinctly, the faint *moo* of a foghorn. Dashing on deck with Reed's *Nautical Almanac* in one hand and a stop-watch in the other, I listened carefully so as to time the next characteristic. Apart from the soft noise of our wash, there was nothing to be heard. Not a thing.

Puzzled, I went below again, and returned to the forecabin. Immediately and clearly, the horn sounded to me again, though the others out on deck heard nothing. Curious, I timed the signal, and ascertained that it came from the Barrells Lightvessel, surely some considerable distance away to port. The much nearer Tuskar Rock should have been far more audible, yet we could not hear it at all. It was all rather worrying, for the tides in that area run rapidly, and if we were even to approach the vicinity of the long lines of shoal banks which now lay – or should be lying – not far ahead, along the eastern Irish coast, an accurate Fix was absolutely vital.

I resorted once more to the little radio set, and immediately picked up the dots and dashes of the Marine Beacon on the Tuskar, apparently fine on the port bow and just where it should be. More than intrigued by this trick of the fog, we sailed on. At 1340 the radio bearing began to swing left, and I shot up on deck just in time to see the ghostly light-tower slide past through the mist about a quarter of a mile away. Landfall! (Map page 132.)

In seconds it was gone, and we then had the task of finding the Blackwater Lightvessel, fourteen miles further north. We should have altered course at once for less cluttered waters, armed as we were with some sort of proof that I *could* navigate blind if I had

'In seconds it was gone . . .'

to. But we didn't, and fortunately the Blackwater Ship turned up as expected, at teatime.

Rain swept in, and the evening went prematurely dark before we had reached the next lightship, on the Arklow Bank. Here the tide races diagonally across long chains of sandbanks which lie parallel to and about eight miles off the Wicklow coast. The velocity varies, just to complicate the matter.

Judy and I located the first two monstrous, unlit, red buoys on the outside of the Bank, luckily missed the third in the darkness, and caught a quick glimpse of the flashing one at the northern end. At once we set a new course to the north-east, aiming for the Codling LV which guarded yet another shoal, further out from the land, and, having handed over to Nicco and Dave, I turned in very tired.

I was deeply asleep when Dave bashed on the cabin door and announced that the ship was becalmed again and that some kind of tide-rip had appeared astern and we were being sucked backwards into it. Quaking with sleep and the suddenness of the wakening, I scrambled aft to the cockpit, hauling on clothes, and blearily stared at the broken water which showed in the early morning greyness, now only a hundred yards astern. Hastily I got the engine lowered and firing, wondering feverishly where the hell we could have got to.

"What course will I steer?" asked Nicco, placidly.

I blinked at him, shuddering in the cold damp air. "Best stick to what you were s-steering," I stammered, and with a thumping heart hurried down to the little chart-table in the port hull. "How long have we been becalmed?" I shouted over the whine of the outboard.

Dave poked his head in, his dew-spangled hair giving him an exotic look. "'Bout half an hour, no more. Going quite well before that."

Half an hour? It made no sense; there simply was no sandbank near us anything like shallow enough to cause breakers. Surely not? I reached up and switched on the echo-sounder, and its neon indicator flickered to life, reading well over six fathoms.

"Did you see the Codling Lightship?" I called.

"No. But we heard its fog signal." Dave consulted the Deck-Log. "Two forty-five. We thought it was about three miles away to starboard."

"To *starboard?*" I gasped. "It should have been ahead." So much for my navigational prowess.

"We heard it again, or thought we did, just about twenty minutes ago," Dave added, but that only helped a little.

"What was its bearing, near as you can guess?"

"Starboard beam, or thereabouts. Hard to tell, really."

I glanced at the sounder again. A bit better, thank goodness; eight fathoms, and gradually deepening. At least the engine was forcing us over the tide and away from whatever shoal it had been. Glaring at the chart, I saw there were many possibilities, inshore of the lightship. We could be here, near the shallowest part of the Codling Bank; or there, further north off the Bray Bank; or maybe had been swept away back down to the South Ridge. But which?

The radio!

Hastily I tuned in to the frequency of the Kish Bank lightship, which in those days was moored some seven miles off the mouth of Dublin Bay – its bearing would surely give us a clue. But no matter what I did, the little DF set was capable only of picking up the staccato buzz of the magneto and sparking system of our high-revving outboard motor. I dared not stop it, for the spring ebb was still running hard, probably at around 3 knots against us, and none of us wanted to find ourselves back with those tide-rips. I would have to 'find' us some other way.

Having thought for a moment, as calmly as I could, I asked Nicco to steer directly into the tide's run, which we obtained from the chart. We were now making through the water at a regular 4½ knots. Allowing for tide speed, this gave us a nett 1½ knots over the ground on a known course, so it was a simple matter to work out that each four minutes' motoring should see us progress one cable's length (1½ nautical miles being 15 cables, and 4 minutes being conveniently a fifteenth part of an hour).

Noting the depth at the end of each cable thus travelled, and using the scale of the chart, I was able then to plot these soundings onto tracing paper. By moving the resulting trace over the approximate areas of chart I supposed us to be on, and keeping it exactly parallel to our course, the line of soundings would coincide with those on the chart itself – somewhere.

They did.

In *two* places. I still had to decide which. Both areas being clear of any immediate shallows, I felt it safe now to ask Nicco to stop the motor for a moment, and almost at once got a good clear radio bearing of the Kish Bank Lightvessel's beacon, which when drawn on the chart nicely crossed one of my lines of soundings. The other was miles out, so once more we knew where we were.

In anything at all of a breeze, we would have continued under sail, happy enough that we would make our home port in adequate time for Nicco and Dave to be back at their jobs by Monday. Strangford Lough however was still over seventy miles north of us, and at the present rate it might be a day and a half or more before we arrived. This would be cutting things rather fine, especially since we carried barely enough fuel for five hours' running. We decided the sensible thing was to motor now either directly to Dublin Bay, or a trifle further north to the snug little harbour of Howth (which rhymes with 'both'). Suitable trains could be boarded at either, but Howth seemed the more attractive possibility. Altering course, I hunted out the Irish courtesy flag, and its presence in our rigging produced the most friendly and helpful welcome one could imagine when, just after midday, *Twintail* came to rest at the quayside.

"Customs?" said the man who took our warps. "Oh yis, to be sure, but isn't he away just now for his dinner? You'll be wantin' showers and tings in the Yacht Club here, so just you come on ashore and help yourselves. The Officer will come and see you later. Don't you be worryin' about a ting. Now, what can I be doin' for you?" His eyes lit on our outboard. "It's a long walk for petrol – you'll be wantin' some of that. Just hold your horses a minyit, and I'll get me motorcar and run you along with the cans."

He subsequently refused point-blank to be paid a penny for doing so. What could have been nicer?

The Customs Officer arrived shortly after Nicco and Dave had rather sadly departed for their train, but, far from being put out about this, he displayed enthusiastic interest in our unusual craft, the first catamaran he had even heard of let alone seen, and was most curious about 'that fonny ting' at our masthead. Indeed he wanted to know much more about what kind of a passage we had than about what we might, or might not, be carrying.

The weather that afternoon remained calm and dull, and on our own now, Judy and I decided to wait for the 1755 shipping forecast before moving on. In the event, it spoke of better conditions due 'later', and as we both needed a really good rest, we gladly took this as an excuse to stay in port for the night.

Sitting, just the two of us, in *Twintail*'s cosy little saloon, with the warming Tilley lamp hissing merrily and a good supper tucked away, we reviewed the passage we had just made. Slow? Yes, very. The average speed over the 257 miles covered from Penzance was a mere 3.3 knots, perhaps not so bad when one considered the half-hearted headwinds when crossing St George's Channel, and the lengthy calms encountered further north. But we liked our new ship very much.

Seven o'clock on the sunlit Sunday morning that followed, saw *Twintail* slipping out between the pierheads. A light air from just east of south wafted us past the rocky islet of Ireland's Eye, and with mainsail and genoa set wing-and-wing we headed smoothly northwards in great contentment, Judy doing the navigating just for practice. (We felt it only sensible to be able to do each other's jobs on board, though I have to admit that her navigating is a lot better than my cooking.) She kept the shore in sight all morning, past the green and humpy Lambay Island, until though the strong sunlight still warmed our backs, the day became hazy and everything disappeared except our own now familiar bright circle of sea. We liked that circle. It was ours, and it came with us always. Now and then a ship or a bird would arrive to visit it, or a plane would fly over it, to depart and leave it all once more to us, our little ship, and the sky above.

That was a glorious sail, slipping along at a steady 4 knots without the slightest effort. The cockpit was spread with airing bedding, drying oilskins, discarded clothing and improving suntans. Around teatime the peaks of the Mourne Mountains, Judy's heartland in County Down, began to show faintly to port above woolly banks of mist, and our pleasant following breeze gradually took off as blue afternoon lengthened out into the golden paleness of evening.

St John's Point Lighthouse appeared from the haze ahead, its banded tower familiar to me since my very first sailing days, when my father took the two-year-old me afloat in his Snipe Class dinghy, from nearby Tyrella beach. Now, as our speed dropped away, there was not even a current to carry us on, or back, for this is a strange place where tides from north and south in the Irish Sea meet and equalise. We stowed all sail and motored on towards the little fishing port of Ardglass, and behind its massive breakwater at twilight we dropped our anchor onto a sandy bottom clearly visible through sixteen feet of still and crystal water.

Next morning brought uncanny silence, and we peered out through blank windows into a dense, white fog. After breakfast it was still as thick, and in flat calm we motored cautiously out with the ghostly shore blurred but bright, showing about a cable off. We were now only a few miles from the hurrying currents of the long narrow entrance to Strangford Lough, and it was a question of catching the remaining hour of flood right now, or else having to wait until evening, when passage up the then unlit lough might be even more hazardous.

Keeping the craggy shoreline just – only just – in sight to port, and a careful watch both on chart and echo-sounder, we hummed along until forced to strike off into nothingness on a one-mile compass course to clear the outlying St Patrick's Rocks off the entrance to Strangford Narrows. Hoping hard we were allowing enough for the powerful tide rushing in, we took a further blind cut right across the tideway to locate the Bar Buoy. Faintly at first, it swayed and swung into sight, the water boiling about its weedy sides as we closed it gratefully, then hard a-port, and the brown shores and dim white tower of the Angus Beacon materialised on either side. We were in.

It was, as I had hoped, purely a sea-fog, and as the last of the flood bore us rapidly five miles inland to the open lough itself, the mist thinned and evaporated into another beautiful and warm day of perfect late spring sunshine. As *Twintail* swept through onto the broadening, island-studded and very blue Strangford waters, a quiet little wind came rippling merrily after her, like a welcoming pat on the back. Making sail at once, we shut off the engine, and silently, delightedly, slid on towards the green, curving humps of the drumlin isles behind which our mooring lay waiting, in Ringhaddy Sound.

Safely and comfortably, our little catamaran had journeyed 728 sea miles at an overall average speed (for time under way) of 4.1 knots. And now she was home, so early in the morning that no one saw us arrive. It was rather nice to share that moment, just Skipper and Mate together.

10
THE SHIP THAT WOULDN'T GO TO SEA

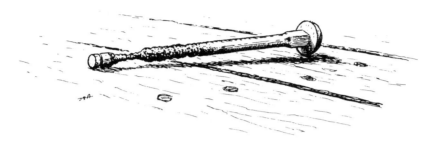

A corroded iron fastening from *Sudvik* – one of the 'important ones'

Time and again we have met saddened mums and dads cruising alone while Granny looked after the kids 'who don't much like sailing, you know, particularly when it's rough'. (Out comes the tale of some wild passage when everyone was seasick and Daddy swore at little Johnny for getting in the way during a sudden gybe – or something of the sort.)

We were utterly determined to ensure that our small daughters could always enjoy their cruising, so we introduced them to it extremely gently, sailing at first in the shelter of Strangford Lough, choosing our weather, and going home if it turned nasty. Gradually, we hoped, the time would come for rougher, more venturesome stuff – and come it did, to the point where *they* wanted to set out when *we* did not. (Photo page 52.)

In the meantime, I was, however, to be offered one major change of scenery, and most memorable it proved to be. And although it took place abroad, I feel it worthy of mention for the lessons it offers.

One Monday evening at home, our telephone rang. It was Jimmy, the little lady we had met and liked so much during our honeymoon cruise in *Ocean Dove*, now four years previously. Calling from Scotland, she explained that an acquaintance had recently bought an ancient Colin Archer ketch, and had asked her to sail the boat back from Norway for him. Would I like to help?

Her voice came tinnily through the earpiece. "We'll have to leave on Friday morning – is that all right?"

"*This* Friday?"

"Yes. If you can."

Panic ensued, but I duly arrived with other members of the crew at the bright little fishing harbour of Risör, nestling in an arm of a fjord on the north-western shore of the Skagerrak, about ninety miles south-east of Oslo.

Met by the owner's teenaged son, we were led along past elegant wooden buildings, where ornamental trees dangled their feathery foliage in the breeze between the smartly painted lapboard gables. On, beyond the low fish quays, the town straggled to where colour-washed bungalows were perched on the bare rock, each with steps zigzagging down the smooth, ice-worn curves to its own private jetty. Nearly all of them possessed a flag-pole, and the national colours were much in evidence.

Everywhere people smiled, and seemed to grab any excuse to practise their English on us. Almost every family seemed to own, as if they were cars, little varnished clinker-built launches, double ended and fitted with a windscreen and a one-lung motor driving a feathering propeller.

At last we came to where a ramshackle set of boatyard sheds covered and even overhung the edges of a small, rocky island a few yards out in the fjord, and there, between it and the mainland shore, lay an elderly, white-painted, and very beamy gaff ketch – like a sullen duck. We were rowed out, and had not been on board her more than a minute before we knew she was anything but ready for sea. (Photo page 101.)

A typical Norwegian-sterned Colin Archer design (rumour had it that the great man himself had once owned her), *Sudvik*, as I shall call her, had originally worked for her living as a pilot cutter, then as a fishing boat. Only a year or two before we joined her, she had been converted below decks for cruising. Fitted and furnished in attractive, varnished pinewood, with a coachroof of the same material, she had also been given a new and powerful diesel engine. Even that was shortly to cause us trouble.

At some stage in her career, the main boom had snapped and, for ease of handling the lost area in the original cutter's mainsail had been reinstated in the form of a large gaff-rigged mizzen,

whose stout mast now grew out of the cockpit smack in front of the tiller. Her bowsprit was new too, and one began to suspect why when a study of the ancient mainmast revealed literally dozens of longitudinal splits. An Aberdonian wit amongst our crew was heard to remark that one of these cracks, near deck level, could usefully have been fitted with a locker door.

During the next couple of days of intensive work, we learned to our astonishment that *Sudvik*'s new owner had not himself set eyes on her. Nor had he seen fit to have her surveyed. We also discovered that when she had been taken for a trial sail about a month before our arrival, the rudder had fallen off. A rescue had been affected and the boat hauled out at the little island yard off which she now lay, and where it was then found that most of her iron hull fastenings had rusted almost to nothing. The 'important ones', we were told, had therefore been replaced; which left us wondering which were the unimportant ones. Moreover, during that brief sojourn under cover, her coachroof had dried out, so that when we had first tumbled below decks to stow our gear, we had found ourselves seeing not merely daylight through its gaping seams, but could actually watch the cars and buses going past on a nearby shore road. Two tubes of sealing compound went into just one seam, as a hasty, temporary measure, for as an amateur crew with jobs to get back to, we had little time to caulk it all properly.

Even more and worse revelations cropped up, one after another. I had been allotted a cosy pilot berth high under the broad sidedeck on the starboard side of the big saloon. Awakening the first morning, I involuntarily stretched, extending my right arm as far as the cramped space allowed. My forefinger encountered and was enfolded by something strangely brittle yet soft, rather like a dry sponge, and I opened my eyes to see half my finger embedded in the middle of one of *Sudvik*'s massive oak ribs. Horrified, I peered at the neighbouring rib. It too was as squashy as an overripe pear, and so was the next. I hastily stopped looking, and in pensive mood, climbed down to the cabinsole to ask the skipper if she knew. She did, and was equally gloomy about it.

"The yard assures me she won't fall apart all the same," she said. "They reckon there's so much excess timber in these ships, a little duff stuff here and there won't make the slightest difference. I just hope they're right."

Waterproofing the old vessel was the prime job, but we spent nearly as much time on fruitlessly trying to correct her steering compass. *Sudvik*'s wheel was mounted on the back of the cabin bulkhead, at the starboard side of the cockpit. Chains led from it through galvanised tubes to the long tiller, which itself was too awkward to use because of the intrusion of the mizzen mast.

The compass, when we had arrived, was still in a cardboard box in the cabin, but as we naturally would need it permanently fixed for the proposed North Sea crossing, we had screwed its gimballed base onto the cabintop, just forward of the wheel. Only when we got under way for a quick engine test did we begin to have doubts about it, but time was pressing, and as the first part of our journey would consist of coast-hopping, we thought we would have ample time and opportunity to check it on different headings as we went, and so make out a suitable deviation card.

At last, with the big diesel rumbling reassuringly underfoot, we headed away southwards into the Skagerrak. It was a bright, completely calm morning, and as we rounded a low headland and found our way back in amongst the 'leads' behind an intriguing string of smooth-rocked islands, a series of quite dreadful bearings warned us that the compass was more than badly in error.

"Perhaps it's the engine," suggested the skipper, and she had us making sail the moment a breeze filled in. Swaying up the heavy gaff main and mizzen, and sweating up the headsail halyards, we hopefully bore away. As Jimmy said, she had no intention of motoring all the way across the North Sea, so if the engine had been setting up some electrical field and upsetting the compass when it was running, who cared, so long as all was well under sail.

The newly risen wind was dead ahead, and though not over-fresh as we hauled in the sheets, I think we were all amazed at *Sudvik*'s extravagant angle of heel. Buoyant and about as stable as an empty eggshell, she lay over till her lee bulwarks dragged through the water, and we forgot all about the compass in forming the opinion that she must have only about half her correct amount of ballast on board. Where the rest had gone not even the owner's son knew.

"Well, she does seem uncommonly tender," commented the skipper as she closed the engine's throttle, and pulled the 'Stop' button.

The diesel gave a resounding *clang* and thudded to an abrupt stop with a loud and alarmingly evil *hissss*. We looked at each other in puzzlement. Burly Ned, our handyman extraordinary,

'. . . amazed at *Sudvik*'s extravagant angle of heel'

came up at once with the likely answer, by suddenly leaning over the lee side.

"Isn't the exhaust outlet down here somewhere?" we heard him ask, just as a sea came up and smacked the side of his head. He jerked inboard, aided by his wife Margaret, who had taken a firm hold on his belt. Brushing the spray from his face, he opened a seat-locker at the side of the cockpit, and peered in. "Thought so," he said, closing the lid again. "Some idiot's gone and led the exhaust-pipe straight down to the engine without a loop in it to act as a water-stop. The outlet's well under water with her heeled like this. My guess is there's sea in the cylinder-block. We'll be lucky if it hasn't cracked it wide open. It must have been pretty hot when it stopped."

"Maybe if we tried to restart it, the piston might blow the water out again," said I, not knowing a thing about diesels. So we tried. There was no provision for a handle, and each time we pressed the starter button we were rewarded with nothing more than a loud metallic *clonk*. The engine was locked solid.

All the while, Jimmy had been trying to take the tubby old ship to windward up an increasingly narrow passage between enclosing rocks and islets, and it was suddenly but definitely

154

time to tack. With everyone at the ready, she fisted the tiny spokes. After a nerve-stretching pause as though to consider what was being asked of her, the elderly boat slowly began rounding up towards the wind. At last the sails commenced to lift, then to flog heavily in the fresh breeze. For a while they continued to do this, then less enthusiastically; and *Sudvik* finally lost way.

"Dammit, she's not going to make it," said Jimmy between her teeth, and the red bobble-cap cast about this way and that as she glanced at the nearby rocks. "I don't think she's got room to gybe round, either, the old cow," she remarked, and laughed suddenly. "I'd never have believed it!"

As *Sudvik* hung motionless, the skipper twirled the wheel the other way, reversing the helm, and got us to back the headsails. Ned ran along the deck and held the clew of the staysail far to weather, not realising its power. It filled and practically shook his arm off as the wind at last forced the wallowing ship's head round. Reluctantly she gathered way, heeling mightily as before; but it seemed barely seconds before we had almost crossed the rocky channel and would have to tack again.

"Lee-Oh!" called Jimmy (with a bit of room still in hand). "And back everything," she added with a chuckle.

This time all went well, but it was soon obvious that beating to windward was not at all practical, for we hardly gained at all before it was time to come about once more.

"It'll take us all day to work any worthwhile distance south inside the leads, at this rate," said the skipper. "She simply won't stand up to her canvas, and the leeway is frightful with her heeled so badly. We'll just have to go back and get the engine seen to."

Choosing the first suitably wide part of the channel, we were relieved when our ancient vessel agreed to bear away on a run, and indeed gave us a very pleasant sail downwind, back towards Risör. With our minds now free to check the compass again, we knew our turning back was right on that account too, for we could make no sense of the instrument at all.

Creaming in towards the boatyard island, we stowed the main and under headsail and mizzen began rounding up towards our mooring buoy. *Sudvik* had another idea. She shot past, having turned nothing like enough, and headed directly for the main road and one of those pretty little houses perched upon the rock under the trees.

"Let go the anchor!" barked Jimmy instantly, her clear voice ringing out only just in time. The cable literally jerked us to a halt with the bowsprit end vibrating just four feet from the nearest stone.

By now the weekend had set in (naturally), and neither mechanics nor compass adjusters could be found. The owner's son at last located a small man with a grin-wrinkled face, who agreed to come and have a look at our 'sizzed' engine. His few words of English had a distinct Scottish twist to them, and were due, he explained, to certain quite regular clandestine crossings of the North Sea in wartime. He had many a yarn to tell, and was highly pleased to learn that most of us had either been born in Scotland, were of Scottish ancestry, or had at least 'the fine sense to livings there'. On being reminded that many places on the Scottish west coast had names in Old Norse, he grinned even more than ever, and with twinkling eyes said: 'Ah – Veekings!' and looked sheepishly at us over his whisky glass.

By unscrewing the injectors and rotating the flywheel by hand, our friend soon had the water out of the engine. It had entered two cylinders, but apparently just slowly enough not to have cracked anything, for when everything was connected up and the starter tried, the machine burst into immediate and healthy-sounding life. Grins all round, and more whisky all round too, which produced even better yarns.

We arranged to prevent water entering the pipe in future by remembering to stop the engine only when the outlet was well clear of the water, and then bunging up the pipe with a wooden plug attached to the ship's rail by a string. In practice the method worked well, for if perchance we forgot to remove the plug before starting the engine, the gases merely blew it out on the end of its line popgun-style, with an impressive and rather pleasing 'bang'.

The compass was our major problem now. Our brief initial sortie had shown that it was grossly inaccurate whether the engine was running or not, and there was no question of it being 'good enough' to get us home. First thing next morning we motored in to the fishquay (where old *Sudvik* looked in no way out of place) and moored very tightly indeed alongside. Then, with a hand-bearing compass, Ned sighted carefully along her fore-and-aft line from the stern.

"Two-seven-oh," said he, eventually. "What have you got, Jim?"

"Two-*five*-five," said I, peering into the binnacle.

"Better check it," muttered the skipper, glaring darkly at the offending instrument.

Ned put his foot on the tiller to try again from the extreme pointed stern of the ship, and the rudder moved, revolving the steering wheel a little as it did so, by means of the connecting chains.

"What have you now?" I called over my shoulder.

"Still two-seven-oh," said Ned, sighting again. "Why?"

"Because I now have a reading of two-seven-er, about eight," I replied. "Now there's a novelty. The ship hasn't moved, but she's suddenly got a different compass heading."

"It's the other way, too," laughed Jimmy incredulously.

"Just a moment, Skipper." I turned the wheel back again to where it had been before Ned's foot had caused it to move.

"Well I'm blowed!" Jimmy looked round at me, her face creased with amusement. "You've just turned the compass!"

The only explanation was that one or more links in the steering chain had become highly magnetised, just where it ran over the gypsy at the back of the wheel, so that each time the links moved from one side to the other, the compass card tried to follow them round. Short of unshipping the chain and bashing it with hammers on the quayside to displace the magnetised molecules, there was only one quick thing to do. The compass was moved forward to a position where its card eventually agreed with the hand-bearer's reading. It was now sited a good four feet away from the wheel, along the cabintop. True, we almost needed binoculars to read it, but at least the thing was now passably accurate.

At last we felt ready to try again, apart from requiring more ballast. That was unobtainable, so we went anyway.

The same weather pattern unfolded as on the previous day; total calm until just before noon, when a brisk wind appeared out of the cloudless sky and blew right in our teeth. We hardly tried to sail at all. We even kept 'inland', following the leads behind the islands as much as possible, for each time we poked *Sudvik*'s almost unballasted bows into open water she bobbed about like a cork and appeared to gain hardly anything over the ground, whether under power or sail or both. Sheltered water was our only hope, or we would never reach the North Sea, let alone get across it, and that in itself now raised certain speculations. As it turned out, we never did cross it.

We spent the first night at the head of a tiny rocky inlet below a rather run-down village, and the second in another creek that bored into the very heart of an extraordinary island in the mouth of the short fjord leading up to Kristiansand. That was a fascinating berth, totally sheltered by reason of a dog-leg kink in the entrance channel and high rocky cliffs all round: the most perfect anchorage I have seen anywhere. Our third afternoon brought us into the winding river-mouth at Mandal, our selected 'jumping off' place, near the southern tip of Norway. Here we tied up to the main street, making our warps fast to the lampposts, and did some last minute shopping.

Next morning was busy with Customs and watering ship, and then we were off, once more motoring, but this time truly westwards, towards Lindesnes, our departure point. The calm and lovely forenoon clouded over as we approached the big headland, still under power. Down below in the pine-clad cabin, Jimmy and I were plotting North Sea courses, and securing loose items. It was as well that we did the latter, anyway.

No sooner was the great dark rock mass squarely abeam than the wind arrived dead in our faces yet again, and we hurried on deck to help the others make sail. Crazily heeled, the ketch was laid on starboard tack, but at once it became necessary to reef, for she was wallowing hopelessly now that we had stopped the diesel (and carefully bunged its exhaust-pipe). She was sailing quite fast, but right over on her very ample beam ends, and her wake told us she was sliding to leeward very badly indeed.

The wind continued to freshen as we worked, and before the job was half done, a shout from the skipper had us fighting to get the mainsail off altogether. The ship seemed to go mad without it. In fact so appalling was her movement that even Ned, who had never been seasick in his life, suddenly erupted. Water cascaded over the decks, and it was all we could do to retain some sort of grip on this wildly bucking, half-ballasted pig of a yacht. Under headsails and mizzen now, she was a little more upright, but still dragged her rail through the water, and made poor speed.

After studying the situation for a few minutes, Jimmy handed me the wheel and went below again to look at the chart. In less than fifteen seconds, her small, cheery, walnut of a face reappeared beneath the drawn-back hatch-cover, wisps of grey hair blowing in the draught.

"I'm going to turn back," she announced chirpily in her high, clear voice.

Surely not again, I thought as I struggled with the little steering wheel. The decision, however, was even more advisable than I guessed.

"For one thing," the skipper continued, climbing out into the cockpit with the rest of us, "the way we're heading, we aren't going to make better than the German coast, and even if we stood on a bit and then threw her about or gybed round or whatever, with the amount of leeway she's making we wouldn't even weather Norway." She paused, and looked from one to the other of us. "For another thing," she added, "she's making water, and it's coming in rather quickly. I could hear it pouring in somewhere around the engine. Better head back for Mandal please Jim, *if* you can get the old tub to bear away. I'm very sorry, everyone; but I just don't think it's safe to continue."

While most of us fought with sheets, bilge-pump or wheel, and got *Sudvik* heading back into the lee of the gaunt headland, the owner's son crawled about beneath us, where the engine lurked. He soon came up again, pale green and soaked to the skin around his shoulders and chest.

"It's pouring in all right!" he gasped, gulping air. "Seems to be where the exhaust-pipe goes out through the hull. I can see daylight around the pipe, and the sea simply gushes in each time she rolls. It must have been coming in at a terrific rate when she was close-hauled."

"*Round* the pipe?" exclaimed Ned. "But it's a tight fit in the hull!"

"Well, not now, it isn't."

"I'm glad it's nothing more serious," said the skipper, no doubt thinking (as I was) of those 'unimportant' fastenings. "We'll be able to do something about *that*, back at Mandal. Really – it's as though she doesn't *want* to go to sea."

"At least with a good following wind like this, we won't be long getting there," said I rather foolishly. I had quite forgotten the pattern of weather that had been repeated daily since our arrival in these waters, and, true to form, for it was now late afternoon, the wind began that very moment to fall away. There were inevitable suggestions that we might turn around and try again, but the skipper wisely wouldn't hear of it.

"The ship just isn't seaworthy," she rightly insisted. "We'll be so and so lucky if something else doesn't go wrong before we get in, as it is."

So on we drifted, gradually closing with the coast and eventually resorting to the engine, which mercifully started and ran as smoothly as ever, for all its drenching.

It turned into one of those unforgettably beautiful evenings, flat calm and with the low, humpy land showing deep blue to port, and each successive little headland ahead of us a paler, greyer shade than the one before it, yet each with a crystal sharp outline. The cottages along the shore were at that distance just dots of white, from whose chimneys hazy blue wood-smoke could be seen lazily spiralling into the still air.

"It's amazing how you can smell the smoke so well, right out here," I mused aloud – and found everyone staring at me, and then sniffing vigorously. In a moment we were all whirling round, some dashing below decks, and others sniffing low in the cockpit.

"Nothing's visibly amiss down here," came a muffled shout from the cabin, "even around the engine – as far as I can see. And the batteries are okay."

Ned lifted a locker lid – that same port side one in the cockpit which opened onto the space along the back of which lay the exhaust-pipe and silencer. As we peered into the twilit gloom of the locker, the smell of burning wood intensified, and we suddenly saw little glowing growing sparks creeping about like those in the burning-off soot at the back of a coal-burning fireplace. The planking of *Sudvik*'s hull all around the silencer was, despite its recent soaking, on the very point of bursting into full flame.

"For God's sake shut the bloody lid!" someone shouted. "One puff of air, and that's going *whoof*!"

The skipper pulled the stop button, and the engine clattered to a halt.

"A bucket, quick!"

As the old ship drifted to a standstill on the pale satin sea, we cautiously reopened the narrow lid, only to find that the worst of the trouble was so high up under the sidedeck in relation to the tiny opening of the locker that, no matter how many buckets of water we tried to chuck in, it was quite impossible to wet it. Neither of the fire extinguishers on board was small enough to do it either.

Sudvik began to rotate in the current. We could not sail her in to Mandal, for there was now not the merest breath of wind.

Crossing our fingers, we gingerly restarted the engine at a tick-over to keep the exhaust as cool as possible, and pushed on over a quietly chuckling bow-wave towards the darkening point around which lay the Mandals River. The sparks in the locker brightened noticeably as we gathered way.

"If only we could get water onto them somehow," said the skipper, without her usual happiness.

"I know!" exclaimed Ned's wife suddenly, and dived for the companionway. "The coffee pot! It's got a long spout. I'm sure we could reach in with that!"

And so it was that we picked up the colour-sectored leading lights as dusk closed in, and worked our way into the river-mouth up to our old berth alongside the main street, with a human chain of coffee-pot-passers busy between galley pump and an open cockpit-locker, from which issued acrid clouds of smoke and steam. It also happened that an observant young newspaper reporter saw us coming in, respected our need for rest after we had finished putting out the last of the sparks, but made an appointment to get our story, such as it was, first thing next morning; which is why we really owe some kind of an apology to Her Majesty the Queen and His Royal Highness the Duke of Edinburgh because, while we were being interviewed (cameras and all), their then ocean-racer HMY *Bloodhound*, came motoring impeccably into Mandal. Admittedly her Royal owners were not actually on board, but she was nevertheless the first foreign Royal Yacht to have visited the little port, certainly since the war (if not ever), and there would normally have been considerable pub-licity.

Even so, '*Sudvik* of the Roasted Sides' got the banner headlines and front page treatment, and *Bloodhound* had a nice little mention on page two.

The sequel to all this was that we did not in the end bring *Sudvik* across the North Sea. She was sailed over much later by a professional delivery crew who were favoured by a fair wind and who abandoned her at the first British port to which they could get her.

It had been a sorry but extremely interesting excursion; one which taught me that one should *never* buy a second-hand boat without carrying out a thorough survey, and also that taking an ill-prepared vessel to sea may be not only foolish but downright dangerous.

I had found southern Norway fascinating, however, and had revelled in the intricate pilotage amongst the many islands and narrow sounds. After all, it was not so very different to finding one's way between the drumlin isles and shoals of my then home waters of County Down's Viking-named Strangford Lough.

11
TWIN WAKES TO THE
OUTER HEBRIDES

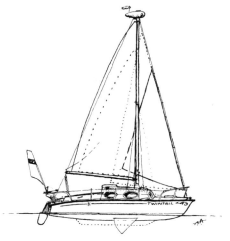

Twintail; changes to rig: smaller mainsail, larger foresail; changes to hulls: drop-keels replaced by low-aspect-ratio fixed-keels, portholes added in both stern-cabins

As the years passed and Judy and I cruised progressively further from home, our three daughters grew older, eating more and needing on board a wider variety of clothes, books, games and so on. The amount of gear we took with us on our annual holidays steadily increased, until little *Twintail* was gradually weighed down, far below her designed marks. In the normal, lightweight trim for which the 27ft (8.2m) Prout Ranger had been intended, her round-bottomed hulls had of course ample buoyancy to keep her riding high, and the lower parts of her 'U'-shaped transom sterns, most effective at speed, dragged only slightly in the water when sailing slowly. But loaded as our catamaran eventually was with all the fuel and provisions required for the particular kind of cruising we liked (mainly in out-of-the-way and totally deserted, shopless places among the Hebrides), her transoms inevitably became more deeply immersed, and seemed to pull half the Minches after them at low speeds.

It therefore became an increasingly rare event for us to be able to work *Twintail* up to any great pace, particularly when close-hauled. If anything of a sea was running, her already low bridgedeck would slam heavily on the crests and further cut down her speed, sometimes so much that her drop-keels would be on the verge of stalling, causing a lot of leeway, and little progress.

Fortunately we were able to give her a new lease of life after the Prout brothers had developed their low-aspect-ratio fixed-keel idea, by removing her wooden boards and fitting a pair of these long, shallow keels, early in 1969. They gave her colossal directional stability, but naturally made her somewhat heavier on the helm, so we also rigged up a simple wheel-steering arrangement. This too was a huge success, especially in heavy going, when the helmsman could sit comfortably forward at the port side of the cockpit, nicely sheltered by the cabin bulkhead and the full height of the cockpit coamings. (Photo page 101.)

Her turning circle was of course now bigger than it had been, but this seemed not to matter, since the process of coming about was altogether more certain than it had ever been with the drop-keels. As before, she would round into the wind readily enough, but whereas previously, getting her going again on the new tack had often demanded smart work on the jib-sheets, the long keels now took immediate effect, allowing her to fill away without hesitation. Not only that; they were considerably lighter than the old wooden boards and GRP plate-cases, and they were also hollow, thereby adding valuable buoyancy just where it was most effective. Once again, *Twintail's* waterline returned to a more acceptable level, and her drag was much reduced – for a time.

Down below, with no thick plate-cases to clutter up the outboard sides of the accommodation in the hulls, we gained a lot of extra space, and were able to restyle the galley to provide more food stowage and a working-top almost four feet long. To port there was (at last!) room for oilskin stowage adequate for a crew of five or six.

During the next two summers, we discovered that our catamaran was now reliably manoeuvrable under jib alone, in anything of a breeze. I began to experiment, eventually learning that, at any rate when working to windward, a sail set on a stay tends to be almost twice as efficient for its area as one set immediately behind a mast. With the steadiness of helm generated by the long keels, it seemed to us that *Twintail* might now happily carry her largest headsail even when her mainsail was considerably reduced by reefing.

After her refit in 1971 therefore, we spent several weekends sailing in various wind strengths amongst the tightly packed islands of Strangford Lough, with the mainsail well reefed, and came to the curious conclusion that she might actually be better off with a permanently smaller mainsail. This, we reasoned, would enable her to carry bigger headsail areas for any given breeze than had previously been possible. We took a deep breath and chopped a wide chunk off the mainsail's foot, equivalent to a full reef. It looked very snug indeed, not to say tiny, and I feared we had overdone things.

A few days later school holidays started, and at last the family could set off together down Strangford Narrows bound for the Hebrides, with *Twintail* sporting her genoa in a far stiffer breeze than it had ever held before. The result, both in speed and handling, was excellent; so much so that I described the alteration and its effects in a letter to the Prouts. They successfully carried the idea a stage further in their subsequent designs, some of which favour huge headsails and very small mains, set on a mast stepped well aft – an arrangement which works superbly, odd and all as it looks. This was all grist to the mill in my increasing role as 'multihull correspondent' to one of Britain's leading yachting journals, so it had been a valuable experiment on several counts.

After an unusually rapid passage of sixty-three nautical miles to Campbeltown on the Kintyre Peninsula, our deck-log clearly stated how well *Twintail* had behaved. It also mentioned how very good it was to be back in Scottish waters and, as the children themselves poignantly put it, 'away from the bangs' of what had recently become Ulster's insanely terrorised and sadly battle-scarred towns and villages.

Working our way next day northwards up Kilbrennan Sound, we anchored for tea in the inlet south of the steeply wooded Barmore Peninsula in Lower Loch Fyne, and were thrilled to see a family of delicate little roe deer, who came to stare timidly at us from the bushes by the water's edge a few yards away. It made us feel there really was at least some true peace in the world. We had no idea even then that within six months we would have left Northern Ireland, to live in a house not two miles down the loch shore from this same enchanting spot. (Map page 76.)

We cruised on, gently and happily, up along the now familiar sheltered waters to Tobermory on the Isle of Mull, revisiting many already favourite anchorages on the way. Tobermory was as ever densely crowded with yachts; the narrow shelf of reasonable anchoring depth next to the town was a continuous bustle of commuting dinghies, and the sparkling West Highland air was torn with the buzz of outboards and the rattle and roar of anchor chains as each newcomer found a gap, or moved to a better one. This was not our idea of peace, so we were glad when Sunday 18 July dawned calm and with a good forecast; just right for the next, more open stage of our journey.

This day, little *Twintail* won her first clump of heather for rounding Ardnamurchan – a traditional 'badge of achievement' on the West Coast – *en route* for the distant isle of Canna.

The 'Small Isles' (their collective name) are really nothing of the sort; but in comparison with Mull to the south and the huge, spectacular sprawl of Skye close to the north of them, they are not large. Past Muc, the first and tiniest, then Eigg with its sharp pinnacle of rock crowning an otherwise smooth hilltop plateau, Judy and I had sailed before, in *Ocean Dove*. In her, we had visited the wild and craggy once volcanic island of Rhum, but little Canna, lying low and long and green to the west of the group, and thus nearest to the Outer Hebrides, was still new to us that evening as we entered the sound dividing it from the steep, seaward cliffs of Rhum. The sky in the past hour had clouded over, and a light drizzle was beginning to fall as we beat in under genoa only, to anchor past the small stone quay among a handful of other yachts.

Almost landlocked, the inlet lay open only to the east, where the north end of Rhum blocked the horizon three miles away. Around us, curiously 'stepped' hills rose, steep and sheltering above the clutch of cottages straggling along the shingly beach, their lights twinkling on one by one as dusk became dim twilight.

166

First thing on Monday morning we rowed ashore past the mostly still sleeping yachts, and explored awhile before telephoning home to breakfasting grandparents. We were amused to find a most polite notice pasted up in the 'phone box, requesting us to be brief, since use of that particular instrument blocked all other calls on the island. It was typical of the courteously considerate and down-to-earth outlook of Hebridean folk, and there was yet another example of this. On either side of the anchorage was a small church; one for the totally Roman Catholic community, and the other a Protestant kirk which the islanders maintained for the benefit of any visitors who might be of that other persuasion. (The island is now owned by the National Trust for Scotland, so the preservation will be continued.)

From the top of the hill by the harbour, beyond the ruin of an ancient stone fortress atop a seemingly impossible pillar of rock, we could see pale glassy water stretching away to the entrance to Loch Braccadale, over on the distant Isle of Skye. Behind us, the air over the anchorage now bore the aroma of bacon and eggs, and already several yachts were getting under way and heading out under power, to turn west – towards the Outer Isles. Well, we had not really planned as much, but here we were, about as near to the 'Long Isle' (the general nickname for the entire string of Outer Hebrides) as we were likely to be. And the Minch was *calm*.

We hastened on board, and hunted out the appropriate charts. While no doubt more heftily crewed yachts were bemoaning the total lack of wind, we, with our complement of kiddies, fully appreciated the stillness of the water, as the outboard took us close under the curious rock pillar of Bod an Stol, a needle-like stack standing 82ft (25m) high at the base of Canna's highly magnetised Compass Hill. Vast 'rafts' of assorted auks lay around us as we took our departure and headed out for the western horizon – a line at first unbroken apart from one low blue-grey hump. Then another grew beside it, and yet another, as gradually Canna, and finally the long coast of Skye, dropped astern.

There is always a wonderful sense of challenge when approaching any land for the first time from seawards. We all enjoyed trying to pick out and identify correctly the various features from the chart – easier with the beautifully printed topographical information on the old-style Admiralty Charts than with the modern 'simplified' metric replacements. These blue islands, however, were like nothing we had ever set eyes on before – a succession of rounded, monochrome bulges, sprouting slowly out of the line of sky and sea before us – and there seemed to be *far* too many of them.

"That high one, for instance, must surely be the top of this mountain marked on South Uist," I told young Rona. "And the one there to port of it would be the hill shown there to the south."

"But what then are that, and that, and that?" she asked. It was quite a puzzle.

Slowly, as we worked across, with our outboard beating its faultless rhythm, the separate humps filled out, stretching towards each other and for the most part resolving into just a few big islands. Over the bows, Loch Boisdale was identified as a distinct dip in the land, and the tedium of steering under power was relieved as all three daughters, then aged seven, six and five, took the wheel in turn now that there was something definite at which they could keep the bows pointing.

After lunch, occasional patches of ripples declared the coming of a breeze which eventually filled very lightly in from fine on the starboard bow. Stopping the motor to sail on in a quieter rustle of sound, we had to bear away a little, and compass-bearing showed that *Twintail* was now heading towards Eriskay, instead of South Uist.

It mattered not that we had set out with Loch Boisdale in mind; Big Harbour, Eriskay, would be just as novel and interesting. We knew it offered excellent shelter, but the Clyde Cruising Club's *Sailing Directions*, without which I can hardly imagine attempting to explore these waters, suggested a tricky entrance to its all but totally enclosed lagoon. Unmarked sunken rocks seemingly lurked in just the wrong places, necessitating an approach very close under the southern point of the outer bay. That was easy enough to identify. But just off the narrow mouth of the natural pool beyond lay another 'awash' rock and, coming in as we were at half-tide, I was relieved to discover that it had recently been given a solid-looking iron tripod and topmark, which made the pilotage much more certain than expected.

Safely in between the bare, stony hills, we anchored in 16ft (4.9m) a minute before 1700. Around us were three sturdy fishing boats, a motor-yacht, and rocky shores on which crouched the low stone ruins of ancient 'blackhouse' crofts. Above these a few prosperous-looking dwellings squatted on the open slopes, their stumpy chimneys emitting the sweet smoke of peat fires, their grounds devoid of fences; who needs a fence when everyone thereabouts knew fine where your own territory began and ended?

Walking round to the head of the harbour to climb the nearest hill, we found Eriskay's wildlife astonishingly tame: rabbits lolloped softly out of our way, not really bothering to hide, and birds paid even less attention, despite the delighted antics of our children. At the top, we gazed out over the evening sunshine glittering across the empty miles of Atlantic Ocean.

"Beyond there," we said to the girls, pointing in 'Boyhood of Raleigh' fashion to the distant horizon, "beyond there lies nothing until America. It would take *Twintail* about a month of non-stop sailing to reach it." I believe Judy and I were almost as awed by the thought as they were. But we knew very well that *Twintail*, grand little boat though she was, could never do that sort of journey with all of us on board, supposing we ever thought of trying. Even with her new buoyant keels, she simply could not carry the necessary stores.

We had used a lot of fuel getting out to the Long Isle, what with the two wonderfully calm but long passages under power from Tobermory to Canna, and from there across; and we were also a bit low on bread. The light to moderate sou'westerly breeze next morning suggested, therefore, a run round from Eriskay to Loch Boisdale where we knew there were shops, rather than having to punch to windward down to Castle Bay, Barra.

It was satisfying to get away quietly under main and genoa after breakfast, but outside there was a surprising amount of swell running, bursting in sudden spouts of foam around the various rocks. We sledged along comfortably enough making 3–4 knots, past the place where the fabled '*Whisky Galore*' ship sank, and by 1045 were approaching the mouth of Loch Boisdale in nice time to shop before lunch, the *Sailing Directions* having indicated that this would be early closing day.

In a while, the fine big white cutter *Solway Maid* came running out under full sail from the anchorage by the pier further up, and as she slid by to port, her owner hailed us with the news that if we wanted stores, everything was shut already 'because of the Highland Games'.

Oh, well. Too late now to wish we had come here direct from Canna! The anchorage looked quite sheltered and we could well have waited a day, but as Judy and I both had a very long-standing desire to visit the twin anchorages known as the Wizard Pool and the Little Kettle Pool in Loch Skiport, further north on this same large island, we decided to use the fair wind and carry on. We could manage without extra fuel and bread for a day or two longer.

We bore away after *Solway Maid*, and Ivan Carr, her observant owner, unfortunately taking our manoeuvre to mean we were trying to catch him up, immediately hove to and waited for us. With immense generosity as we drew abreast of him, he offered us food from his own lockers – a wonderful gesture to complete strangers. Glad that we did not have to accept, all the same we found it hard to thank him adequately for such kindness.

Beautifully handled, *Solway Maid* then let draw to head south, while with friendly waves to her crew we gybed and began a magnificent if increasingly cold reach northwards, along the spectacular South Uist coast. Deep glens and steep mountains sloped firmly out of the sea, many with fine-sounding Norse names to them. Five-year-old Eileen was less impressed by these scenes than the rest of us, but with the offshore wind allowing no sea to upset the steering she happily sat at the helm, competently conning us past the mouth of Loch Eynort, until lunchtime called her to the cabin table with her sisters.

Usinish Light came abeam at 1415 – a lone tower on a bleak headland at the foot of 2,000ft (609m) Mount Hecla – and in minutes we were trying to sort out the various islands at the mouth of Loch Skiport. The lighting that afternoon was grey and flat under the lowering clouds, so it was hard to tell which piece of rock stood in front of what, or whether this or that grass-topped protuberance was a promontory or an islet. Close-hauled, we stood warily in, then with two *very* short tacks, slid slowly through the narrow sound east of Shillay Beg, into the still water of our long-sought Wizard Pool.

And we were not disappointed. It was a lovely, yet at the same time weird and desolate place – especially so in those dour conditions. The smaller of the two Shillay islands closed us in on the one hand, while to the south and east, rough ground swept untamed up to the glistening heights of Hecla.

Despite the rather creepy atmosphere, after tea we all enjoyed a scramble ashore to the top of the steep, craggy hill just east of the anchorage. Remarkable views spread beneath us over the watery fingers of the entire Loch Skiport complex, to where the indented coastline of the Outer Hebrides stretched away northwards past Benbecula's flat wet expanse, to the misty outline of North Uist. Close below us, nestling in a dark land studded with tiny freshwater lochs, the Wizard Pool was a silver pond with a toy catamaran moored just beyond the stony hump of Wizard Isle. From there, a short rocky cleft with vertical sides led westwards like a canal into the adjoining Little Kettle Pool, which despite its name is a bit bigger (roughly two and a half cables across), and which opened again at its far side into yet another way through to Loch Skiport itself.

Before returning to *Twintail*, we had of course to land our girls on the rough and heathered Wizard Isle, to let them pay proper respects to the Wizard, should he be about. Susan, our 'middlest one', was convinced that he may indeed have been, for close at hand an invisible duck kept quacking at us, over and over again – 'himself' in disguise, no doubt!

Just after breakfast next morning, following a damp but quiet night during which the only sounds had been those of drips falling from the rigging and the restless rushings and surges of the sea outside, the wind suddenly swung nor'nor'west, and a heavy swell soon began working in through the rocky entrance, narrow and all as that was. It was nevertheless much wider than the steep-sided 'canal' to the adjoining Little Kettle Pool, through which we were shortly squeezing.

A sleek but elderly white sloop, named *Torridon*, lay there behind the good shelter of Shillay More, her crew still fast asleep after making a night passage and dawn arrival out of Tobermory. We puttered softly by, checking the depths with our echo-sounder before going on and out into Loch Skiport proper, through the other end of the pool.

Setting sail now to the freshening breeze, we reached quickly back seawards round the north side of Shillay More, and out in the Minch found a stiff headwind and steeply breaking seas. We have always tried to cruise for the fun and pleasure of the entire family, so when the slamming of the bridgedeck became unbearable and the heavily confused waves started producing

'We puttered softly by . . .'

rejected breakfasts in spite of the usual pills, we had no hesitation about turning back. The supplies to be had further north at Loch Maddy could wait.

Anchoring again, this time abreast of *Torridon* under the lee of the island's hill, we spent the rest of the morning rambling ashore among its rocks and summits, while the sky cleared and the wind blew with added vigour, mixing the tang of salt spray with the strangely feathery smell of heather. That afternoon, while Judy baked soda bread in the galley, I went off solo in the semi-folding Puffin sailing dinghy we carried, to explore a bit of South Uist. Up among the hills above the southern side of the pool I climbed, and in the strong sun and chilly wind, took an invigorating bath in the brown, peaty waters of the Gull Loch. Neither from there, nor from the anchorage, could house or road or any sign of other man be seen. All around spread only the yellow-greens of grass, the lushness of bracken and soft purples of heather and ling, alternately lit and shaded by the racing clouds. Dark peaty earth showed where the Atlantic storms had scoured plant-life away from the steep overhangs around the naked grey of the ice-worn rocks; the call of land-birds mingled with those of their sea-going brothers, and the wind soughed and hissed in the heather stems. Running about to 'drip dry', for I had no towel with me, the sun and wind on my skin and the roughness of the ground under my bare feet made me feel somehow totally at one with nature that day – an unforgettable experience.

By evening it was blowing much harder, and we ran our invaluable Chum anchor-weight down the cable on its traveller to increase the rope's catenary, for on the very steep-to bottom here, we feared that the CQR might otherwise trip out and literally roll down the hill underwater.

Such is the weather pattern on this exposed edge of the northern ocean that it continued to blow hard for the next five days without let-up. Bitterly cold, never below Force 7, and peaking on Force 9 for hours at a time on several occasions, the wind threw salt spray in soaking wraithlike streaks clean over the 90ft (27m) rounded top of Shillay More, and coated our decks with twinkling crystals.

Without a radio transmitter, we had now been a long time away from a telephone, and were very aware that back in Ulster the girls' grandparents might be getting anxious. Even in normally expected weather conditions, there was often an element of potential danger associated with this constant need to 'phone home to say we were safe. Indeed, we had more than once put the ship into some exposed and obviously risky anchorage or bay merely because it was the only one in the vicinity with a call box – occasionally to find that the thing was out of order, or even that on getting through, there was no one at home at that hour anyway. But here, in this totally uninhabited place, there was no way of communicating at all.

We resolved that in future we would arrange instead to keep a sort of 'running letter' going, ready to post at the first reasonable opportunity, and unless we literally happened to walk past a convenient telephone no one back home should expect us to ring. The system, once we had explained it to those concerned, worked admirably in later years, and turned out advantageous to both parties. Letters were hardly expected more often than once or at most twice a week in the first place, so there was much less cause for worry if we were a day or two finding a post box. But the best was that when a letter eventually did turn up, it presented far more detail about our exploits than a few hasty words over a bad telephone line could possibly impart. Even more, the letters we had sent were kept for us on our return, and formed the basis of the narrative version of our cruising logs, written up later in the year.

At last the wind eased, but the seas were still boisterous when, with our holiday time thinning down, we left the Outer Isles and headed across the Little Minch towards the remarkable 1,000ft (305m) cliff of Dunvegan Head, which lies roughly half-way up the west coast of Skye. We had just enough fuel to motor-sail the last bit of the journey, up the long inner loch to the village, where at Dunvegan's general store we found all we required.

There was a considerable fetch along that part of the loch, so, wanting a peaceful night, we dropped back down to the snug bay below the pale walls of Dunvegan Castle, the impressive stronghold of the Clan MacLeod. The sun set in a yellow calm, gleaming back like flames from the ancient windows, while around us the water reflected the golden-green of trees. What a change from South Uist! And not only was it beautiful here, it was *warm* as well!

Rona had especially asked if this year (just for a change) she might have her birthday 'on land', so we *had* to be home early in August. Conditions next morning, however, seemed simply ideal for heading off round the north of Skye, and possibly visiting the island of South Rona between it and the mainland, before we headed south. If we did that, there was considerable risk that we might not get back to Ulster in time, so we suggested that Rona herself could, if she wished, decide our next move. Quite a responsibility for someone not quite eight years old. She hesitated, but only for a moment.

"My island," she said firmly; and that was that.

It had been a 'crack of dawn' decision too, for we were under power by 0630, hoisting the mainsail as we steered out. A light sou'easterly air let us add the genoa as we cleared the loch, increasing our motor-sailing speed to just over 5 knots. The tide was strongly in our favour too as we rounded Vaternish Point; and with Skye's most northerly headland, Rudha Hunish (pronounced 'Roo Un-ish'), now in our sights, we rushed merrily on, the kids playing 'Happy Families' in the sunlit cockpit.

By ten o'clock, the strangely pointed rock of An-t-Iasgeir was abeam close to port, and its stink of fish and guano was overpowering. For all that, the razorbills, guillemots, and particularly the funny little puffins which sported around it were well worth seeing. And so indeed was a decidedly odd-looking bird, swimming along like, but considerably bigger than, any ordinary seagull hereabouts, and equipped with a most unusual kind of beak. We had trouble finding it in our reference books, and no wonder, for of all things it proved to be that singularly rare and apparently quite accidental visitor from the southern hemisphere, a black-browed albatross. (The poor lonely thing's presence in these waters was later confirmed officially by other sightings.)

Our navigation now needed to be quite a bit more accurate than that unfortunate bird's, for the passage inside the reefs and skerries off Rudha Hunish is not without excitement. Tide-rips, shoals, columnar basalt cliffs and the general aura of harsh, untamed northern elements kept us agog and busy until we were safely around the corner and able to come on the wind.

Under sail only now, we beat more peacefully southwards, past the staggeringly spectacular eastern Skye shoreline, with the altogether different outlines of South Rona developing on the port bow. It was nine whole years since Judy and I had sailed into Acarsaid Mor, at Rona's sou'west corner, and we enjoyed picking our way between the hazards to anchor once more behind the islet at the head of this delightfully secluded inlet. This time, however, five other yachts were already in, and there was not over-much swinging-room.

Proud of having accomplished a forty-two mile passage by mid-afternoon, we were soon ashore to let our eldest daughter lead us on an exploration of the nearer parts of 'her' island. Its rosy and rugged core, rearing in abundance through the thin soil, glinted and twinkled in the sunshine, even more attractively than Judy and I had so fondly recalled. (Map page 76.)

With time so short, we had to leave next morning and chose the 'sheltered' route between the island of Raasay (immediately south of Rona) and Skye's high coast to the west. By 0900 we were already some miles on our way when we began to encounter an increasingly lumpy head-sea. Though trying to remain close-hauled, we were so much slowed up by our once more quite heavily laden little catamaran's dragging transoms and banging bridgedeck, that we were forced to ease sheets to keep way on, and so could no longer lay directly down the Sound of Raasay towards the distant mountain peaks of the Cuillin.

Soon the wind which had been causing this swell arrived, or rather we arrived in it, where it funnelled down from the mountains; Force 4, then 5. We changed to working jib Force 6. We rolled a biggish reef into the already small mainsail. That was better – for a while; then even that became too much for her as the wind increased sharply to Force 7 and we started really battling through heavily breaking seas. Admittedly they were not very big, but incredibly steep and streaked with long, trailing tendrils of foam.

The bridgedeck slammed very severely now. Clipping the end of my safety harness to the track on the cabintop handrail, I edged forward to the juddering foredeck with the minuscule storm jib tucked under one arm. On setting it in place of the working headsail, I discovered that the clew of the latter had become badly strained, so that the metal thimble had partly opened. A non-heeling sailboat puts incredible strain on her rig in a blow.

I spent the next while sitting on the foredeck with portable vice, palm and twine, repairing the clew as best I could, while Judy steered and *Twintail* hammered on under close canvas. I only just had the repair completed when the wind quite suddenly dropped to Force 4. Down storm jib; up mended worker; shake out reef in mains'l . . .

Meanwhile, as their mother continued expertly sailing the boat to windward, down at the cabin table the kids played 'Snakes and Ladders' (to judge from the alternating cheers and groans I heard sounding up the ventilators). They never felt deserted or ignored when the two of us were busy with the ship, for not only could they see out almost in every direction, but with the saloon sited on the catamaran's bridgedeck, they were of course on the same level as the cockpit, and could always speak to one or other of us. We for our part could equally readily assert parental authority if fighting broke out in the 'mess deck', which was sometimes a most appropriate term for it.

Tack, and tack; and tack again; and the sound gradually narrowed about us. A sloping rock strata would come close under our lee on the Raasay side . . . a quick squint at the plastic-cased chart held by shock-cords to the bulkhead in front of the helmsman, then "Lee-Oh!", and round she would come with a sudden rattle of canvas and swirl of the twin wakes and the ring and clatter of a sheet-winch. The smallest of lists (perhaps six degrees at most) would develop to starboard as she filled and accelerated away, perhaps this time towards some soaring cliff on Skye.

Back aft, the rushing maelstrom would begin sluicing out like a millrace from between her transom sterns, then as the breeze once more faded, it would slacken to a disappointed burble. Ten minutes later, still Force 2; so forward Skipper, down jib, and up genoa. Then back along the sidedeck to help tack once more. Thirty minutes later, I would likely be changing her back to working jib.

We worked hard all morning, slowly but certainly altering the scenery as we crept south towards the Narrows, at the far end of Raasay. And then, when lunch was barely over and the town of Portree was just dropping astern behind its steep-sided guardian hills, the wind fell yet again. On with the engine now, to burst over the foul current squeezing through Raasay Narrows, and at long last we were able to bear away with a free, fresh wind on our quarter. Tilting the toe of the outboard clear of the water, we sledged eastwards touching 8 knots in the strong gusts coming off the nearby mountains. Good, yes; but we knew it was nothing like what the boat really should be making in that wind strength. Her designers would have expected *Twintail* readily to top 10 knots in those conditions, as indeed she sometimes had for us in the past, but carrying so much gear, plus a heavy pile of charts, and several days' supply of provisions, fuel and water for the five of us, was clearly asking more of the little cat than they had ever anticipated.

The inescapable conclusion that we had outgrown her, and outgrown her modifications too, came home to roost that day, and very sadly we knew then that if in future we wished to extend our cruising, or to include longer passages to even more out-of-the-way islands as the girls grew bigger and more adventurous, we must seriously begin to look for a yacht designed with that sort of loading in mind. Judy and I, who often think the same thoughts simultaneously, both felt that this could be the last time our beloved little *Twintail* would sail those

177

northern waters in our hands. Even so, there was one more moment of unforgettable magic to come.

At 1840, having motored the last four miles, we rounded the off-lying rocks and turned to starboard into Plockton Bay in Loch Carron. In spite of its unglamourous name, Plockton is perhaps the most beautiful of all Highland anchorages, and that evening it excelled itself, with the blue and mauve mountains making an almost dreamlike theatrical backdrop across a sea-loch fringed with pine trees and rocky cliffs.

As our anchor splashed down to lie in full view on the pale sand two fathoms beneath us, and our engine stopped, the scented air brought music to our ears. Sitting against the clinker planking of an upturned boat beached half a mile away below a neat row of white cottages, a young lad was playing the bagpipes, his lilting pibroch echoing romantically over the anchorage. All five of us sat on the cabintop and listened, totally enthralled. As a sheer treat in sight and sound and smell, this was ample compensation for all the effort that had brought us there that day – and exactly what makes cruising off the West Coast of Scotland so uniquely what it is. It remains for all five of us the most perfect memory of what indeed proved to be our last cruise in *Twintail*. And we did (just) get Rona home to Ulster in time for her 'birthday on land'.

12
THE WANDERING SPIRIT

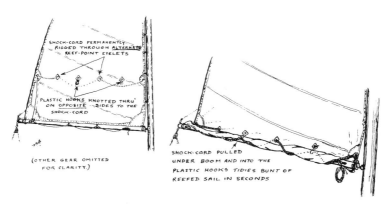

The Andrews' shock-cord 'reef-tidy' (other gear omitted for clarity)

"She's all yours."

A thrill always wells up within me whenever someone offers
me the helm of a new or different sailing boat, but Tom Lack's
wide grin and twinkling eyes seemed to suggest that this time I
was about to find out what the term 'sailing' really meant.
Among a mixed selection of craft which I was sail-testing for
'*Practical Boat Owner*' magazine that spring, this strange-looking
9 Metre Catalac was just one of four quite varied fibreglass
cruising catamarans.

My first glimpse of her, as she rode squat and squarely on her
mooring in Christchurch Harbour, had at once interested me, for
she was unlike any other production cat I had so far seen. Just
over 29ft (9m) long and 14ft (4.2m) wide, she had flaring motor-
yacht-style bows which curved out above upswept chines, and
her much-windowed cabintop looked a very long way off the
waterline as a result of an unusually high bridgedeck. At least
that one shouldn't slam, I thought. However, despite high,
somewhat slab-sided, 'V'-bottomed hulls, she looked purposeful
rather than pretty.

The Catalac's class name derived from her development by the Lack family, long successful in marketing the popular plywood O'Brien-designed 8 metre 'Bobcats'. Unlike them however, this new boat's transom sterns were vertical and partly recessed, so that the lifting rudders were neatly protected by an overhanging extension of the deck and outer topsides. Far more intriguing was the way that the bottoms of these transoms were tucked up, well clear of the water. Compared to my *Twintail*'s deeply immersed transoms, there could be little drag at low speeds here, I reflected; though I confess I doubted if such a bulky vessel could *ever* attain much speed, even in the jolly breeze ruffling the bright, sunlit water of Christchurch Harbour that morning.

Her designer having thoughtfully given her a broken sheer-line, the deck was 'stepped' to a sensible height aft for boarding from a dinghy, and with my cameras and notebook, I climbed up to find a veritable playground of a cockpit enclosed by a sturdy teak-capped taffrail. And the lockers! Never had I seen such enormous lockers. Those either side of the cockpit measured 6ft by nearly 4ft (1.8m × 1.2m) internally, and when I stood in one for fun, its lid was at chest height.

While Tom and his cheery wife Mary steered us out under outboard power through the Run, and made sail in the more open water of Christchurch Bay, I explored below and discovered how carefully their 'family cruising' kind of thinking had been applied to the new boat's layout.

A splendid 'U'-shaped settee embayed the saloon table on the bridgedeck amidships. Seated comfortably there the view to each side, as well as forward via large openings in the main bulkhead and on through the forecabin windows, enabled me to watch our progress with ease. Good handholds were provided where one stepped down into the hulls, which led forward to a pair of bright, airy sleeping cabins, one double and one single, with the bunks situated on the bridgedeck.

In the port hull, a vast galley with a wealth of lockers stretched almost 7ft (2.4m) long, abaft which a door closed off a neat, single-berth quarter-cabin. The starboard hull contained a comfortable passage-berth and a separate washroom more than spacious enough to take a shower installation. Up above, firm guardrails enclosed sensibly broad sidedecks, as well as the 12ft wide (3.7m) foredeck, and there was that gigantic cockpit. How marvellous it would be for children, I told myself.

But best of all, the helmsman was provided with an upholstered folding chair in a snugly recessed steering position forward of the main cockpit, just alongside the cabin doorway. A huge sliding hatch before him acted almost like a 'sunshine roof' over the after part of the saloon, and that entire area right back over the helmsman's head could be sheltered under a big sprayhood in wet or cold weather. The incredible thing was that all this was encompassed in a ship actually a few inches shorter on the waterline than *Twintail.*

As I took over the varnished wheel from Tom, I knew within seconds that I was in control of a true sailing vessel. She manoeuvred with unexpected ease and precision, tacked readily without the need for a backed headsail, yet was quite steady enough on the helm for single-handed sailing. There were no concessions whatsoever towards racing; her Bermudian sloop rig was completely ordinary and basic, and none of her fittings had the expensively complicated look one associates with cruiser-racers. For all that, her ability to sustain astonishingly high speeds and to make to windward satisfactorily in spite of a total lack of any sort of external keels, was a considerable surprise.

It was as we came sliding back towards Christchurch that I felt a tingling, tight sensation growing behind my ears and in the pit of my stomach. Without having at all consciously looked for her, I had found our next boat.

Although a new Catalac would cost quite a bit more than we could expect for our second-hand Ranger catamaran, Judy and I had been living quite modestly for the last seven years. We seldom ate out, or expensively even at home, and had spent our family holidays completely free on board *Twintail* for no more than the price of a few gallons of fuel and the food we would have consumed at home anyway. In fact, what with the numerous weekends we had also spent afloat, we had all become very attached to little *Twintail*, and only with the greatest of difficulty did I finally accept the cheque and hand her over to a new owner. None of us could bear to watch as she departed for her new home near the mouth of Carlingford Lough, though just recently we were consoled by the news that she is still well looked after and loved – a pleasure to someone yet, in the troubled land of Ulster.

We ourselves were then living not far from Belfast, and the extremes of terrorism which had now plagued Northern Ireland for three over-long years were becoming increasingly unpleasant. Eventually, when a building in our local village exploded into the main shopping street in a cloud of flame and flying debris, just after Judy had walked by on her way to pick up our schoolgirl daughters from the next bus stop, we did a lot of very serious thinking. Ulster, in its state of near civil war, seemed to us no place in which to continue bringing up three small girls if we had no real reason to do so. Apart from that, I had been having less to do with our family business, and as a more or less established author and journalist I yearned for somewhere peaceful in which to get on with my writing.

It all added up, and with a sister, aunt and sundry cousins living in Scotland, a move there suddenly seemed entirely sensible, especially since – and what better reason – it would take us to the doorstep of our most favourite cruising ground. A good friend from Campbeltown in Argyll sensed exactly what we wanted when we told him of our intention, and found us a most attractive stone-built house perched on a rocky spur on the edge of Lower Loch Fyne, just outside Tarbert harbour. The Gaelic name on its gate translated as 'the Fort of the Little Ship'. For the likes of us, nothing could have been more appropriate – the miniature Scottish baronial 'castle' (four tiny bedrooms and two reception rooms) I had often romanced about, complete with a mountain burn cascading through its little garden.

Thus it was that when I finally journeyed down to Christchurch on England's south coast, early in the spring of 1972, it was not to sail our new boat to the Strangford Lough that *Twintail* had known, but to the land and sea-lochs of my ancient ancestors.

We had decided on a Polynesian name for her, since after all the modern concept of catamarans had originated in the Pacific. Those who have read Thor Heyerdahl's fascinating book about Easter Island and the giant stone statues to be found there, will recall mention of the *aku-aku* or 'wandering spirit' which every Easter Islander possesses and which can transport his thoughts to distant lands. The idea appealed to us, and so we hoped that Catalac No 7, *Aku-Aku*, would similarly carry us to exciting and faraway shores. So she did, though the start of her delivery trip was a short-lived affair, in both time and distance. (Page 132.)

With Mary Lack and two friends on board as crew, I employed the big 33hp outboard motor to thrust us clear of Christchurch Harbour and out into the hazy Channel calm of that sunny May morning. There was much chat and jollity, for in Mary's company there is never anything else, but we were rounding Hengistbury Head before enough wind filled in to let the kingfisher-blue sails do the work. At last we could turn westwards without having to talk over the rumble of the engine, yet only an hour later the wind died away, a dense fog materialised out of nowhere, and we perforce had to think again. Turning to starboard, we buzzed into the nearby security of Weymouth, and that 'fits and starts' kind of progress was to typify our journey down west during the following days. The fog turned into a short, sharp gale, and windy weather also plagued our crossing of Lyme Bay when the worst was over.

Successfully remembering and allowing for the ingoing tidal set that I had experienced during *Twintail*'s delivery, we made a quick passage to Dartmouth, then were forced in turn to seek refuge in Salcombe, Plymouth, Falmouth and ultimately Penzance, where my brand-new ship got covered in coal-dust and grime. At least by then I knew I had bought a very able sea-boat, whose only real weaknesses lay in the mainsail's roller-reefing system, and an engine that tended to suffer from cavitation problems when used in anything of a head-sea.

The subsequent passage north up the Irish Sea showed off her speed potential, for she easily outsailed *Twintail*'s earlier efforts in virtually identical light headwinds, as far as the Tuskar Rock. Then in only slightly firmer following breezes, she swished non-stop right up the Irish coastline and on across the wide mouth of the Firth of Clyde to the Kintyre peninsula with the greatest of ease and comfort, to delight us with an average speed of 5.3 knots over the total of 396 nautical miles from Penzance to Campbeltown. Our time under way was just 2 days, 23 hours and 35 minutes, port to port, with a best 24 hour run of 143 miles and a highest logged speed, held for a couple of minutes off Arklow, of 12.5 knots.

There was a lot of mutual thanking as I saw my crew off to the airport, before telephoning home with news of our arrival in Scottish waters. Then I returned to the harbour and panicked when I gazed down on the grubby vessel below. The next hour of that sunny, welcoming morning, was spent in a frenzy of sweeping, swabbing, scrubbing and polishing, so that before the family got their first glimpse of *Aku-Aku* she would look again as sparklingly new as when I had first set eyes on her, down at Christchurch. Mostly because of the move to Scotland, neither Judy nor the girls had ever seen a Catalac, other than in photographs. They had touchingly relied on me to buy them the right boat, and I confess I wondered how they would take to her. One look at their faces when they came tumbling out of our little car on the quayside told me. They were thrilled. (Page 102.)

The remaining sunlit sail, twenty miles up the narrow Kilbrennan Sound and round the mountainy shore of Loch Fyne, with the children trying each bunk in turn and peering excitedly into all the huge lockers, and their mother revelling in the excellent steering qualities and speed of her new ship, was a happy way indeed to bring *Aku-Aku* home to Tarbert.

Time showed the new boat to be ideal for family cruising on the rugged West Coast; she took all the vagaries of Highland and Hebridean weather in her stride – and that is saying quite a lot. I used to think that in an area so plentifully strewn with excellent natural harbours, one need never be caught out on passage in a bad blow, because there would always be somewhere to tuck snugly into, and wait till it was over.

Take, for example, the first two blustery weekends of our family holiday in 1974, when *Aku-Aku* had most successfully dashed from bay to inlet and from loch to rocky gut, dodging a veritable procession of gales and lesser blows, any of which would have seemed grossly unpleasant under way. We had carefully 'read' the different levels of cloud, noting the movements of the higher layers which always foretold the next windshift's likely direction and strength; we had heeded the glum and steady all-day drizzle which as often as not heralded the next gale, as warm-front cloud-belts lowered on the advancing wings of depression after depression. And in spite of it, we had still managed to enjoy an interesting and pleasant holiday.

One evening, however, when lying to our hook in a rather open bay, we were particularly perplexed to see not two but *three* cloud layers, each going in a very different direction. The shipping forecast had spoken of nothing more than usually untoward, and the barometer was reasonably steady. Not understanding, but yet feeling that something peculiar was about to happen, we cleared out early the following morning (in another suspiciously soft blanket of fine rain) and high-tailed it to an anchorage which we knew offered all-round shelter.

Safely there, we had spun a web of cables to various trees and our two anchors just in time to experience the sudden start of an exceptionally violent, but totally unforecast storm. Indeed, it was already gusting gale force from the south-east as I rowed the final warp back to *Aku*. A large, well-manned yawl sharing this excellent spot went dragging by, gunning her engine and heeling over with her rigging shrilling. Yet, no sooner had they got sorted and re-anchored, than the wind died right away.

Judy, clutching *Aku*'s pulpit as we completed the adjustment of our ropes, suddenly pointed sharply skywards.

"Jim! Just look at that cloud!"

It was the only time either of us had seen such a sight. An individual cloud, lower than the others, had just come blowing over the hill to windward of us, and was visibly slowing and writhing round just above us. As we watched, it suddenly began retreating, right back over the same hilltop! Within a minute, the surface wind had switched viciously through 180°, and began blasting at storm force out of the north-west. Our warps now lay uselessly out the wrong way, and I had a frightful tussle lifting and hastily relaying the kedge to what was now windward, as the catamaran swung precariously towards what *had* been some sheltering rocks – a salutary lesson in always having more than one anchor on board!

So unexpected and unpredicted had this particular and baffling storm been that only a few miles south of us a well-found yacht was lost at sea, moments after the windshift, both her crew-members unfortunately having been swept overboard.

Between two further, and I'm glad to say boringly ordinary gales, we managed to continue our cruise as far north as Loch Torridon and Loch Gairloch, which nestle spectacularly and very picturesquely among the steep mountainous mainland of Wester Ross. Deciding that was far enough, we then battled our way back south through the Kyles of Lochalsh and Rhea, to spend a windy night snugly isolated in the little bay behind Sandaig

Light, in the Sound of Sleat, where Gavin Maxwell had once lived and written his bestseller *Ring of Bright Water*. Exploring ashore, we visited the waterfall where his beloved otters had once played and the cairn over Edal's sad little grave, while white against the deep blue sound *Aku-Aku* waited at anchor, yawing this way and that to the squalls. (Map page 76.)

I suppose we were by then becoming a bit blasé about these strong winds, and the capable way our sturdy rectangular boat seemed to handle them. The forecast on the morning of our departure from 'Camus Fearna' spoke of nothing worse than '*North-east, backing north, 5-7*', so the fact that it was currently in the nor'nor'*west* should have immediately warned me that the weather was once more failing to 'work to rule'.

During lunchtime the penny dropped, and we decided it might be as well to run on southwards, and round into Loch Nevis. Should it then come on to blow really hard, we would have good shelter under the high hills surrounding the old shooting lodge at Glaschoille.

We motored up to our anchor with the mains'l set, then adding and backing the working jib, bore away to clear the arms of the bay, and in moments were swooping along on a broad reach out in the open Sound of Sleat. I wanted to keep us well clear of the gaping mouth of Loch Hourn and the craggy shore beyond it, for it was under our lee, and breaking seas were already tumbling right across from the distant entrance to Loch Indaal, away over on Skye. At first the catamaran was unperturbed by the motion, and rushed along at 7 knots or so without any fuss at all. Within the next twenty minutes, however, the wind increased dramatic-ally, and I was soon up on the cabintop struggling to reef the mainsail.

During the previous spring, Judy and I had developed our own version of slab-reefing to replace the Catalac's original roller system. Our scheme was conventional enough in concept, apart from replacing the reef-point idea, which would normally have to be laboriously tied down, with elastic shock-cord and hooks led through the eyelets across the sail. This enabled a neat reef to be pulled down and tidied, and the sail reset well within sixty seconds – in the ordinary course of events. Today, with the wind aft and very strong, *Aku-Aku* was beginning to rock and lurch and surf on the steep, quartering seas, and up there on the high coachroof the job of heaving down on the clew pendant lines demanded all my strength and caution.

Triumphant at last, I dropped back down into the cockpit and was greeted by a rightly irate wife, who rebuked me in seamanlike phrases for not having first put on my safety harness. As an afterthought, she added that I'd just be in time for the 1355 shipping forecast, if I went below.

Duly chastened, I dodged down to the chart-table and switched on the radio. This time it gave an uncompromising statement of fact: '*Malin, Hebrides: north 6 to 8, locally 9, imminent.*' We were already having nor'west 7, it was freshening by the minute, our speed was up to 8 knots and the steering getting difficult in what I now saw were very big seas indeed, for such relatively sheltered waters.

Even wearing my reassuring safety harness, the decision to take in the second of the two deep reefs in the mains'l was enough to cause momentary butterflies in my stomach as I clambered up on the bucking cabintop and felt *Aku-Aku* go into a long, surging plane off the face of a wave. I reached the mast and began easing the halyard. A rushing squall hissed and shrilled about us, flattening the sail against the port shrouds. Stooping so that she could see me through the spray hood's window, I motioned Judy to close-haul the mainsheet. This was no time to bother with reefing. I let go the halyard and clawed the entire mass of fluttering, blattering blue Terylene down round me, stowing the whole thing as best I could along the boom.

Stepping back down to the sidedeck just as the ship leapt forward on a bursting crest I almost lost my balance, and the line of the safety harness, hooked into its slide on the cabintop, sprang tight and steadied me. One glance at Judy's watching face told me more than words could say, and it was a very sheepish skipper who joined her in the steering recess, forward of the cockpit.

"How's she handling?" I bawled over the roar of our wake, for despite the massive reduction in sail, our speed was still around 8 knots.

"Better again, but it's still not easy," she shouted. "I've never known her so hard to hold." That should have warned me that something was amiss, but it didn't. Another squall howled down, and *Aku-Aku* launched herself forward like an accelerating sports car. Inwardly concerned for our children, I ducked to see Rona and Susan still playing 'Ludo' at the cabin table. Only Eileen, the youngest, was looking a bit quiet and pale. She was often seasick, poor kid, yet always stoutly maintained she didn't mind. By the looks of her it wouldn't be long, but there was nothing I could do about it. The appropriate bowl was waiting on the seat beside her. Beyond her, on the shelf at the fore end of the saloon, our usual vase of wild flowers stood, its delicate plant-heads dipping, lifting and vibrating to the quick, jerky movements of the catamaran. One might otherwise have thought it was the cabin of a peacefully anchored yacht, for it all looked as still and normal as though we were indeed at rest in some snugly sheltered berth.

"Nine knots," said Judy, behind me. "No – ten! I can only just hold her!"

"I'll take her for a bit." As I placed my hands between hers on the small wooden wheel, I felt the full power of the twin rudders, for at that very second *Aku* tried to broach, swinging round to starboard as a wave rose under her weather stern. Wriggling onto the seat as Judy left it, I was astonished at the force needed to correct the swing, and it took longer than I liked before the cat was back on course, parallel to the jagged cliffs.

Glancing over my shoulder to a Sound of Sleat looking like a snowfield, I saw another sea smash at our sterns, and again the boat tried to turn as she scurried before it. I felt sure that the steering should *not* be so difficult, but that did not alter the fact.

"I think I'll have to reef the jib, Judy," I shouted finally. "It's still strengthening, and we *must* try to reduce this speed."

With my harness once more clipped to the track, I worked my way forward again. We had had reef-points fitted to the working jib during the spring of that year, but apart from once for trial purposes had never actually used them in anger. I now found that I had to lower the sail almost to the deck before I could unclip the sheet from the clew and transfer it to the reef clew-cringle. Changing the tack position was easier, but I made a poor job of rolling the excess up and tying in the points, so that the result was far from tidy. From time to time as I worked, *Aku*'s bows would depress slightly and she would commence another of her soaring, surging sweeps forward, although now only under mast windage. It did not make the unaccustomed task any easier.

With the rehoisted sail showing barely 75sq ft (7m^2) of area, I returned to the cockpit, and for a further while we continued relatively comfortably down the coast. I can normally judge wind strength quite accurately in light or moderate, even strong, conditions, but over Force 7 I am never too certain. It *was* over Force 7. Salt-spume had risen like a shallow mist, fogging the outlines of the land ahead, and even blurring the lower parts of the changing cliffs abreast of us as we tore on, holding 8 or 9 knots and frequently surging far higher.

At last, even that tiny amount of sail felt too much, for steering had again become very hard work. A call from below announced that poor Eileen had finally lost her lunch. Judy went to the rescue, and a rather pasty-faced Rona appeared, kitted out in oilskins and her own safety harness. She took a sudden, wide-eyed look at the seas astern, gasped and said "Wow! I'd no idea it was *so* rough!" – an impressive tribute to the steadiness of the catamaran. All the same, when Judy returned to the helm I got everyone into life jackets, more for my own peace of mind than anything, and donned my own before once more going forward, this time to replace the reefed headsail with the 50sq ft (4.6m^2) storm jib – the smallest sail we possessed.

Brilliant yellow, the tiny scrap of a triangle filled with a thud and wavered and shuddered as we sheeted it home. It would be easily seen by anyone who might have been watching, even in those poor conditions, and for us it was like a bright flower on a waste-land of watery grey rubble, cheering us up in the gloom of the gale. And to our astonishment, *Aku-Aku* continued to career forward at around 7 and 8 knots, and several times held 9½ for many long, thrilling seconds. She was in no way over-canvassed like this, for we had only been made to shorten sail so much because of the heaviness of the steering. And that thought kept nagging at me.

Here, on reflection, were all the danger signals a better skipper would have heeded *and* acted upon. I heeded them all right, but it wasn't all that far to shelter now, and I admit I just hoped like hell that whatever was wrong would not get any more so before we got in – potentially the most easy way any crew can slide into untold hazard – just hang on and hope. How many ships have driven blindfold into fog, and on into cliffs, because of navigators who had got lost but just hoped? How many masts have broken because of skippers hanging on to unreefed sails, just because it wasn't more than a short way to harbour? And I, normally so conscientious about my young family being on board, just hoped too.

By now the breaking seas were even larger, extremely steep and still very close together. Laced with lines of foam churning over the flood tide now inexorably coming against us up the sound, I thought that heaving-to to inspect the steering might cause more problems than we had, skating downwind like this. The strain, I told myself, might snap something, and then we'd really be in trouble. So far, very little spray had come aboard; there were only a couple of wet patches on the big open cockpit floor, and although I kept expecting water to enter the steerage lockers via the lids and through the tiller slots in the transoms, repeated checks showed that this was not happening, nor could I see anything wrong with the steering gear. We tobogganed on.

Soon we were able to make out the rock-strewn entrance to Loch Nevis appearing through the mist not far ahead. I took the wheel again to give Judy's arms a further rest, and found myself actually enjoying the situation – for the moment. Then it was suddenly time to gybe and begin working across the seas towards the entrance. That was no trouble in itself, but I realised that we would eventually have to turn beam on, to avoid a couple of dangerous rock-groups in the approach, and it would have to be *before* we could gain any shelter from the land. I cannot say how hard it was blowing then, but the seas were like walls of tumbling, careering water, some seven feet high, and all but vertical on the leading faces. We would soon see if what Tom Lack had always claimed about the stability of the Catalac was correct.

The moment came.

Judging it as best I could, I eased the helm, and *Aku* swung her yellow jib in towards the loch. A white cataract reared alongside. She lifted, rolling crazily to starboard, then skidded bodily sideways and instantly lurched back upright, only to find another crest about to collapse on her. It too somehow vanished under the weather hull, flinging her over and then back the other way as it passed on to lift her lee hull. Then it rumbled off downwind, leaving a broad roadway cobbled with foam in its wake.

The next sea was even less trouble, and reaching on at a

Force 8 'and the flower vase had fallen over'

sustained 9 knots, the catamaran bore us joyfully into the smoother water ahead. Susan, now efficiently acting as Eileen's nurse below decks, afterwards assured us that the inclinometer on the cabin bulkhead had achieved a record angle of twenty-five degrees at one stage, though possibly some of this was due to its pendulum being lurched sideways, rather than by a true angle of heel. In either event, it was well below the boat's theoretical 'point of no return', so we had been nowhere near achieving anything dangerous. All the same, she said with a touch of awe, the flower vase had fallen over and spilled at that same moment. Gosh!

Rona's only complaint about this unruly behaviour was that a dash of spray had had the audacity to wet her face. And that, in *Aku-Aku*'s cockpit, actually was somewhat noteworthy.

We were now virtually into Loch Nevis, and my superb shipmate of a wife was fitting the large-scale detailed chart into the plastic case on the back of the cabin door, by my side. We needed it, for in the fog of driving salt around us, we could make out none of the leading marks, and had constantly to check compass headings. Even the large stone beacon which stands on a particularly ill-placed rock there was quite invisible in the smother of white water and spume-laden air, so, stifling a very strong temptation just to head in and hope, I steered well out to starboard of the dangers. This would of course mean that once properly inside the loch, we would be a long way downwind of our objective, for the small bay of Glaschoille was tucked behind a couple of islets half a mile to port of the entrance. It could not be helped. At least there was much less sea running now, and, apart from the violent whistling gusts that repeatedly wuthered down off the crowding mountains shredding the surface into rushing sheets of mist, it all felt relatively bearable.

After a while we reckoned it was safe to start tacking up towards the bay and, as Judy winched in the sheet until the little storm jib was almost flat, I edged the catamaran more and more into the wind. To our amazement, despite its minute size compared to the bulk and windage of the Catalac's high bows and superstructure, not to mention 40ft (12.2m) of bare mast, that tiny sail had all the power necessary to haul us along on a close-reach at speeds of up to 5½ knots in the gusts. In the lulls our bows tended to fall away badly, however, and in the end we lowered the outboard and added petrol power to take us the remaining distance up to the anchorage; but it had been a most interesting experiment.

Had the engine failed for some reason, and if we had still been in heavy seas, it might have been impossible to sail the craft to windward without some kind of balancing canvas set abaft the mast, and I set to wondering if we might perhaps have rigged the working jib as a kind of trisail. Possibly we could, but it occurred to us that it was hardly designed for use in such fierce winds anyway, and might well have blown out. Rather ashamedly, I admitted to Judy afterwards that without a proper storm trisail on board, we had perhaps been risking more than we should.

We both remembered a previous occasion when we had been left without a mainsail on a windy day in restricted waters. The two of us had been bringing *Aku-Aku* down Loch Craignish from Ardfern to the Crinan Canal, near the end of the previous season, and were sailing her hard so as to arrive at the sea-lock before the canal closed for the night. It was blowing a gusty Force 6 from the sou'east, and we had therefore chosen the narrow, inshore passage between a string of islands (past our 'Bay of Noises') and the mountainous weather shore of the loch, in order to shorten the final beat up to Crinan.

It is odd how it sometimes blows harder in the *lee* of a

headland or promontory. As we neared the mouth of Craignish a truly shrivelling squall shrieked suddenly off the hill to wind-ward, whisking the surface into a scattering blizzard of white spray. The catamaran shot forward to I don't know what speed, close-reaching though she was, and for a fraction of a second I wondered if she was perhaps going to fly a hull in the air – or worse.

Nothing of the sort! Tom Lack and John Winterbotham had designed the Catalac's hulls to remain safe even in these vicious conditions. Without proper keels to stop her, she merely skidded sideways in a rush of foam, thus relieving the pressure, but alas, too late for our mainsail. With a noise very like an extremely rude 'raspberry' being blown through a megaphone, it split smoothly from leach to luff. Something had had to go since the boat would not capsize, and had barely heeled at all which of course would have been the monohull's way of spilling excess wind. Com-fortingly in a way, it was neither the mast nor the rigging which had failed, but we were shortly faced with an extremely steep head-sea out in Loch Crinan, in which the outboard, added to help us on our way as soon as the damaged main was stowed, cavitated so much as to be almost useless. The no 2 jib on its own had been barely man enough to keep us going, and we only just made it. Then too, we could have done with a trisail.

Our arrival in Loch Nevis, however, was very different, for this time there was virtually no sea once we were in, and no deadline to meet. All the same, soundings right up to the shore under the old shooting lodge are very deep, and even with the engine doing its best, it was extremely difficult to control the boat in the gusts as we hunted for the shelf of shallower mud off the burn-mouth. A large, if rusty, metal mooring buoy came enticingly ahead of us as we yawed to a particularly heavy squall, and Judy and I both had the same thought. Then she shook her head.

"Better not," she called, wisely. "Goodness knows how long it's been there. Could be rusted away to nothing down below."

It certainly seemed unlikely that such a mooring would get much use, or be often checked or maintained in this all but uninhabited spot, for there was not another boat in sight. Nevertheless, I agreed it might be better to trust to our own ground-tackle. We caned the engine again, crept forward with the rigging whistling overhead, got 20ft (6m) on the echo-sounder and let go, swinging back nicely clear of the mooring and the nearby shore.

We spent quite a while clearing up on deck. The storm jib was unhanked and bagged by the children, and Judy and I busied ourselves with shaking the reefs out of the working jib and mainsail, and making a neat and proper stow of both. I need hardly add that as far as I was concerned such meticulous attention to detail was partly an excuse to stay on deck long enough to be sure our anchor was holding securely. The squalls which repeatedly jerked us back on our cable did seem to be getting rather less nasty now, but even so I wondered if we had been silly not to have taken that big mooring, bobbing astern of us there.

"Good heavens!" exclaimed Judy suddenly, and I looked up. Coming round the point and turning directly towards us was a small car-ferry. On and on it came, the short waves exploding under its overhanging and flatly rectangular bow. A crewman came forward with a long boathook, picked up the rusty mooring and secured it in a well-accustomed manner, while the skipper stopped her engines. Within seconds, the two of them had departed shorewards in a dinghy.

Now, if we *had* been on that mooring, all snugged down and oilskins off, settled comfortably below having tea, just imagine the shouting and fuss and pandemonium to get clear. Some of the thought must have transmitted itself to my mate.

"How about hot drop-scones for tea?" she asked suddenly.

There was a concerted race for the cabin door.

And Eileen won.

As usual I had raised the steel rudder-blades clear of the water so as to keep them from being noisily jiggled by the wavelets overnight, and I was duly letting them down again before getting us under way for a bit more home-going next morning, when I discovered why *Aku-Aku*'s steering had been so abominably heavy during the gale.

A downhaul line was arranged so as to pull each rudder-blade slightly forward of vertical, so that a small portion was then ahead of the pivot-line axis, thus achieving a partly 'balanced' effect. This advantage could not be retained, however, unless the downhauls were very tight and well secured. When I tugged on it, the port line simply came away in my astonished hand, its frayed and broken end coming up after it through the fairlead on the rudder-head. Exactly when it had parted I do not know, but it seems more than likely to have happened before we had sailed very far down the Sound of Sleat in the gale, thus allowing that blade to tilt back and up and become very 'unbalanced' indeed. The strain could well have snapped the steering wire. When I looked, I found the starboard downhaul also showing signs of chafe, so I replaced them both there and then, scolding myself roundly for not having checked the two of them more regularly. Once again my boat had taught me that if I did not look after her she might cease to look after us, and would likely choose a really awkward moment to do so.

Once outside the loch later that morning, we found conditions still so unpleasant with the wind now strongly back in the south-west (and therefore dead on the nose for our intended course to distant Ardnamurchan), that we chickened out and fled instead into the fishing port of Mallaig – again, alas, minus Eileen's latest meal. I truly hated 'making' her ill by driving through rough water; it was after all supposed to be *her* holiday as well as ours, and on this occasion we were not yet short of time. In any event, it was pleasant enough to visit Mallaig again, at first. During the next five days of being cooped up there in appalling weather along with an increasing number of other yachts who were also trying in vain to work south, we changed our minds. *Aku's* decks were plastered continuously with seagull excrement and covered with fish-scales and other unpleasant rubbish blown off the fish quay above us. In fact Mallaig, in our eyes, lost its charm for ever.

I used the time to design that storm trisail we had talked about, and the following winter it was beautifully made for us by Cranfield's. In the years to come we used it gratefully on plenty of occasions.

Meanwhile, back in Mallaig, the wind blew and blew, always and maddeningly from the sou'west.

At last one evening after a very correct show of ritual reluctance on his part, the Harbour Master was persuaded to come aboard for a 'dram', and while comfortably ensconced in our saloon, told us that he had just seen the televised Atlantic weather chart. Although the radio forecast had mentioned nothing of the kind, the impression was that during the night the wind might start veering west; or even north-west. And *that* was a possibility which earned the good HM a third dram, for cheering us up. If we didn't think much of his harbour from a yachtsman's point of view, we decided *he* was all right.

Sure enough, by 0830 next morning the wind had indeed worked round into the west, and the track of higher clouds ran even more from the north. We lost no time in motoring clear, and, to make what speed we could, set full main and working jib *and* kept the engine going. With its help we could just lay the Sgurr of Eigg, that mighty pinnacle of rock towering over the distant island. There was still a rough and sloppy sea being knocked about by the persistent Atlantic cross-swell, causing the propeller to cavitate now and then, but progress was good all the same; and Eileen could be heard singing away to herself, harmonising with the note of the outboard, so *that* was all right, too.

After a while the breeze freshened and veered slightly under an approaching black and heavy cloud, but I felt that if we could only gain the lee of Eigg, which lay rather to windward of our direct course to Ardnamurchan, all would be well. We reefed the mainsail and kept pointing as high as possible, towards the island's northern extremity, for there is nothing like being able to steer a trifle to windward of the desired course; it instills confidence. (Photo page 119.)

From time to time, heavy rainstorms came marching out of the west as clouds ripped open on the jagged mountains of Rhum, seen dimly to seaward of Eigg. The visibility came and went repeatedly, and there was a lot of wind in the rain-belts. In one squall we stopped the engine as it was being outpaced at the 7½ knots we were now making close-hauled, and we sailed on with the humpy seas coming more and more round onto our beam. Then at last we were feeling the shelter of the first great cliffs, and soon the wind went fluky and light. I had overdone it and come in too close.

Shaking out the reef in glorious sunlight now, we watched the sea turn a brilliant translucent green, and suddenly we were surrounded by countless shoals of pink, purple, yellow and vivid-red jellyfish. Great numbers of razorbills and guillemots dotted the surface, barely attempting to dive, swim or fly out from under our twin bows. We took this quiet spell to enjoy an early lunch, and then restarted the motor until the breeze came through once more as we cleared the southern end of the island. I was still a bit wary of the long white cirrus 'wind streaks' we could see in the western sky, and especially doubtful about a vast sun-halo which had formed, but both were false prophets.

With sheets at last eased a few inches, we now aimed to keep the distant pencil of Ardnamurchan lighthouse a safe space to port of our track, knowing that after such prolonged bad weather the backwash off the massive cliffs would be severe. All the same, sailing even that little bit freer made a world of a difference. The catamaran fairly flew over the big, windblown waves and the huge sunlit swell, each blue hill of which, rolling in from the Atlantic, bowled along in a glittering, living line. Like great dunes, they were, and they further increased in magnificence as we swept past the small isle of Muck, four miles south of Eigg. Everyone was on deck, enjoying it. Judy even sang at the helm; a singularly rare occurrence!

"Look astern," said Rona suddenly, from her corner by the taffrail. Assorted sails were spread right across the horizon in the direction of the Sound of Sleat and Mallaig – waters where one seldom sees more than a couple of yachts at any one time.

"Everyone else is escaping from Mallaig, too," commented Susan with a grin.

By 1255 the wind had steadied slightly over our quarter, and it was time to replace the working jib with the genoa. Sweeping and soaring grandly over the waves, maintaining a speed always well in excess of 6 knots, we brought Ardnamuchan's lofty light-tower abeam one mile off, and altered course to port, for the Sound of Mull.

A large white ketch came leaping out to meet us, ploughing and lurching to windward in clouds of flying spray and with the American flag rippling from her mizzen masthead. On seeing the crowd of other craft hurrying along after us, we wondered if they had the feeling that they were for some reason going the wrong way . . .

Goosewinged at last, we ran upright and steady as a steeple into the sound itself, glad we were not aboard some of the heavily rolling monohulls astern. We made such good time that *Aku-Aku* was off Tobermory's secluded bay by 1500, and even Eileen agreed it was far too early to stop. Besides, we asked ourselves, who would be daft enough to waste a fair wind down the Sound of Mull?

The answer seemed to be fourteen of the fifteen other boats in the gaggle closest astern, for only one followed as we trundled on between the sloping mountains of Mull and Morvern. If the other boats had tired their crews with excessive motion, ours certainly had not, and if only the strong tides some eighteen miles further on down at Duart Point had been fair, we would have continued in due course across the Firth of Lorne, away beyond that. But, well, it would have been a slow and unpleasant battle, bashing over the inevitable tide-rips at the southern end of the sound. So instead, since we were very quickly right down to where the narrow entrance to lovely wooded Loch Aline ran in to port among the Morvern hills, we stowed sail and motored our way gently and luxuriously into the limpid green calm under its crowded trees, and brought up far in on its northern side.

A seal played around us as we anchored, then hauled himself out on a nearby rock with contented humpings and snorts to dry his long whiskers and warm himself in the afternoon sun, while only slightly after the approved hour, the family of us took tea and home-made fruit-cake, served in the cockpit. We had done just over forty-eight miles at an average of 5.7 knots – not our fastest ever, but definitely a passage to remember.

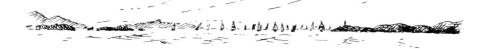

13
SAILING FOR PROFIT

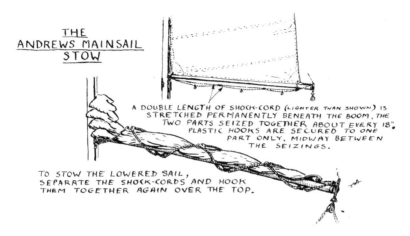

THE
ANDREWS MAINSAIL
STOW

A DOUBLE LENGTH OF SHOCK-CORD (*LIGHTER THAN SHOWN*) IS
STRETCHED PERMANENTLY BENEATH THE BOOM, THE
TWO PARTS SEIZED TOGETHER ABOUT EVERY 18",
PLASTIC HOOKS ARE SECURED TO ONE
PART ONLY, MIDWAY BETWEEN
THE SEIZINGS.

TO STOW THE LOWERED SAIL,
SEPARATE THE SHOCK-CORDS AND HOOK
THEM TOGETHER AGAIN OVER THE TOP.

The Andrews' mainsail stow: a double length of shock-cord (lighter than shown) is stretched permanently beneath the boom, the two parts seized together about every 18in, with plastic hooks secured to one part only, midway between the seizings; to stow the lowered sail, separate the shock-cords and hook them together again over the top

In the years between 1972 and 1976, *Aku-Aku* provided our family with the most comfortable, easy-going and trouble-free cruising we had so far experienced. The exceptionally vivid light-weather performance of her keelless twin hulls enabled us to wander where we liked with relatively little use of her outboard motor among the West Coast's myriad isles and lochs. So reliably did she manoeuvre under sail alone, that we were often able to wriggle our way confidently into the narrowest of anchorages, enjoying that supreme satisfaction which only such a silent approach can achieve.

There were many simple trips out of our home port across Loch Fyne, perhaps to a favourite swimming beach on the hotter days, and lazy drifts home when in the fading air of the evening we could sometimes sail slowly right through Tarbert's tortuous islanded entrance. If we were lucky with the fluky puffs off the surrounding hills, we might even manage to work our way, still engineless, between the other moored craft to our embayed mooring in the tree-reflecting confines of the tiny, northernmost corner.

There were Saturday 'Cruises in Company' with assorted small ships from the little yacht club, when we would all anchor at some selected venue and have a bonfire and sausage-sizzle (with toasted marshmallow 'afters' for the younger crew-members), by way of tidying up the local tideline. (Map page 10.)

Other times, maybe with some visiting friend aboard, we would slip away northwards to the horseshoe-shaped lagoon of Loch Gare, beyond the Ottir Narrows in Upper Loch Fyne; or else bowl merrily before a spanking breeze down-loch to double the low, rocky spur of Ardlamont Point into the land-locked channel of the Kerry Kyle. There the rounded green hills of the Isle of Bute would lean ever closer to our course as we reached swiftly over the still water, fizzing along past Kames and Tighnabruaich. On, beyond the rows of yacht moorings, the wild pine-covered crags would then loom steeply above us and the wind would come and go in slamming, wayward puffs, until it settled down again where the dark trees rose in tiers, by the mouth of Loch Riddon. And here indeed lay enchantment.

"Glen Caladh, or Wreck Bay?" the Mate would ask. If the children were with us we knew the answer, for around Caladh's completely sheltered pool, formed behind a rocky wooded islet, were the intriguingly abandoned remains of a once elegant country estate. Up tangled pathways one could explore to where its great house had once proudly stood overlooking the Kyles, or else push through the rhododendron bushes to discover its lovely old boathouses, slipways and (gem of all childhood gems) the miniature stone lighthouse perched on the point by the southern entrance.

If our daughters were away at school, and only the two of us were on board, or if beloved beautiful Caladh was too crowded (it nominally held just about twelve yachts, though we recall one windy night when an incredible nineteen swung wildly to their anchors there), we would head across to Wreck Bay instead, just to starboard round the northernmost tip of Bute. Here, under the heather-covered hillside, was a different and more open kind of peace; and with the hook down nicely clear of the tide, we would watch curlews feeding in the shallows, while busy oyster-catchers rushed importantly about, pecking at mussels clustered on the weedy bones of an ancient wreck, half-sunk among the pebbles. Pure, crystal-clean drinking-water could be collected in cans from a burn which cascaded in a series of leaps down through a nearby copse of tiny oaks. Or one could walk sea-booted over the marshy, bracken-scented slopes above, for miles if one cared to, with never another soul in sight. And on returning to the shore, there she would be; our white cat, with her blue waterline and matching sailcover, waiting, swinging lazily on the inverted reflection of the mountains beyond.

As time passed we came to know *Aku-Aku* so well that when clambering aboard at the mooring and taking her wheel again after a week or two ashore, it was for all the world like shaking hands with an old friend – a most heart-warming sensation.

But bliss is so often short-lived . . .

One after the other as they grew, our three girls went off to boarding-school, and our increasingly strained finances were suddenly stretched past the limit when the Labour Government abolished the grant which that and other such educational establishments had hitherto enjoyed. A freelance writer, albeit with other valuable strings to his bow, needs more than ordinary success to become rich, so I had quickly to think of a further supplement to our funds. Except as a final frantic recourse, selling *Aku-Aku* was not a good idea for, sentiment apart, she presented us with almost the cheapest form of holiday a family of five could have, not to mention lots of copy for my typewriter.

In 1975 we worked it out, accounting for every last penny spent on sailing from the cost of the annual refit to harbour and canal dues, replaced equipment, insurance, engine maintenance, fuel, gas and so on. We even included the total of our Yacht Club and Class Association subscriptions. Leaving out only the price of food eaten on board (since we would have consumed that anywhere), it all came to just under £350, for the full twelve months. Cheap? Even at 1975 prices it was. But of course we still did all work ourselves as far as possible, laying her up afloat at her well-sheltered moorings, and putting her on the local beach to scrub and antifoul.

And for our £350 that year we had had just under three full

weeks of family cruising in the most beautiful of scenery, and enjoyed countless evening sails and weekends afloat as well. Compared to a four-day visit to London where we had all stayed in a modest hotel, enjoyed a little sight-seeing by public transport and flown back home to Scotland for a shattering total of £310, our kind of sailing was unquestionably good value for money, particularly where annual holidays were concerned.

It seemed only sensible now to try and convert cruising into actual profit, and chartering, however unappealing at first sight, looked the best answer financially. But could we compete satisfactorily in an area already well supplied by established charter firms? Knowing we could never let our beloved ship be sailed away by people about whom we knew virtually nothing, we settled for doing only skippered cruises, with me as 'Master under God'. This decision immediately put us in a unique position compared to our competitors, for although there were one or two catamarans for hire on a 'bare boat' basis we at that time would be alone in offering skippered cat-cruising in Scottish waters. It appeared likely that we might thus attract folk who, though they felt like trying a catamaran, were nevertheless hesitant about doing so for the first time without having someone else on board who knew about this strange, unballasted sort of vessel. My book *Catamarans for Cruising* and magazine articles on the same subject might further help with the advertising.

We were in for many surprises. The first was that Judy and I, then lawfully man and wife for fourteen years, now had to pay a fee to become 'Legal Partners'. Then there was the perplexing discovery that, whereas under the existing Government Regulations of the day it was apparently perfectly in order to hire one's boat to utterly incompetent strangers without putting *any* safety equipment on board, the moment one went along as skipper to see that the ship was properly handled and to look after one's guests' welfare, this was considered dreadfully unsafe by the powers that be, who then insisted on the boat carrying all sorts of elaborate emergency gear.

Proper *round* lifebuoys; Officially Approved life jackets; a six-man liferaft; massive distress rockets, fan-ventilated bilges; the list seemed endless. Out in the cockpit, our Government Inspector even wanted us to have the two lifebuoys fitted differently – one with an automatic flashing light (which we already had), and the other made fast to the rail with 30ft (9m) of *floating* line. That, however, was where I began to get awkward, for with floating rope about and the outboard's propeller only inches below the surface I could envisage a truly disastrous situation building up. Anyway, the thought of someone going overboard when perhaps the catamaran was sailing in excess of 8 or 10 knots, and some helpful soul chucking them the tied-on lifebuoy, was too appalling for words.

"Why," I protested at once, "if the poor chap caught hold of the buoy, the moment the line came taut it would pull his arm out. Worse, if he had just got his *head* into the thing!"

"Ah!" exclaimed the Inspector patronisingly, "but that one is not for throwing when someone falls in *under way*! Dear me, no. You must throw the *other* one, with the flashing light, for that purpose. The one with the line is only for when somebody falls over in *harbour*. That's why our Regulations insist on thirty feet of line, you see – because of ship's freeboard."

I regarded him solemnly for a moment, then leaned over the side of our cockpit to touch the water with my fingers. "Our freeboard is thirty inches," I said firmly.

After a lengthy pause, he assumed a sour expression and began closing up his expensive briefcase. In abrupt, clipped phrases, he then announced that since we would not actually be offering 'individual berth bookings', but chartering solely to one person and his party of guests (though he had not thought it necessary to say so earlier), none of these Regulations in fact, er, um, really applied to us. He had wasted almost an entire morning.

I rowed him ashore in a determined silence. Disgusted as we were by this nonsense, Judy and I nevertheless felt that in order to try and build up regular business it would be worth doing the best we could for our clients-to-be, so most of the recommended equipment was installed anyway during the very thorough refit in 1976. For my own peace of mind, I wanted to have no doubts about any item of gear or rigging or machinery, so everything from marine loo to masthead light was overhauled and refurbished. Provisioned and fuelled for a week, *Aku-Aku* thus set out in very fine fettle on her first charter, through the Crinan Canal and away up the West Coast to the lovely loneliness of Loch Sunart.

A lot of lessons were learnt, I have to admit, and in particular culinary ones. Normally our menus were quite sophisticated, but we did have a couple of plebian dishes, the juxtaposition of which, I quickly discovered, was definitely better avoided. Serving one's guests with a 'sweet' course of prunes for supper is acceptable, but it is then singularly unwise to give them baked beans the following breakfast-time. Apart from that little error, we had few disasters, although our first year taught me to appreciate the true wisdom of the charter-skipper friend who had initially advised us.

"A cruise duration of one week at a time is quite long enough," he said, "because though sometimes you get a bunch of folk with whom you could gladly spend all summer, on other charters and with the best will in the world, things may not work out so well. One can at least remain civil for a week – but perhaps not a lot longer."

We also learned that a 'quick turn-round', unloading one crew on Saturday morning and going off with a new crowd the same afternoon (with the ship in the meantime cleaned from soup to nuts, watered, refuelled and reprovisioned), while possible, is extremely hard work indeed, and that during the subsequent second week I tended to become more tired than was safe.

For another thing, I rapidly found that while one could happily 'allow' one's guests to do the washing-up, it was wiser to insist that not even the ladies of the party did any of the actual cooking. For some reason it seemed that a few people could manage to make more mess in the galley than it was worth. Others failed to grasp the very real dangers of butane gas in boats, turning the tap on first and then fumbling about with matches, instead of doing it the other way around. It wasn't difficult to assert one's authority in these matters pleasantly, though. If a lady was kind enough to insist that it didn't seem right that I should do all the cooking as well as everything else, I found I could always insist back (Master under God, after all) that this was supposed to be *her* holiday, you know, and that she was just to sit back and relax. It always worked!

In a way, being chef as well as Skipper was no great problem, partly because when cooking the same things week after week one gets quite slick at it, but mostly because Judy, bless her, had worked out a delightful set of dishes with ample trimmings, which were easy to make attractive and tasty. She also used to provision the ship in such a way that the food for Saturday's supper (always the first meal of the charter week) was stowed at the fore end of one of the Catalac's long galley lockers. Next to those came the things for Sunday's breakfast, and so on aft to the final Saturday morning's 'put-you-on-the-road' repast. She also saw to it that we had lots of ready snacks and home-made goodies, and I think these last often accounted for those of our clients who so keenly rebooked and came again. It was sad that owing to home commitments and 'minding the office' Judy herself was only able to come along on two occasions.

For me as skipper, the hours and responsibility did prove rather long and exhausting. One has to be very fit. Each morning began with the 0630 shipping forecast, listening to which gave me time to choose the day's possible anchorages, for a fixed-route itinerary is a nonsense in a small sailing craft. After dressing I would clean the decks, this operation being partly designed to waken those still asleep below me; then I would get breakfast going.

Once under way, I had to remain on my toes, often literally, until the hook went down again, for our clients were frequently novices with no steering experience who could not, initially at least, be counted on to hold a steady course. Then there was morning coffee; lunch usually at anchor in some convenient bay; afternoon tea as like as not served in style on trays out in our huge cockpit, and finally on arriving at the evening's anchorage I had maybe to row everyone ashore if they couldn't do so themselves, and either show them some place of interest or return for a quick sweep round the cabin carpets before preparing the full three-course evening meal. When that was all cleared away, one was most likely expected to join in some card or board game, or to keep everyone amused with yarns under the cabin lamp until it was time to turn in.

What with having also to keep a constant eye on pilotage in an area thick with strong tides and unmarked rocks, and teaching people to handle the ship, it all amounted to an exerting *minimum* of sixteen hours a day, during which one had to be continually keyed up at least to 'bright conversation' level. Then if a gale sprang up in the night, one sat up through the hours of darkness too, because probably this coincided with a crew new to the game, who could not have recognised the sound or feel of a dragging anchor had it happened.

Usually, after bidding my charterers farewell at the close of their week, helping Judy to clean out, change the linen, and stow the next lot of tinned goods, then finally driving home, I would sink into a hot bath and go to bed to sleep the clock round.

Maybe I took the whole business rather too earnestly and painstakingly; we certainly did our very best to give everyone the most interesting and smooth-running holiday we could, but it paid well. And word got around. By the end of our second season, we were getting more requests for bookings than we needed, without having to advertise at all. And with *very* few exceptions, we were blessed with a delightful, fascinating and often jolly bunch of people, some of whom have become firm and lasting friends.

Our brochure, admittedly, was carefully written to discourage would-be pub-crawlers or 'night-spot' hunters, for it emphasised the likelihood of spending most of the week amongst the wild, uninhabited places, often miles from the nearest road never mind shops or telephones. My idea was to take people where they could not possibly go by car; where they could study seals, birds, porpoises, etc at very close quarters, and maybe watch deer on the skyline (if not on the beach alongside), or with luck the odd pair of golden eagles soaring over the barren peaks above some silver, silent loch.

I soon discovered, however, that to cover a reasonable distance and still be certain of returning to base on the final day *in all weathers* called for much more use of the engine than did normal family cruising. On one ghastly occasion, early in our first season of chartering, we inadvertently got caught by a gale too far north, then fought continuous, strong headwinds as we struggled to beat south again. Another even worse rush, following tragic news from a client's home, was also performed to windward and in very heavy seas. Each time I was compelled to use engine and sails together in order to achieve the maximum possible speed, but in such conditions the inner bow-waves of the catamaran threw so many bubbles between her plunging hulls that the outboard's little propeller, confounded by the stream of hopelessly aerated water, cavitated so severely it produced very little thrust.

There were other awkward moments, such as when attempting to enter the sea-lock at Crinan in heavy weather, or manoeuvring into a berth in vicious squalls, when the boat's windage coupled with a reverse gear of very low efficiency became exceedingly embarrassing. Charterers do not expect one to make a muck of things, and it was very soon obvious that for this type of work, where reliable and trouble-free timing is of the utmost importance, we would be far better off with inboard engines. By this time (1976), most 9 metre Catalacs were in fact being produced with what came to be dubbed 'twinboards', the propellers of which were tucked far underneath the actual hulls, and never suffered from cavitation.

Another problem was our already five-year-old spray hood, which covered the helmsman and also, by extending forward over the huge sliding hatch, provided an area of full standing headroom on the bridgedeck at the after end of the saloon. It was no longer weatherproof. Faded and leaky, we felt it let down our ship's carefully cultivated air of smartness and efficiency. A rather boxy hardtop, or wheelhouse, had for some time been available as an 'extra' for these boats, but now a much better-looking more streamlined version was on the go, and would be the perfect answer. The drawback was that this fixed wheelhouse meant also having a new and taller galvanised-iron tabernacle fitted, so that the mast could still be lowered clear of its roof. '

Carefully we worked out the cost of having the recommended pair of RCA Dolphin two-stroke engines, their electrical systems, controls and propellers, as well as the new wheelhouse and the tabernacle, all transported to Scotland from the south of England and then locally installed by professionals. The result was dismaying, but I knew I was not competent to do the fitting myself.

"So why not sell *Aku-Aku* as she is, and buy a new Catalac with the engines and hardtop already installed by us?" asked Tom Lack suddenly, during one of our lengthy telephone discussions. "The total difference between what you can expect for a boat in her nice condition and the price of a new one with all the trimmings, won't be such an awful lot more than you'd pay to have the conversion done up there in Argyll, when all's said and done."

For quite a few seconds I couldn't answer. *Sell* our beloved

Aku-Aku? Unthinkable! All the same, the advantages of having one of the latest boats were obvious. Apart from anything else, the accommodation details were now being finished in 'wipe clean' fibreglass (a worthy consideration when chartering in rough waters!). But even more to the point, the twin rather strange little 'reversing' engines and their complicated switch-gear would be installed by experts who had fitted dozens of them into this kind of boat, with the controls put in at the building stage – a 'proper job', in other words. It was very tempting, and in the end we agreed.

The final passage Judy and I made, taking *Aku-Aku* from her home port down Loch Fyne and across the Firth of Clyde to the marina at Inverkip, was an extraordinarily beautiful one. A November haze lay freezing over a thin film of ice on East Loch Tarbert, and we had to smash a pathway out to her from the dinghy. Like a thick white fur, hoarfrost coated her decks and cabintop, and as we motored slowly into the pale calm of Loch Fyne, the golden ball of the rising sun caused every crystal to shimmer, so that she seemed encrusted in diamonds, sapphires and rubies. Poor *Aku-Aku*; she managed to delight us right to the end, and I have never in my life felt so like a traitor as when after berthing and stripping her of our personal things we finally and tearfully turned our backs on her, and walked away.

In spite of coming from exactly the same hull-mould, our next ship, with that sleek-lined wheelhouse projecting above the aft end of her cabintop, looked definitely larger. 'Big *Aku*?' In the Gaelic tongue still spoken in the West Highlands and among the Hebridean isles of her cruising ground to be, 'big' translates as *mor*. Thus *Aku Mor* was named at a Scottish/Polynesian-style ceremony, when Judy and I simultaneously poured seawater (collected from Loch Fyne) down each of her curving bows, and instructed her to be a safe and happy ship, full of fun and empty of seawater.

We had been concerned, I must admit, lest her sailing performance might be poor in comparison, spoiled by the drag of her twin propellers, for in *Aku-Aku* we had always swung the outboard clear of the water when it was not in use. Our carefully kept average-speed records, however, suggest that less than half a knot of sailing speed was in fact lost by the new craft in light going. In stronger winds she proved curiously faster under sail, perhaps because the weight of the inboard engines right down in her bilges helped her to punch through seas and to carry sail more powerfully than the older boat. (Photo page 119.)

Once we became used to handling her under power (one had to be quite careful, if turning her with one engine going ahead and the other astern, not to throw people off the foredeck), she demonstrated time and again the value of the Dolphin inboards. Working together, they could shove her dead to windward into a solid Force 8 gale, and either one of them on its own would let us cruise for mile after mile in a calm at around 5½ knots, burning barely half a gallon of petrol an hour. This represented a sixty per cent fuel saving over the 33hp outboard's much less efficient efforts in *Aku-Aku*.

Throughout the next two seasons, *Aku Mor* proved herself a luxurious and highly reliable little charter craft, but she pleased us better still as a private yacht, when, following one of those strangely unpredictable changes in family circumstance, it became sadly necessary to cease trading. Still, this did give us a chance to try something we had not dared before, during which experience two more valuable lessons were drummed into her skipper's rather lazy head.

Some years previously, I had rashly vowed that 'sometime' the entire family would sail out to where my sister then lived crofting on the tiny Outer Hebridean isle of Grimsay. A great idea – except that detailed inspection of the appropriate chart and *Sailing Directions* showed up the disturbing fact that the pilotage required to get into any kind of sheltered anchorage near Grimsay was intricate in the extreme. The entire area is spattered liberally with unmarked rocks, shoals and narrow gaps through which strong tides boil and swirl. And in those days these hazards were but scantily shown on an elderly Admiralty survey of inadequate scale. It is true that I had once – only once, and from the land – seen the approach to the Grimsay anchorage, but my vague memories of a rocky maze through which the island's small open fishing boats twisted and wound, checked only approximately with that 1902 chart. Not encouraging. However, having at last a highly manoeuvrable ship with twin propellers about 7ft (2.1m) apart, I had suddenly lost my excuse about 'only having an outboard, you know', and had to agree that at least we should now go and look at the place. (Map page 76.)

With the girls collected from their boarding-school at the start of the holidays, we worked our way northwards via the Sound of Mull and rounded into a favourite anchorage in Loch Sunart which, surrounded by mountainy stillness, was often our 'jumping off' place when bound north or west. Departure day dawned calm but with poor visibility and by midday we were beating gently into light, tentative airs barely two hours clear of a haze-hidden Ardnamurchan headland. A few sums at the chart-table made it clear that at this rate arrival off our destination would be in the darkest part of the night, so altering course further to the north I split the distance by heading instead for the island of Canna. Even at that we had to motor a good deal to get in before sunset.

The mist was thicker than ever next morning. There was not a sign of the nearby and craggy skyline of Rhum, and no hint either of the southern cliffs of Skye, less than five miles away. Canna itself faded quickly astern as we crept gingerly out on one engine, and I remember feeling glad of our big radar reflector, hung as it was in the correct 'catch-rain' attitude, just clear of the mast below the inner forestay. A fair bit of shipping uses the Minch, and they at least would be able to see us; of course they would.

Thanks to the generosity of my father, we now had a fine little VHF transmitter aboard *Aku Mor*, and being an Auxiliary Coastguard at that time, I was keeping a full-time listening watch. Half an hour out on a compass course for the westernmost tip of Skye, where the Neist Point Light sported a useful foghorn, we overheard the skipper of a motor-yacht which had also spent the night in Canna, telling someone that he too was just leaving. When he had finished his chat, we called him up to ask if he could see us on the radar set we knew he possessed. To our dismay, he could not. No, not a sign of us, yet he had confirmed that he was on exactly the same course as us, and should be dead astern.

Now, although our reflector (one of the flat-plate, octahedral sort) was quite a bit wider than our mast, it was forward of it, and I began to wonder if the curvature of the mast's alloy sides could perhaps be deflecting his radar waves, so that he received no echo from us. I asked Judy to alter course ten degrees. Almost as soon as *Aku Mor* began turning, our friend came on the air with the news that 'a very large echo' had suddenly materialised three miles ahead of him. When we returned to our previous course, again placing our mast between him and our reflector, he at once reported that we had 'completely vanished'. The discovery that not even our metal mast showed at that range was something of a revelation, and, since a great number of small craft hoist their reflectors hopefully in their rigging, there must be many with a similar and equally unsuspected 'blind spot'.

We motored on rather thoughtfully.

Just occasionally, we got enough wind to be able to stop engine and maintain course close-hauled at 4 knots, but with real fog now forecast we wasted little time. The mist in fact flattened a little in the early afternoon, for at 1430 land recognisable as the top of Mount Eaval, North Uist, showed through above it on the starboard bow and, before long, barren, humpy outlines of an island ahead materialised as Ronay, round the southern end of which we had to go to get into Kallin Sound at the eastern extremity of Grimsay.

Fine, except that the breeze began freshening rapidly, and gaining the lee of Ronay we stowed all sail to motor more cautiously in over the shallow, rock-encumbered waters. Off Kallin's few buildings, it was quickly obvious that to anchor here would mean leaving the boat exposed amid very strong currents. The wind was still rising, and clearly shore-going by dinghy was likely to become hazardous. Even if we succeeded, as I recalled from that earlier 'land' (and car-ferry) visit, we would have quite a walk over to my sister's house on the north side of the island.

Again I peered at the chart, studying the faint possibility that we just might work *Aku Mor* further through and round into the sheltered loch behind Grimsay. This, however, would mean negotiating the barrier of islets and reefs ahead, between which we could see the current fiercely ebbing over sunken rocks – mostly through one tiny dog-legged sound. On the chart this showed as a totally blank gap perhaps 60ft (18m) wide. I thought it might not be entirely uncluttered, so as we approached, Judy and Rona stationed themselves, one on each bow, ready to point directly at whatever rocks might threaten our shallow hulls. Through the clear Hebridean water we had already seen several dark-looking patches on the way in.

With wheel and throttles in hand and heart in mouth, I

Visiting Grimsay – not at all a seamanlike business

cautiously steered *Aku Mor* into the first left-hander, skidding her crabwise over the 4 knot stream. She seemed far too wide to fit the gap opening ahead between the high heathered rocks as she strove forward, trembling to her engines' thrust. A tiny baylet opened now, and we spied the next turn to one side of it; hard a-starboard round a steeply flanked, rockbound isle. I opened the throttles wide for the next turn, now to port, and was at once involved in a line of broken water, dotted with rock-heads and discoloured by sinister black weed patches, swaying over the sandy green just below our slim hulls. Judy and Rona both pointed vigorously towards a rock apparently streaking across our path. Jerking the wheel over, I wriggled *Aku Mor* past the end of it, and we were suddenly through, racing out over a clean sandy bottom into an ever widening stretch of beautiful, still water.

Weak at the knees, I gratefully eased the engines to a crawl. It was utterly perfect in there. Eaval's conical peak soared grandly over the silver loch ahead like something out of a Japanese painting, and we found superbly sheltered anchorage at the mouth of a little glen. And there was my sister waving to us from the shore.

After an admittedly enchanting visit, with the menagerie of hens and hungry goats delighting our daughters, we were of course faced with the inevitable problem of how to make a similarly unscathed departure. This time a fresh wind on our tails did little to aid control, causing one very nearly disastrous moment, but we squeezed through and gratefully rounded the last of the reefs off Kallin.

No sooner were we clear than *Aku Mor*, with an impressive sense of timing, decided to deflate her skipper's ego with a second lesson. Her starboard engine cut out. Only seconds earlier, to help make that tightest and most tide-torn turn, I had required, and mercifully achieved, full power on that very same motor. If it had failed us then . . .

The full meaning of this metaphorical rap over my knuckles was only made really apparent when after making sail and settling the catamaran on a direct course back to Canna, thirty-five miles to leeward, I inspected the offending machine. The fault had been entirely mine, for its plugs were badly sooted up. Apart from cleaning them, I could only curse myself for all kinds of an idiot, for not having checked them *before* getting under way that morning. Many years of two-stroke engines of various sorts should have warned me that a plug-cleaning session was in any case long overdue, quite regardless of the fact that I had known both engines were about to be needed in those singularly dangerous waters. I had been so concerned about the pilotage, however, that I had forgotten all about the things. I felt very abashed, but the family kindly made no remarks, and *Aku Mor* herself had let me off very lightly indeed, mindful though she no doubt was for her own safety.

The passage she gave us back to Canna was a majestic and fast one, running like some clipper-ship of old over a mounting sea, with her blue and brown wings spread before a steadily freshening nor'westerly. The wave-fronts were very soon long enough to get even the well-laden *Aku Mor* surfing merrily and for long periods on their forward faces, for sledging downwind under a press of sail like that is an easy and perfectly safe business in a well-designed catamaran. There is no rolling whatever, and therefore little risk of an accidental broach or gybe.

By the time Canna's dark cliffs were starting to loom out of the murk, high and close on the starboard bow, we were continuously holding around 10 knots, steering as though on rails, and still under full working canvas. Exhilarating, yes, with bursts in excess of 12 knots, but soon we would have to round up into the wind and reduce sail for the final beat into shelter. This was where another piece of equipment we had given *Aku Mor* would come into its own.

From my occasional job of test-sailing various yachts, I had long known that the most important sail in almost any modern catamaran is her jib, for set on its own without the mainsail a reasonable foresail will let such a boat manoeuvre readily in any direction, whereas few cats I have tried can be guaranteed to tack under mains'l only. Apart from it being the most powerful sail, the jib's area can be very critical; too much and a multihull will become overpowered; too little and she will not drive to windward as she should. *Paradis* and *Twintail* (one with single forestay, and the other with twins) had both confirmed this, and fitting twin stays had also made a world of difference to *Aku-Aku*, enabling us to change to the correct size of headsail fairly quickly. That of course did nothing to minimise the actual *number* of sail changes which we were so often forced to make in these delightful but mountain-girt and therefore squally northern waters. The west of Scotland is notorious for un-announced, often dramatic shifts and changes of wind strength, and anyone who cruises there has to work hard to keep up a presentable average speed.

The increasing fashion for reliable, well-engineered roller-reefing headsail systems had seemed to us like a gift from the gods. Basically, there were then three types of gear. In one, the sail was permanently stitched round a solid rod forestay which could be rotated (but I disliked this on the grounds of not being able to lower the sail for repairs). Alternatively, there were two employing alloy spars which had the sail hoisted in a groove. One of these was arranged so that the load was taken at top and bottom by ball-bearings, and the other so that the bearings were instead clamped round one's existing wire forestay. Not being of a mechanical nature, I mistrusted the thought of our entire rig being held up by a ball-race, and plumped for the kind which left the forestay doing its normal work, while the spar simply turned about it, operated by a line from the cockpit. Before launching *Aku Mor* we had selected the equipment made by Cooney

Marine, which when properly adjusted proved entirely adequate for our needs.

We then had to decide which sail to apply to it. Some of the modern gears have twin tracks and halyards, permitting choice in the matter, or even allowing two genoas to be set wing-and-wing for downwind work, but our relatively inexpensive set-up had just the one track. We could of course have chosen the ghosting genoa (a vast sail overlapping most of the mainsail), thus theoretically providing the fullest range of areas; but a roller headsail is best cut flat to minimise distortion when reefed, and a good light-weather sail *must* be cut full, to give maximum drive. Also, because the same sail would perhaps be used in gale-force winds, it would need to be of tough, heavy material which would inevitably hang uselessly in light airs, whatever its area. Finally, while in shape our genoa was almost an ideal isosceles triangle and would not require its sheet-lead to be adjusted as the sail was rolled, when deeply reefed its centre of effort would be very high up, and not at all where one would like it in strong winds.

In the end, we set our smaller and tougher working genoa on the roller spar, hoisting the ghosting sail flying on a separate halyard whenever we needed it.

The joy, therefore, of terminating *Aku Mor*'s wild, surfing run back across the Minch to Canna was great, and untroubled. Little *Sea Cat*'s lesson of long ago about not carrying too much sail downwind was bright in my mind as we prepared to luff towards the entrance, and realised it was now blowing a lusty Force 6. This time, however, there was no need to worry. We simply eased the jibsheet, pulled on the furling line, and in seconds had a more appropriate sail area. It was marvellous! And we particularly appreciated not having to risk going forward in those leaping seas to smother a mass of slippery, flogging canvas on the bucking foredeck, wide and all as that was on *Aku Mor*.

Undoubtedly it was mostly when manoeuvring that our roller-headsail gave us the greatest satisfaction. Arriving off a chosen anchorage, we would often drop the mainsail outside, and come sliding in under jib alone, rolling it progressively smaller to adjust speed, until it finally disappeared around itself just as we reached the selected spot. This left the foredeck clear for anchor work at the right moment, and although all sail was thus tidily stowed away even before the boat was fully at rest, enough could be reset within seconds, should the need arise.

Getting under way was even easier. Frequently we would haul up the anchor with dormant engines and sail still neatly furled, and with rudders reversed would allow the boat's head to pay off as she made a sternboard under mast windage, while I sloshed a couple of bucketfuls of water over the deck. A pull on the sheets, and lo! Instantly enough sail was set to work us clear of other craft and out to sea. No fuss, no frights, and, best of all, no shouting.

At long last, though it had taken me something like twenty-eight years to accomplish, I knew I had won total confidence in myself and my boat. I knew her ways in all weather, and could judge to a few centimetres exactly where she would go in response to the helm when manoeuvring, how far she would carry her way, or how smartly she would spin round when the headsail has backed or an engine reversed or revved up. I was – and my beloved family were too – completely 'at one' with the boat we sailed, and our delight was intense.

Then fate struck again.

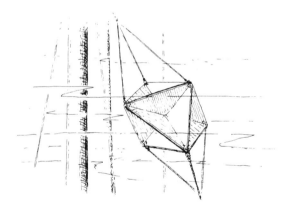

14
THE FUN OF 'SQUARE ONE'

Urr estuary

For some months I had been experiencing some very unexpected sharp pains in my knees and fingers. Medical examinations and X-rays had shown nothing, but one day I suddenly felt as though I had been viciously stabbed, right between the shoulder blades. The sensation eased as I was on the point of passing out. A day or two later, on board the boat, it happened again; the trouble had reached my spine, and the resulting loss of sleep each night, as much as an increasing difficulty in moving about, soon made charter work almost impossible. We had no alternative but to close down our flourishing little business.

Whatever it was spread through me like wildfire, affecting my wrists and elbows, and I was soon having to use a stout stick in order to walk more than a few steps. Sailing ceased to be practicable. The action of steering had become agonising, handling ropes or winches was out of the question, and the slightest movement of the catamaran under way hurt me like hell. Even ashore, I now had to be helped up and down stairs, and in and out of the hot baths which provided the only slight relief. At last a new set of X-rays confirmed what deep down I already knew. A rapidly developing form of generalised osteoarthritis had set in, and the medical profession had little to offer other than pills with nasty

217

side effects. In my forty-fifth year, I had suddenly been transformed (despite my best intentions) into a grunting, bad-tempered old man. None of us could bear the thought of *Aku Mor* lying unused on her mooring, and we made the ghastly decision to sell her. With her went our whole sailing life style.

At least the proceeds of the sale took all the worry out of financing the remaining years of our daughters' education, which was a good thing, especially as I now wondered what on earth I should find to write about. Even the thought of continuing to live in that fairly remote part of the Western Highlands, just to be near a now unusable cruising ground, suddenly lost its point – and a lot of its appeal. Besides, to get to our old stone house meant climbing a very steep and narrow gravel path, and the house itself was anything but suitable for someone with more than half an eye on wheelchair advertisements. Judy was absolutely marvellous, and much though she too loved the Highlands agreed that, with the girls' boarding-school away over on the Ayrshire coast, and my business connections still involving me in frequent if now somewhat difficult visits to Belfast and Manchester, it seemed only sensible to move south. Our whole world was being brutally changed – or so we thought.

Life, like the sea-waves, always has its ups as well as its downs. By chance, Judy came across an article in *Here's Health* magazine about the relief from arthritic soreness and stiffness to be had from a diet evolved by the Chinese-American doctor, Collin H. Dong. As I was then taking up to eighteen aspirins a day, loaded with muscle-relaxant pills and gaining nothing, I had got to the stage where I was willing to try anything that would do me no harm, and decided to give this cranky-sounding diet a go. To our utter astonishment, within just five days I was visibly moving more freely. Doing without fruit, dairy products, most animal foods, and avoiding any kind of chemical additives, not to mention pepper, was not easy, especially as that left only what were then my two most unfavourite foods: fish and vegetables. One soon learns, however, that if something is going to hurt, there is no temptation to touch it, and taking even a tiny quantity of 'the wrong thing' often had me in agony within thirty minutes. After only two weeks of strictly following the diet, I was once more able to go for gentle walks and generally fend for myself. It was like a miracle.

That autumn, although we knew there was no chance of my handling a boat of any weight or size, we nevertheless bought a second-hand Skipper 12 dinghy in which to potter about, and found to our huge delight that coping with her tiny sail area in smooth water was just about feasible.

Our luck remained good, for we soon discovered a most suitable riverside house on the Urr Estuary, at Kippford on the Scottish shore of the Solway Firth. An equidistant one and a half hours' motoring from the school, the ferry to Ulster, or the English motorway system, it could not have been more convenient. Within months of settling in, we were already heavily involved with the Solway Yacht Club and its cheery fleet of Mirror dinghies, and before long we were wondering if when our daughters were away us two relative oldies could manage a Mirror. An elderly one came available, and in due course, with M29767 all agleam, we arrived on the club slipway accoutred in our sea-going oilskins and huge life-jackets, and were naturally regarded with some amusement by our sleekly wet-suited young rivals. Old skills nevertheless returned within a race or two, and we somehow contrived to win a modest collection of trophies over the next two seasons. (Map page 224.)

For good reasons, however, Mirror Class Rules forbade the use of jamb-cleats or ratchet-blocks to take the strain off the mainsheet, and I had not enough grip to hold the sheet in fresh conditions. Judy, of course, was perfectly capable of taking the helm, and of winning races, but ducking under the low boom and kicking-strap in a crewing position designed more for supple youngsters than for stiff, middle-aged men, proved more than my partially rigid spine would allow. Even Judy found it awkward. Besides, I knew that inwardly what she really wanted was a boat she could brew a warming cuppa in, and a proper cabin in which to relax after a day's gentle coastal exploring.

Dinghy sailing was great fun, and it had been rewarding to discover that in spite of a gap of some twenty years away from racing we could still gain the odd 'gun', but since none of the girls had really taken to the racing scene, we began to wonder if perhaps I was now sufficiently recovered to think once more about a cruising boat. A tiny trailer-sailer, maybe?

After three years of sticking carefully to Dr Dong's diet, I was to a large extent free of arthritic pain – and very healthy otherwise –

so once the racing season ended, Judy and I began taking daily walks along the waterfront or up through the woods behind the village in order to keep fit, and the renewed possibility of cruising was a frequent topic of conversation. For myself, I felt that provided the gear was light and the sails none too large, I could probably cope well enough in a small monohull with Judy's help. Catamarans, with their brief but jerky motion, no longer seemed so ideal, and the thought of winching home large headsails would simply not be 'on' at all. Nor would excessive heaving on warps or mooring lines. It looked as though an overall length of 20ft (around 6m) would be the most we dare contemplate.

On one of the last remaining school runs to Ayr with Eileen, the two of us drove on up the Clyde coast to have a look at any small craft for sale in the marinas at Troon and Inverkip. Alas, all the available boats of that size or a bit larger either offered too little sitting headroom for my long and now pretty inflexible back, or else were much too 'racing orientated' and demanding; and in general their bare, four-bunk interiors looked depressingly cramped and unhomely. Somewhat discouraged, we returned to Kippford, and went for yet another forest walk – this time returning via the rear of the Solway Yacht Club's premises. There, in a corner between the other laid-up craft, a purposeful but badly faded blue bow slanted out over the tow-arm of a rusting road trailer. Such high freeboard looked to be that of a considerably larger boat than we wanted, and we had passed her by many times without a second glance. This time, however, I hesitated, for beyond her shallow central keel and twin bilge-fins I had suddenly spotted a three-bladed propeller, and it didn't seem all *that* far away from her soaring bow.

"I do believe she's a little motor-sailer," I said pensively.

"Do you know, that might be just the thing!" exclaimed Judy.

It was quite a thought, for with a really powerful inboard engine that could take over if the loading on the sheets became too much for me to handle, such a boat might indeed solve the problem very well. We both knew we would be bored silly by a pure motorboat, but a motor-sailer? Yet surely she was an unusually small one? And then I plucked at Judy's elbow.

"Come on love, let's take a closer look. There's something familiar about those lines."

And indeed there was. She turned out to be one of the old 19ft (5.8m) Mirror Offshore diesel yachts sponsored back in the mid 1960s by the *Daily Mirror*, but outmoded by today's lightweight 'performance' trailer-sailers. Designed by Eric van de Stadt, famous for world-beating ocean-racers, the rounded, buoyant sections of the little boat betrayed more than a hint of sturdy Dutch ancestry, and the curved sweep of her cabintop, though once thought radical to British eyes, was now quite in keeping with the latest trends. There certainly appeared to be reasonable headroom below decks. However, with less than 2ft (0.6m) draught, and that big three-bladed propeller, driven by what we later learned was a heavy, 7½hp diesel, and a mast even shorter than herself, she seemed unlikely to sail very well. The concept, as I now recalled, had been that of a simple-to-handle 'package deal', primarily aimed at newcomers to the sport of cruising. Well, neither of us had contemplated a boat with such apparently limited windward abilities, but – nothing ventured . . .

"She's surprisingly spacious inside," said Judy, peering through the grimy windows. "The little galley seems to have quite good storage lockers and shelves, and a proper sink, as well as a gimballed cooker. But there are only two bunks."

I had a feeling that these boats had originally been produced complete with a large boom-tent, so that children could sleep in the cockpit. I reflected that by now anyway our daughters were naturally starting to go their own ways and quite properly preferred mostly the company of their own generation, so perhaps a two-berth boat might be a reasonable enough idea. Then I noticed the frosted glass in one of the windows.

"Look, I do believe she's got a separate loo compartment, Judy. Tell you what; she'd make a grand little changing room and restaurant for taking swimming parties down to the beaches at the mouth of the estuary." I clambered onto the crumbling trailer and peered over her coamings. "The cockpit's quite large enough to seat four or five, *and* it's self-draining." I eased myself carefully down again, and thought for a minute. "I'm sure I remember seeing a write-up of these boats in an early issue of *Practical Boat Owner*. Let's go home and look it up."

What we read not only fitted quite remarkably with our own ideals, but spoke of a degree of seaworthiness unexpected in what was after all a very small 'beginner's yacht'. It seemed that at least one of these tubby little craft had made a safe double-crossing of the Atlantic, and several had found their ways to Spain, Gibraltar and the Mediterranean, by sea as well as by road or canal. Not that *we* aspired to anything of that sort. Not now.

We got the keys from her owner, and spent a cold but happy morning making a thoroughly detailed inspection and survey. The first thing we discovered was that at some time she had obviously half-flooded, and over a year had then gone before we came upon her, so her Volvo MD1 diesel was in a terrible state. When I poked it, quite a lot of it fell into the bilges in a cascade of rust. That at least would probably have to be replaced, as would her roller-headsail, the leech and foot of which were badly weakened by ultra-violet bleaching. The tiny alloy spars, stainless-steel rigging, and her bright-red mainsail, on the other hand, were all in excellent shape; the mainsail having apparently hardly been used at all during her twelve summers on the Water of Urr. Indeed, as we subsequently learned, none of her three previous owners had ventured much further than the river-mouth, and even within the shelter of the estuary she had for some reason seen very little action.

The fibreglass hull (moulded at Dell Quay near Chichester, in 1969) was in passably good condition, even if the twin iron bilge-keels were somewhat pitted with rust. True, the blue topsides were bleached and scratched, and there were a couple of star-cracks in the white deck-moulding. Nothing really that a bit of careful attention couldn't put right.

Below decks, we found the little cabin without any kind of insulation to cut down night-time condensation on its bare GRP surfaces, but we could probably do something about that, too. It was, however, bright and amazingly roomy, with acceptable headroom. Very importantly, the bunks proved delightfully comfortable. So we lay on them, and looked across at each other, and knew we both felt that she was as 'right' as could be for our present needs.

We approached the owner with a silly offer, just to test the ground.

"Well, that's a silly offer," said he pleasantly, and the usual ritual of adjusting the amount was duly performed, resulting in adequate satisfaction for both parties. Thus, on a damp but joyful autumn day, Mirror Offshore M359 became ours, and we wondered what on earth all our multihull friends would think of us.

Choosing a boat's name is always a problem. We had struck lucky with *Twintail*; everyone had liked that. *Aku-Aku* had not proved so easily accepted by people unfamiliar with its origin or pronounciation, though it had 'hailed' well. (We could never forget hearing a man in sailing gear standing among a puzzled crowd of holiday-makers on an Oban pier and yelling at a group of anchored yachts *"The Country Cottage*, ahoy!") *Aku Mor* had been better than that, though even it had sometimes raised baffled looks. This time, inspired by our 'new' boat being just about a quarter the size (in area) of the catamaran, we named her *Farthing*. Derived from the ancient Norse *farl*, meaning a quarter, the word was not only familiar to Britons of our generation, it could be split up to read 'Far Thing', which to us conjured up pictures of distant horizons. (Photos page 120.)

Yes, we said, *Farthing* would be just right. And it was – until we eventually managed to repair her old engine enough to make it function after a fashion, launched her into the Urr, and sallied forth to act as nannyboat to the dinghy racing fleet that next summer. The club youngsters listened for half a minute to her raucous, spluttering exhaust note and thereafter pronounced her name without the 'h'. We only managed to cure the habit when the gearbox finally failed and we replaced 'old rusty guts' entirely, with a new and very much quieter-running Japanese Yanmar diesel, a year later.

From the start, though, we were completely captivated by our microscopic motor-sailer. With a mainsail no bigger than that of a small racing dinghy, and a genoa jib which could be reefed or furled at the pull of a string, I soon discovered I could manage her entirely single-handed if need be. The loading on the sheets was so light that adjusting them presented few problems for my faulty joints, in spite of a total lack of winches. In the sheltered confines of the Urr Estuary, therefore, or up the further reaches of the river among the fields north of Kippford, she was just right, and had all the power required to thrust over the strong tides of the area if the wind was too light or too ahead to do so under her modest sail area. We were as pleased as Punch with her. But whether I could cope as well in a jump of a sea in the open Solway Firth, was a question not answered for several weeks.

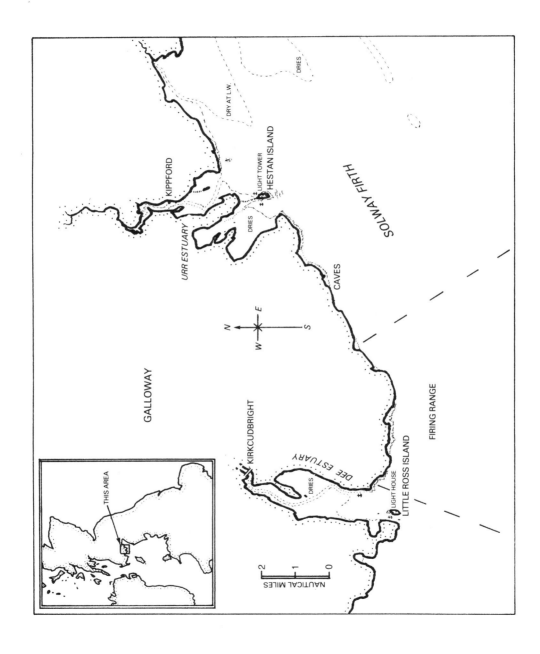

The first real chance came on a brisk and sunny day with a huge spring tide, and on the Urr maximum rise is an impressive 26ft (8m or so). Motoring down over the last of the flood, we set sail and headed out past Hestan Island's bluff slopes, close-hauled into the Irish Sea on a sou'westerly course.

The wind was a lusty southerly, Force 4, touching 5 at times, and there were more than a few breaking crests tumbling off the typically lumpy, uncomfortable chop that the shoal waters and hurrying currents of this area so often produce. Judy eyed me anxiously as I braced myself in the little cockpit, but all was well. Even though *Farthing* was being bucked about and heeled well over in the puffs, her motion proved surprisingly 'well sprung'. In the same seas, a small catamaran's movements, though no doubt less in actual extent, would have been decidedly jerky, and jolts caused agony in my spine. This, on the other hand, I found perfectly bearable. So far.

We plunged on, motor-sailing at 5 knots, with the big flaring bows keeping all but the lightest of spray off the decks. I felt absolutely fine, elated beyond measure to be off shore once more. After two hours, we turned parallel to the Galloway coastline, and cut the engine. Under sail alone now, the little boat charged gamely along until lunchtime, rolling far less than we ex-catamariners had expected, so by way of experiment we then hauled the jib a-weather, and with mainsheet eased and tiller lashed slightly a-lee, hove her to and ate our meal in relative comfort while she lay steadily, and drifted gently to leeward.

In fact, we were so impressed by *Farthing*'s docile behaviour out there that when we let draw again we fully intended to sail on and visit the Dee Estuary inside Little Ross Island, whose lighthouse we could now see beckoning only a few miles ahead. The afternoon shipping forecast made us hesitate, however, and when a distinctly ominous blue-black bank of cloud began drawing over the sky to windward, we realised that some meteorological nastiness genuinely was on the way. Family commitments just then made it preferable not to be more than the one night away, so rather than risk getting weather-bound, we put prudence before panic, and gybed round for home.

Broad-reaching now, our course took us much closer inshore than on the outward leg, and the brown cliffs, great sea-caves and occasional weird rock formations of this fascinating coast lent an air of drama to the increasingly strange lighting conditions. A variety of seabirds soared and swooped around us, and the binoculars were in constant use, though not always easy to hold steady as *Farthing* corkscrewed on the overtaking seas.

It was almost a disappointment when Hestan loomed ahead and our journey's end drew near, but there was one final test to come. A considerable little tide-rip roared and tumbled off the island's southern extremity, mushrooming right across our path. I think Judy expected me to steer round it, but it was too good a chance to miss, and I aimed right for the middle of it. Steep-sided unstable cones and ridges of water started hurtling this way and that, with crests leaping and exploding brilliantly white in the last patch of sun. *Farthing* bounced and plunged, but took never a drop on board, and again that well-cushioned motion caused me no undue discomfort. Within minutes we had swept through and were able to bear away for the Urr.

Later, with sails stowed and supper on the stove, the two of us relaxed in the cockpit with drinks, thrilled with the knowledge that I was 'seaworthy' once more, and that we could now look

'. . . 'seaworthy' once more . . .'

forward to 'proper cruising' once again. What a relief!

There was much to do first, however. Now that we knew we wanted to keep her, and that she was no longer 'just an experiment', it would be well worth trying to make her just that little bit more efficient and homely. Besides, part of truly getting to know any boat lies in altering this and that, and fitting up gadgets or ideas, until everything about her is just the way you like it. We had already managed to buff the faded topsides back to something like their old colour and gloss, and had repaired the cracks in the cabintop and hatches; even given her a properly hung cabin door. When this was opened right back, against the cabintop, a system of shock-cords on its then exposed face held a plastic case for the area's detailed chart, where the helmsman could easily study it.

Below decks a folding dining-cum-chart-table went in, as did a full-width shelf across the forward bulkhead for books and oddments. The condensation problem was dealt with by the application of Fleeceline, a synthetic woolly fabric in a pleasing buff colour, which went very well with the blue bunk-cushions, varnished bulkheads and glossy white fibreglass furniture. The job of sticking it neatly in place with the recommended Thixotropic resin was not as difficult as we had feared before starting, but although we worked with all the hatches wide open, we both suffered appalling 'hangovers' from the inevitable quantity of glue vapour we had sniffed in the process; *exceedingly* unpleasant.

The final touch was to cover the floor of both the cabin and the tiny heads compartment with cork tiles which, apart from being lovely underfoot, glowed most attractively after the necessary five coats of Ronseal – a finish that lasted well and was singularly easy to keep clean. The whole result was most pleasing, and felt warmer and welcoming.

On deck, our first necessity was a new roller-genoa. By an extraordinary piece of luck, Jeckells, her original sailmakers, had chosen just that moment to clear out their loft, and were offering a couple of unsold Mirror Offshore headsails at a reasonable price, one of which duly became ours. I wish now I'd had the sense to buy them both, and put one aside for the future, but at least we now had a new and beautifully cut sail in the same 'Viking Red' as the mainsail.

The second job was to improve the rigging, which for simplicity's sake consisted only of a forestay and two shrouds. Like most owners of these once highly popular little craft, we had found that in a strong breeze the pull of the mainsail caused the middle of the mast to bow aft. Apart from weakening its rigid strength, this resulted in unwanted fullness in the sail, as well as a slack forestay – neither being desirable in heavy going.

At last it dawned on me that with the mast stepped so far aft (it was, after all, right in the middle of the boat), this left a very wide foretriangle which would be absolutely ideal for cutter rig, and the inner forestay would also solve the mast-bending problem, especially if a light pair of lower shrouds were also added. Back to Jeckell's clearance sale – and this time they came up with a little low-cut headsail in a pretty shade of pale blue; exactly right for the available space. With its low foot, we were able to set it on a tiny boom, making it self-tacking so that even when beating up the narrow channels of the Urr Estuary it did not complicate handling.

The first sea-trials with our new staysail surprised us, for although we had hoped for some increase in performance we had not expected the gain to be a whole extra knot, yet in certain conditions it was indeed all of that. In view of its tiny area of just under 20sq ft (about 2m^2) its effect was extraordinary, as well as offering a most useful alternative to the jib when for instance approaching an anchorage or getting under way, with someone on the bow.

Back in my youth in East Anglia when I had had only a very small boat to play with, someone said to me "So what? The smaller the ship, the greater the fun!" Well, so it seems. Later on, another sailing friend had trotted out the equally old saying that the ideal length for a yacht was 'a foot for every year of your life'; a grand idea, no doubt, but I must somehow be getting younger, because I don't think that to be nearly so true.

Admittedly a very small boat suffers from inevitable short-comings in headroom and stowage capacity, not to mention the comparably greater effect of waves in a given wind strength. But I have come to believe that the real criterion for choosing the right boat is simply that her hull and keel configuration, and her sail plan, should suit what you personally wish to do with her, and that she should be *just* big enough to carry comfortably those you wish to have aboard, with the necessary provisions for the passages you intend making. Above all, such a boat should be as uncomplicated to rig, get under way and handle as you can make her, for that way there will be less to go wrong, and a lot more to enjoy.

For the next two seasons, little *Farthing* gave Judy and me the greatest of happy, relaxed fun around the Solway and, although very different compared to the other boats we had cruised in, somehow what she offered delighted us with its utter ease and simplicity.

With the local seawater warmed to a most agreeable temperature as it came flooding in over the sun-heated flats of the Urr Estuary, bathing trips to the various sandy beaches were extremely popular with us, as well as with our holidaying daughters and their successive strings of boyfriends. At other times, with visiting relatives and friends, day-cruises round to little coves where only a shoal-draughted vessel like ours could go, were considered a great treat. Lovely too, were the many excursions she made with just the two of us on board, when we would explore in detail far into next-door Orchardton Bay, or perhaps spend a day or a night dried out comfortably level on her stubby little bilge-keels in some secluded spot, enjoying the calls of the wild birds for which the Solway is so justly famous.

For us, the peak of satisfaction and pleasure came when in June 1983 we hauled out and towed *Farthing* by road over the Galloway hills and launched her into the Firth of Clyde, at Inverkip.

The actual business of getting her on and off her trailer was one we had gradually learned to get right. I suppose most people start with a launch, having bought their boat on its wheels, and after one or two nasty moments, we discovered that with *Farthing* the best method is to ease her down the beach or slipway very gently, controlling the movement all the way by means of the towing vehicle, or using very stout ropes (plural) and tackle. We like then to stop her when the trailer is immersed but before she tries to float off, while I row a kedge anchor out to the extent of its warp, and drop it either directly astern of the boat, or slightly upwind or up-current if that seems likely to be helpful. Then as the rising tide (or lowered trailer) allows her to float, one can very easily pull her clear to where she will lie quietly moored until the trailer is put away. The boat's engine can then be started or sail made without hassle or rush, and when all is ready and the rest of the crew is brought on board, one can get quietly under way.

Hauling out can of course be more fraught with difficulties than many a beginner may imagine possible, but again, the answer is to think out every move in advance, and make sure that everyone involved knows what to do when. Not liking to drive my car into the water, I usually lower the waiting trailer using those same heavy ropes, until the 'waterline' marks painted on the tall guide-arms at each side of it are just immersed. Looped over hooks at the top of each arm is a coil of tough, pre-stretched rope, the business ends of which are attached right at the very front of the trailer, and when the boat is gently driven in, I simply unhitch each coil and take it back to a cleat near the stern of the boat. Using sheet-winches would be better, but *Farthing* has never heard of such elaborate machinery! By adjusting the two ropes, the boat can be pulled forward until her bow is over the right spot, and the bow downhaul fished up with a boathook, and it and the stern-ropes tightly secured. That way there is no risk of one's pride and joy slipping back and falling when the car, on the other end of the tow-ropes, takes the strain and hauls her out.

At Inverkip, of course, we had no such complications, for our little ship was craned in by the marina's travelling hoist. To our great glee, we were then allotted a berth right next to a friend of ours called Tony, who actually lives all year round aboard *his* Mirror Offshore, *Luisa*. He too enjoys getting things the way he likes them, and had given his boat a larger rudder, as well as cutter rig, though in his case the latter was complete with gaff main and topsail, and a long and jauntily raked bowsprit. Detained in the marina overnight by fierce southerly winds, we both had plenty of time to swap visits, yarns, and ideas.

It was late the next afternoon before the weather relented enough to let us go a-sailing – well, a-motoring in fact. Stowing our warps and fenders as we headed out into the Firth, we plugged purposefully down into the dying wind for Toward Point, averaging a steady 4½ knots. Turning to starboard along the shore towards Ardyne we crossed Rothesay Bay and trundled on into the sunset up the narrow East Kyle, with the Bute hills on one side and the higher mainland mountains rising sharply from our quarter-waves on the other.

Dusk crept softly around us from under the steep, tree-clad slopes as, enchanted by the fondly remembered beauties of Glen Caladh's tiny natural harbour, we nosed *Farthing* past its toylike stone lighthouse to anchor in what had always been our most favourite spot. We stopped the engine, and sat together in the silent cockpit. The dim bloom of rhododendrons reflected pinkly in the half-light on the motionless pool around us, and all was peace. We stared at it, a very middle-aged couple holding hands like honeymooners, for that which we had been so certain we had lost for ever, was ours once more.

ACKNOWLEDGEMENTS

I wish to thank the past skippers of yachts *Oread, Maid of York, Merrymaid* and *Sudvik*, and sailing barges *Centaur* and *George Smeed*, who made me so welcome aboard their respective ships, and who taught me so much about handling boats under sail.

For unwittingly introducing me to the art and pleasure of cruising through their inspired writings, and thereby passing on the principles of sensible seamanship, my gratitude is particularly due to the late Arthur Ransome, to Maurice Griffiths GM, and to Eric Hiscock.

To my friends, and most of all my wife and family, for putting up with being written about, to all who at David & Charles aided the production of *Twelve Ships A-Sailing*, and to you who read it, I humbly and most gratefully dedicate this book.

Jim Andrews
Whiterock, 1985